Hope, Trust, and Forgiveness

Hope, Trust
& Forgiveness

ESSAYS IN FINITUDE

John T. Lysaker

THE UNIVERSITY OF CHICAGO PRESS
CHICAGO AND LONDON

The University of Chicago Press, Chicago 60637
The University of Chicago Press, Ltd., London
© 2023 by The University of Chicago
Published 2023
Printed in the United States of America

32 31 30 29 28 27 26 25 24 23   1 2 3 4 5

ISBN-13: 978-0-226-82789-6 (cloth)
ISBN-13: 978-0-226-82791-9 (paper)
ISBN-13: 978-0-226-82790-2 (e-book)
DOI: https://doi.org/10.7208/chicago/9780226827902.001.0001

Library of Congress Cataloging-in-Publication Data

Names: Lysaker, John T., author.
Title: Hope, trust, and forgiveness : essays in finitude / John T. Lysaker.
Description: Chicago ; London : The University of Chicago Press, 2023. | Includes
    bibliographical references and index.
Identifiers: LCCN 2023004295 | ISBN 9780226827896 (cloth) | ISBN 9780226827919
    (paperback) | ISBN 9780226827902 (ebook)
Subjects: LCSH: Hope. | Trust. | Forgiveness. | Ethics. | Life. | LCGFT: Essays.
Classification: LCC BD216 .L97 2023 | DDC 179/.9—dc23/eng/20230419
LC record available at https://lccn.loc.gov/2023004295

♾This paper meets the requirements of ANSI/NISO Z39.48-1992
(Permanence of Paper).

For my mother,
Yvonne Bernadine Lysaker,
who helped me believe I could

Why do I go on writing lyrics of the small occasions . . .
JOHN KOETHE

Contents

Preface

I know I cannot tell it all forever and so I want to tell it.

ALICE FULTON

1. FOR SOME OF EVERY ONE

I've heard a lot about you. Mostly general things, the stuff of demographics: gender, race, social-economic status, ethnicity, national identity, native language, generational character, subcultural character, profession. Quite an assemblage. Me too. We are positioned in various ecosocial networks suffused with synchronic and diachronic relations that are geographic, interpersonal, interspecies, institutional, semantic, syntactic, even atmospheric in character. Dazzling. Dizzying.

How do you inhabit these currents, conduct them? What do you embrace? What do you refuse? Where do your emphases fall? What eludes your detection? What do you interrogate, ignore, reinvent, or simply endure? What wearies you, bemuses, thrills? If I knew, I would know you better. I would know or begin to know your *bearing*, which denotes: a general character—say, a generous or cowardly bearing; the carrying of a weight (What loads?); an enduring (whether you grin or not); a kind of orientation, as when you find or lose your bearings; and a generation—as in "to bear a child."

Hope, trust, and forgiveness are some of the ways in which we bear what befalls us. They orient one toward particular and general ends: what we hope for, who we trust with what, who we forgive and why. Each also endures a limit. We trust because we depend and do not know. We hope because we do not know and cannot secure what we desire. We forgive not knowing what reconciliation will bring or even if it will transpire. Hope, trust, and forgiveness also conduct relations that define social, dependent beings whose conduct carries histories, modulates relations, and initiates futures. And each can be a defining trait of one's character.

I am drawn to such phenomena because they name dimensions of our overlapping existence. People meet there. Trust and forgiveness are principally concerned with interpersonal relations. And our hopes inevitably involve others. Note, too, that we consider and care for one another through the language of hope, trust, and forgiveness. "What a terrible betrayal!" "Their hope is inspiring." "What a saint! I don't think I could forgive him." Not that such phenomena are univocal. Our why, where, and when often vary, even when we seem to respond in kind. And no doubt you might despair when I hope and forgive when I refuse. Your trust may be stronger or weaker than mine in the same situation, and one person's healthy mistrust may contrast with the privileged ease of another. But the challenges that await those considering whether to hope, trust, or forgive nevertheless have common contours. Moreover, what distinguishes each from its contraries (despair, distrust, ongoing resentment) is a manner that also proves legible and so generalizable, which is what makes a philosophy of any of them possible as well as valuable, presuming it helps us navigate the straits that await whoever hopes, trusts, or forgives deliberately.

But there are generalizations and then there are generalizations. I do not believe in "the general reader." Or I do, but I do not write for such a thing, and it is a "thing," a way in which reification, *Verdinglichung*, operates. The general reader is a demographic composite to be approached with lines of thought that one predicts will land with desired effects. I am not addressing you in that way. If I were, I only would write for those I know (or think I know). I am writing for someone else, Emerson's "unknown friend," Mandelstam's "secret addressee."

"What?"

Let me begin by saying, "What, but also who"; that is, you in your bearing, your negotiations of the multiple currents we find in our way. Also, to write for an "unknown friend" or a "secret addressee" is to extend an invitation. "Accompany me," it says, and "consider this"—namely, certain dramas in our overlapping existence and ways of negotiating them. "And if you can, let me know what you think." The intimacy of my address is neither accidental nor ornamental, therefore, but a way of offering generalizations about matters that individuate us. Outside the purview of the universal (and thus of the particular), one generalizes to empower, not replace.

For us to meet in terms like those under review, you will have to let me in, and that is a big ask. You can, of course, refuse the invitation. You can refuse even while reading every word. To my mind, this is part of philosophy's fragile beauty. It aspires to an intimacy it cannot manufacture.

One might be skeptical about whether such meetings are possible. Before we write or read, hear or speak, even form our thoughts, discourse at the level of semantics, syntax, and pragmatics is overdetermined by what Braudel terms material life: "Countless inherited acts, accumulated pell-mell and repeated time after time to this very day become habits that help us live, imprison us, and make decisions throughout our lives. These acts are incentives, pulsions, patterns, ways of acting and reacting that sometimes—more frequently than we might suspect—go back to beginnings of mankind's history" (Braudel 1977, 7). Perhaps the currents of material life inevitably displace the sites I have imagined for us, those I count on when I address you. One goal, particularly in the first of two interludes that lie ahead, is to offer reasons for containing and possibly refusing such doubts (which is different than refuting them). But more generally, my attention to usage and my reliance on examples—that is, my replay of certain facets of material life, raw towns that we believe and live in—is integral to my argument that generalized accounts of phenomena like hope, trust, and forgiveness are possible. Sometimes the examples are simple, even easy. But they open scenes in which we might begin to recognize the hope, trust, and forgiveness of one another, even in their differences. And through them we might know a range of their characteristics as possibilities for ourselves and/or tasks, even challenges. They also open a playing field within which questions and counterarguments can arise, some of which I anticipate.

Divergences and disagreements arise in all moral-psychological phenomena, particularly among agents positioned differently. Respect for these phenomena requires respect for this polyphony. But while I observe several differences in usage and viewpoint along the way, and while I note a range of disagreements, my goal is not to survey a scene but to intervene on behalf of certain valences, and to account for that intervention. I want to offer you something definite to bear, not fill a box of curiosities. My accounts of hope, trust, and forgiveness thus belong to ethical life, to me and you in our overlapping existence. They concern ethical phenomena. They also consider how best to navigate situations in which we are answerable, and they aim, in themselves, to be answerable. Ethical or moral theory is evenly stressed across these pages, as "aesthetic theory" is with Adorno.

II. THE APHORESSAY

What is an essay in finitude? You are. I am. We exist in streams of ongoing interpretation and intervention, some reflective, most not, and finitude characterizes each step: our temporality, our epistemic capacities, our vulnerability, the limited reach of our agency. We are experiments, collisions that witness and intercede in their own unfolding, a swipe in a swerve. Over the course of a life we anticipate, behold, assess, and redress results expected and unforeseen.

What is an essay in finitude? A refusal to dilate thought to the point where it tries to catch itself, its allies, and its rivals in figures of necessity or law, even of the historical sort. Lyotard's suspicion of metanarratives came by way of a "report on knowledge." The report character of his analysis entailed his refusal to drift into yet another grand tale. Nancy, for a time, practiced "literary communism," which exposes the being-in-common that metanarratives obscure. An essay in finitude takes the recurring presence of metanarratives—and here I follow Cavell—as flights from finitude. Thoreau attempted to live deliberately beside a pond. Such things can be surveyed, but only in the knowledge that they are fed from elsewhere. The near draws the far, but only so far.

What is an essay in finitude? An explicit attempt to recount and so further the experiments that we are, to conduct them, as it were, from inside the curl. (Like Nietzsche, or perhaps because of him—Whitman too, his electric body—my thought is called from the shore to the sea, particularly where it is fed by rivers.) I have gathered my strokes into what might be called an aphoressay. (*Philosophy, Writing, and the Character of Thought*, which I published in 2018, provides reasons for this form, in part by way of exemplification. Please consider it a preface to this Preface.)

Intimately voiced and topical in scope, the aphoressay generates portraits of phenomena from decentered points of observation in order to navigate them. Such points are texts and usages brought into conversation, with examples generated to explicate how common dispositions and lines of thought are enacted. Eschewing views from everywhere and nowhere, the aphoressay experiments with occurrences that are less instances of universals than moments in a historical dissemination. And the aphoressay sounds them out for what they might hold in store if we enact them.

As a rhetorical whole, the aphoressay, like the essay, is occasional, responsive to encounters with people, texts, words, and images whose representativeness remains in question. I thus speak of the (r)essay to mark the responsiveness and ecstatic temporality of my thought. And like certain moments in the essay tradition (I think of Emerson's reliance on the stark, arresting sentence), the aphoressay, outside systematic recuperation, responds to its own development. It chases the suggested as well as the entailed. While accounting for itself, it also seeks the unanticipated and indulges the counterintuition. The whole thus fragments into multiple vantage points, and unlike the personal essay or the professional article, it refuses to weave them into an autobiographical trajectory or polemically navigate the polyphony. Marking usages, it intensifies them to test their worth for a further (r)essay. The propriety of that offer cannot be secured ahead of time, however, and so the aphoressay's experimental character is thorough. Replication is left to you. Each aphoressay is thus an offer to a future—yours, my own, ours, such as we are. "We?" Those who meet in this address, if only to decline an invitation or, upon accepting it, refuse or refine or embrace what is offered.

While the aphoressay enters philosophy obliquely, let me stress that fragmentation does not preclude generalization or scholarly contestation. Each aphoressay ventures an account in the context of others, favoring certain claims and emphases. Scholarly usages thus appear alongside examples of so-called ordinary language, including idiomatic sayings and song lyrics. I do not have the perspicuity to fathom where the first or final word lies, or who is worth our shared time. I take material life as I find it in my way, to paraphrase Emerson. Having been astonished in several corners, I (r)essay what pulses—that is, what makes me pause, listen, ponder, and reply.

Elsewhere, I have argued that forms, which include genres and logical-rhetorical operations, are modes of historical bearing, and can be read as such—namely, as exemplifications. Through such ventures, we bear history, or fail to; we can become disoriented, buckle under its weight, tire, or prove unable to bear fruit in its currents. In this, the aphoressay is no different than generative music, a painting or poem, or a dialogue or treatise. As Kant himself notes, his *Critiques* are the work of enlightenment. The aphoressay leaps before it looks. "I seemed, in the height of a tempest," Emerson writes, "to see men overboard struggling in the waves and driven about here and there. They glanced intelligently at each other, but 'twas little they could do for one another; 'twas much if each could keep afloat alone. Well, they had a right to their eyebeams, and all the rest was Fate" (Emerson 2003, 11). The power of this passage lies in not knowing whether one is looking down or up, a bearing I enact through quotation and conversation, without polemics or forced resolutions. The experiment thus flows between texts even as it flows between me and you (and within me and within you). This has analogues with musical compositions that initiate processes toward unexpected results, many of which are left to listeners (and to composers insofar as they are willing to become listeners). But here the composer is also a reviser (hence improviser), and so some results are reworked (sometimes more than once) to resound more intensely or draw out different resonances. Is this appropriate to ethical life? I recount and elaborate my "yes" in a second interlude.

Musical analogies do not free me from accounting for my inclusions and the terms that govern them, however. But in an essay, only so much can be said about such matters; at root, they are occasional. Nor have I tried to survey the whole of any literature or field hereby engaged. What I have done is introduce and engage distinct moments in the history of each concept to establish a scene of found, articulated proximities. The initial result is a field of possibilities that I negotiate toward working conceptions, which I offer to you, in turn.

Committing to the essay (and then dispersing it) means that worthy interlocutors are bypassed or treated abruptly. Both Kant and Locke, for example, are subjected to concentrated engagements, as are Epictetus and Rorty. When I move through broader currents of thought, I favor touchstones that resonate with other currents also moving through the text. Writing in a perfectionist vein, I focus on Emerson, Cavell, and Glaude, for example, which does not do justice to transcendentalism, ordinary language philosophy, or contemporary Black thought. I say this by way of acknowledgment rather than apology. Thinking in the currents of ethical life and their individuations, broad traditions or disciplines become texts in their nonsubstitutability, and that holds too for "perfectionism," a term I try to come by honestly.

One might object that this kind of particularism (I prefer "singularism") occurs less often than the above admits: "Texts by black thinkers and women seem engaged to evidence inclusiveness vis-à-vis those very terms." To the degree this is true, broad traditions or disciplines operate—that is the way inclusiveness, as a general project, becomes legible. I feel the weight of this objection. But it misses my bearing. The stakes of "whiteness," I argue, should concern perfectionists. And that requires engaging the swirls in which whiteness swims, which include conceptions of Black life. Various texts bear those currents differently, however, which opens a differential conversation that spills over without erasing the borders of traditions. Moreover, where whiteness is not the issue, texts are considered as they bear upon what calls for thinking regarding hope, trust, forgiveness, being-in-common, truth, shame, the scene of address, improvisation, etc. Not that positionality is ignored. But neither is it reified. Instead, it, or rather they—our positions are many—are set within dispositions, usages, and scenes that ethical life must navigate. Finally, whatever common ground I claim to find, I survey rather than presume. And that involves something more than the identities among us, a claim I develop in the first interlude.

III. PROVISIONS

I do not enter ethical life as an expert. Nor will I establish terms of engagement in the manner of discourse ethics. The second person remains a strong current in material life, but it must be constantly cultivated and modulated rather than simply invoked. Moreover, without abandoning them, what lies ahead does more than exchange validity claims. A forebear is Nietzsche, who approached "deep problems like cold baths: quickly into them and quickly out again" in the belief that there are "truths that are singularly shy and ticklish and cannot be caught except suddenly" (Nietzsche 1974, 343–44, 345). But the point is not only that, in an essay, conceptualization is neither jettisoned nor allowed to function as a simple universal, as Adorno observes (Adorno 1991). The occasional, experimental character of the aphoressay envelops the scene of address on which it relies.

Usages and examples are my plunge pools; passages as well. They are the "particular cultural artifacts," to use Adorno's phrase, that prompt an essay. This might have initiated a phenomenological reconstruction, but the scenes evidenced by those phenomena did not disclose eidetic structures. The breadth of acceptable usage surrounding each term, as well as that term's historical variety, opens a garden of forking paths whose differences can only be resolved at the level of conduct—that is, electing to hope, trust, and forgive in a particular manner. What an essay initiates must be elaborated elsewhere.

Consider an anticipatory example. Some distinguish hope from desire. Others are less inclined, even opposed to it. I side with the opposition. Should someone hope for something but not want it to come about, I would struggle to recognize their hope. But I think it a mistake to simply declare myself the winning party in this dispute. Some might have a narrower conception of desire than I. By establishing "desire" as a limited species of "wanting," they effect a distinction. In that affectation, one could imagine desiring something that one hopes does not come about—say, a liaison or some job that risks unhappiness. But to regard these distinctions as discoveries of eidetic structures is excessive. Each term is an ensemble that flows from a shifting center of uncertain gravity. What sometimes looks like a question to be settled theoretically is, when set back into ethical life, a scene of possibilities to consider and navigate, even in metaethical contexts. Since Aristotle, ethical theory has had ethical goals, even if it has handled them poorly. One is: don't mislead with overly neat distinctions or directives. Inclining people to believe that hope is categorically distinct from desire leaves them unduly interrogative regarding their hopes. It is better to worry about whether my hopes reflect my better desires than to isolate hope with the sealing wax of stipulation.

It remains customary to propose a general definition that gathers all that is said and done under a given term. My goal is not neutrality, however. Philosophy, at least as I would have it, refuses to defer to usage, even when clarified. I may begin with how people speak of hope, trust, and forgiveness, but only to establish scenes in which to play favorites toward an articulation that accounts for its nutritional value. When an essay enters ethical life, it does so as a fighting creed.

Down to its bearing, the book aims toward a representativeness, but in a manner that neither presumes nor guarantees that it will prove so. But that, I insist, is one dimension of being representative. Ethical life individuates us to the point of nonsubstitutability. Rather than insisting "that thou art," an aphoressay, while accounting for the scope and character of its confidence, proposes thoughts that, if successful, strengthen another's working feel for associated challenges.

It sounds overly grand, nostalgic even—*a venture in ethical life*. As if an author might, through a sculpted address, puncture convention, stated or unstated, and turn the rudder for another. Adorno insisted that "since the overwhelming objectivity of historical movement in its present phase consists so far only in the dissolution of the subject, without yet giving rise to a new one, individual experience necessarily bases itself on the old subject, now historically condemned, which is still for-itself but no longer in-itself" (Adorno 1974, 16). I know that unhappy feeling—subjectivity disappearing in an objectivity that *I* glimpse. By way of reply, Adorno used the aphorism to recognize the "evanescent as essential," if only to prevent the complete dissolution of subjectivity into the world of things. At the level of form, the sentences of *Minima Moralia* announce their author by way of negation. "Wrong life cannot be lived rightly" takes a stand and withdraws in six words (Adorno, 39).

I have refused that path. Certain hopes account for why, as does my trust, both in myself and known friends. I also have taken Adorno's realization that "the whole is the false" full circuit (Adorno, 50). As the first interlude shows in a general manner, staying true to that thought undoes its scope and the bravado behind which Adorno often hides. Unable to clearly mark the whole's emergence, descent, and departure, I find the evanescent neither inessential nor essential. An occurrence in its singularity marks a moment wherein we are for what we are in for; it puts us into question. That incipience is the foreground of ethical life and the site where text and reader meet if they prove equal to the occasion. And when they do, I will not gainsay reports of transformation.

IV. TUNING FORKS

Philosophy is morally serious if one allows it to be. The serious are willing to be happily surprised. "Every man has to learn the points of compass again as often as he awakes," writes Thoreau, "whether from sleep or from abstraction" (Thoreau 2008, 118). And not just regarding first-order questions. Like Bernard Williams, I, too, think that the "problems of finding a convincing, adult, and unmechanical way of approaching the subject must be found on each occasion" (Williams 1993, xiv).

To sharpen my interventions and improve their legibility, two interludes are offered. I have alluded to both already. You could skip them, I suppose. Or start with either. Each aphoressay can be read on its own, though it does not stand on its own. No intervention is self-sufficient, and to the point that a purely situational ethic is neither. Epistemic, ontological, and metaethical issues course through ethical life. I raise and pursue some because I am confident that no matter what, the questions they address will come between us. Even if we disagree, it's better to meet you there than presume my way is yours.

The first interlude concerns ontological and epistemic issues. It replies to questions concerning the historicity of thought and its impact on both our being-in-common and the status of truth. Clarifying what I have been calling our "overlapping existence," it situates my explorations of hope, trust, and forgiveness and provides them with a validity term that also proves relevant to the challenges that hope, trust, and forgiveness pose. Without such, whether "truth" or something else, generalizations do little more than warm the room.

Moral perfectionism orients each section of the book. Through show and tell, the second interlude accounts for it as a mode of moral philosophy by diving into the discretionary, imaginative dimensions of ethical life that come to the fore in hope, trust, and forgiveness. Each requires us to account for what we do without complete deference to conventions or principles or anything final. And yet, in each, we remain accountable. The second interlude characterizes that activity.

An essay in finitude acknowledges limits in our situatedness, including our control over what befalls us and what can be done about it. Living nevertheless proceeds. What is on offer in the pages that follow is thus something of an image (or series of images) of ethical life as well as an argument for its irreducibility, something that hope, trust, and forgiveness disclose. These tasks will not go away, a fact I celebrate throughout.

Hope

Life is interruptions and recoveries.
JOHN DEWEY

POST-ITS

Writing is always a sign of hope, even when it is pessimistic. Something, from me to you, wants saying. Without hope, there is no point.

A PHILOSOPHICAL LARDER

What is a philosophy of hope? Something provisional. A stock of needed materials or supplies. Something to chew on, convert into energy. Less strictly, a measure taken beforehand to deal with a need or contingency. Such a task less leaves the world as it is than readies us for what impends.

KEEP HOPE ALIVE

1988. Jesse Jackson is in Atlanta, addressing the Democratic National Convention: "Keep hope alive!" The phrase—more imploring than imperative—culminates the address, resounding four times in the last six sentences. Watch or listen to the speech. Beneath Jackson's vigor you can hear the timbre of desperation. 1988 is a long way from the 1964 Civil Rights Act, which sought to end segregation in public places as well as discrimination in matters of employment. It is also a long way from the Voting Rights Act of 1965, which sought to secure or at least protect voting rights for racial minorities. Looking back from 1988, such advances stood in stark contrast to the undertow of Reaganomics and the GOP's emerging "Southern strategy," which sought the allegiance of disaffected white voters with the promise of investment alongside a culture war that draped Black America in images of welfare, crack, and crime. ("You'd be better off if it wasn't for *them*.") That night in Atlanta, approaching the podium, Jackson could not have ascended in a current of felt progress or surveyed the crowd against a horizon of dreamlike possibility. "Keep hope alive!" As if it might die.

HAND IN HAND

Dyads, antitheses, and dichotomies measure the expanse of human possibility. Critical thought relies on various continua—good and evil, justice and injustice, truth and error, knowledge and ignorance. But sometimes we forget how terms work in tandem, stretching a horizon against which actions and beliefs, lives and institutions, are enacted, perhaps deliberately. Hope is bound to despair, like struggle to surrender. I say that because of the brutality of despair, which can manifest in phrases like "whatever" or "why bother," or an inability to get out of bed. The heaviness of despair is that of cement. We freeze as we twist toward missed opportunities, losses, and laments. Hope looks after the future, reaching out toward what might still be. When it seems impossible, tomorrow does as well.

A SUCCESSION OF FAILURE

Emerson's essay "Experience" confronts the loss of his son, Waldo, who died from scarlet fever. The boy was only six years old. (Having had it twice, at seven and then again at eight, I have some feel for what a fever can do to a tiny body.) But it is not Waldo's death that claims Emerson so much as the trial of living in its wake. A kind of survivor's guilt wracks certain passages: "The only thing grief has taught me, is to know how shallow it is" (Emerson 1996, 472). The guilt follows a bit later: "So it is with this calamity: it does not touch me: some thing which I fancied was a part of me, which could not be torn away without tearing me, nor enlarged without enriching me, falls off from me, and leaves no scar. It was caducous" (473). But there is something of a scar—the isolation that completes the paragraph: "The dearest events are summer-rain, and we the Para coats that shed every drop. Nothing is left us now but death" (473).

Emerson's recollection belongs to the opening of "Experience." The essay handles many topics, including chance, temperament, the limits of reflection, and, in the opening section, illusion, the "evanescence and lubricity of all objects," which Emerson terms the "most unhandsome part of our condition" (473). But "illusion" and the epistemic may be too staid to name the gut punch of loss. "Nothing is left us now but death." But maybe the point, the task, is to think them together—the epistemic and the existential. When one despairs of accord with the world, whether with oneself, another, even objects, experience drifts into a succession of failure, which is little more than a succession of accidents—"all our blows glance, all our hits are accidents" (473). The pun is acute: losses, wounds, but also the insubstantial—our attempts to grasp our world show us to be, predominantly, beings out of touch. And in the grip of loss and error, time falls into allegory, a recurring present without possibilities leading elsewhere. "Nothing is left now . . ." There might remain a succession of such presents, but therein, the "what" in what comes next is evacuated. Nothing arrives but our repeated failure to grasp where we find ourselves.

Emerson's scene contrasts a living succession from a lifeless one. Hope is one thing that makes the difference. In living succession, what arrives has not yet been fully determined but belongs to a scene of possibility that hope not only might arrange—in part—but also preserve. I add "preserve" because Emerson, as the essay itself aims to show, was wrong that "nothing is left now." But his hopelessness made that too difficult to see. "Experience" is, in part, an attempt to transform hopelessness (and a resulting isolation) into a comportment that conspires with its world toward a better one. The essay's close makes this plain and underscores the vital importance of hope: "Never mind the ridicule, never mind the defeat: up again, old heart!" (492). For what? The line is famous: Emerson imagines what he terms not just *a* but "*the* true romance"—namely, the "transformation of genius into practical power" (492). If hope dies, so, too, that dream.

HOPE IS A TROPE OF THE POSSIBLE

Hope is a way of inhabiting scenes of possibility, of being disposed toward possibilities. It occurs as what Emerson would term a mood, even a temperament if one is characteristically so, and brings with it epistemic effects, meaning it renders various aspects of the world more salient; others less so. I agree with Katie Stockdale, therefore, when she says that in hoping, the "situation appears a certain way to the agent," although I would hasten to add that the agent, being part of that situation, also appears in a certain way (Stockdale 2021, 17). One way to say what I have in mind is to rely on Heidegger's sense of moods, *Stimmungen*, which modulate how our being-in-the-world is disclosed at the level of comportment, which not only includes possible actions but their contexts and our own capacities and character, all in dynamic interaction. When we comport ourselves in hope, the possible glistens and we ready ourselves, even prove more inventive than we otherwise might be. Where nothing is possible, hope fades, and we contract.

But I do not want to say too much. There are other orientations toward possibility—calculation, optimism, or the rote confidence of habitual life. Moreover, moods come and go. Much of the day I do not find myself along a continuum of hope and despair. Hope is thus not a condition for the possibility of possibility but something of an intensifier, a way of bearing possibilities, of spinning them, sounding them out.

IN TURN

Hope's future is not without a past or pasts. What might prove possible does so not just against but through what has been. My future is drawn from who I have been, personally, socially, physiologically. (If you think otherwise, think about what leads you to think otherwise.) But hope resists mere repetition. It draws upon or springs from what has been, moving away from even as it pulls us forward or toward. Hope could almost be a trope of troping—

> turning into my own
> turning on in
> to my own self
> at last
> turning out of the
> white cage, turning out of the
> lady cage
> turning at last
> on a stem like a black fruit
> in my own season
> at last
> (Lucille Clifton, "turning," 1987)

Hope enables movement, away and into and away again. It is inceptual, recurrently, like Clifton's closing images—fruit, season, "at last" refusing a period.

PLAYING OPOSSUM

Cynicism: despair masquerading as knowledge.

AFTER DU BOIS

Co-work in the kingdom of culture crisscrosses the color line without erasing it.

WEATHER REPORTS

The hope of the hopeful falls outside the grammar of prediction, which concerns futures that one expects will come to pass. "Hope is not prognostication," Václav Havel writes, "it transcends the world that is immediately experienced and is anchored somewhere beyond its horizon" (Havel 1990, 181). Prediction moves among possible variations on known themes, their foreseeable interactions and likely results. Cautious optimism is oriented in this manner—"Signs are good, I think he'll come." So, too, resolute pessimism, which believes that the future will fall in line with the past or prove worse. Prediction does not trope the orders it surveys but lines them up or lets them brew like storms whose more general contours it forecasts. Hope, however, has its fingers on what is just out of sight and stretches to pull a possibility into view.

POCKET BOOKS

"As if all words weren't in fact pockets, in which now this thing, now that, now several things all at once, have been put" (Nietzsche 2013, 172–73). Ordinary language suggests something similar regarding "hope." Some usages bind it to definitive expectations: "The hope is that there will be a settlement soon." Others suggest something more amorphous: "The drug brought hope to thousands of sufferers." And others are even less definite: "When they started their life together, they were full of hope."

I will not try to locate a reality behind this whirl of appearances, nor turn one against the other. As Husserl argued, phenomena like memory—and hope, too, I think—do not appear as spatiotemporal objects, namely, through qualities that adhere to some thingly-substratum. This has methodological implications. Controlled experimentation usually relies upon a surplus of instances subjected again and again to the same conditions, with only genuine predicates surviving the melee. But one can't fill petri dishes with hope or cage it like an animal destined for nonlife. Thoroughly phenomenal, the appearing is the real in the case of hope.

Ever one to make life harder (and more remarkable), Derrida has shown (convincingly, I think), that phenomena of this order need threads of ideality to perdure and thus prove available to phenomenological analysis. (Before it arrives and departs a scene of reflection, the thoroughly phenomenal is inflected with well-traveled terms and phrases.) "Hope" is thus very much bound to usage, and without an enduring ground to which each usage refers. The term's polysemy reflects the phenomenon's disseminated character. It thus seems wrongheaded to offer a theory of hope that would sort through ordinary language like goats and sheep.

For the same reason, it also seems wrongheaded to explore hope without a sense for the many ways in which the word is used, as if, after the words were set aside (or seen through) *hope* might remain, pure and resplendent. I thus draw a sterner lesson from ordinary language philosophy than Tony Steinbock, who absorbs it into a phenomenological account of hope and other moral emotions. He finds usages as leading clues for an inquiry into the generative structures of experience and self-world interaction (Steinbock 2014, 23–24). But ordinary language philosophy also relies on usages to check undue generalizations as well as overly confident distinctions. Steinbock, for example, claims that "the hope experience" precludes a scenario in which "[we] first encounter dire circumstances and then . . . hope (for a different possibility)" (Steinbock, 165). But this says far too much. We are driving, gripped by neither hope nor despair. If anything, we feel listless because we are both hungover. Suddenly a storm rises and a twister fills the horizon. "I hope we get out of this alive," you say. Usage should not only initiate philosophical inquires but check its results.

But if some *sache selbst* does not await an inquiry into hope, the term still seems to name a deep current of human life. Victoria McGeer suggests that this is one reason why hope is described in so many ways—it is a "unifying and grounding force of human agency" (McGeer 2004, 101). I would prefer less centrifugal language—my hopes also multiply my futures and pluralize my present, expanding beyond a conceivable unity—but I see the point. Even if hope is not univocal, we are bereft if it fails to appear in any of its guises.

GETTING THERE FROM HERE

Hope may belong to despair in more than a semantic sense. "I believe that there is no such thing as hope without an experience of despair," Cornel West has written, adding, "All genuine hope has to go through the fire of despair" (West 1997, 57). And Rochelle Green concurs, working from Marcel (and in alignment with Kierkegaard): "Hope requires that the tendency to despair be present lest hope be an empty and meaningless expression" (Green 2019, 115). I see the point, I think. If one's longings are always within reach or foreseeable, one will get by with predictions. Only when the bridge is out (or not yet built) does one rely on hope for safe passage. I doubt that necessarily entails despair, however. Genuine uncertainty and doubt—vulnerability, too—may be enough, and human finitude provides them in abundance.

IN THE KNOW

"Ah, you're hopeful." I have heard this delivered with smug condescension on more than one occasion. As if I were hiding from something, some black hole sun closing all horizons. As if my accuser had braved a darkness beyond my ken or courage.

Perhaps. I cannot be certain of what they know, what they have undergone. But I wish they would return the favor.

Hope can be dirty, pugnacious, almost erotic in its refusal to answer to who knows best. Some wake up fighting no matter what the night portends.

A LITTLE KNOWLEDGE IS A DANGEROUS THING

Cynicism: metaphysics on the sly.

THINKING-IN-COMMON

Hope is individual. If you turn hopeless, my hope cannot take the place of yours. But individuals are social. My hope may rub off on you while another's despair brings you down. Or your struggle may shame my fears, my doubts, my excuses.

Hope is individual. It orients people, maybe you, maybe me, toward possibilities. And the course of expansion (or contraction) is singular. But people are social. When *I* hope, *we* are inevitably part of the future thereby fingered across our nested activities—home, work, a park, a neighborhood, each woven of social labor unfolding in ecosocial history. The sociality of my hope also circulates outside the jangle of causes and effects, however. If *we* become explicit, *we* become the object of a social hope: "The couple hoped renewed vows would save them."

Hope is individual, even when shared. It flickers and surges differentially, an uneven current distributed across a network of outlets, hence the exhortation: "Keep hope alive!" I wonder how the people gathered in Atlanta heard what Jesse had to say that night. How did his voice land? Were all those timpani identically struck? Or did some think: "Too late"? Others: "Yes . . . yes!"? And still others: "That's what I'm talking about!"?

No doubt some were cynical: "Good speech. But it won't get him the presidency."

But individuals are social, and hope can be shared. *We* can hope and thereby manifest what Ronald Aronson has termed a "sense of collective human capacity," which "presumes," he thinks, "that people have the energy and will to carry out such a project" (Aronson 2017, 14). Indeed. Consider: "The friends hoped their vacation would exceed expectations." But what does it mean for such a project (and the hopes it carries) to be ours? If only some of us bear the fruits of the project, including you, do you still feel unfulfilled? If so, there we are. Social hope is thus not merely an aggregate of individual hopes: "The goal raised the hopes of the team."

Can a "nation" hope? I don't consider it a mistake to say so, but it seems to mean something like: many citizens hoped X in a variety of ways. But I struggle to imagine a nation pulsing with the same hope. So do not let Aronson's "collective" conjure a macrosubject wielding a general will, which is why I prefer the term "collaborative" to "collective," although I am not denying the existence of collective hopes—that is, shared objects of hope, or distributed events of hoping. "The energy in the studio was electric. The band hoped the recording would capture some of what they were like live." But the distinction might have practical implications. If I want to nurture or sustain hope in the context of collective action, I might do well to ascertain and respond to the diverse character of my colleagues or comrades or teammates or neighbors. My experiences on teams, in bands, in neighborhood associations, and within academic units, small and large, suggest that a nuanced and differentiated feel for who we are (even when we are headed in the same direction) energizes. But the more general point is that we rely on each other, hope for each other, even hope together, because we do not exist as one.

STILL LIFE

I tend toward the future, turning toward it, imagining it, playing with it in and through my hoping. Not that I am unhappy to be here and now, but here is also always a beginning, and I would be there as well, anticipating, poised to pivot.

But then I run into Scott Parker's succinct insistence: "The past has weight." It does, and he is right to continue: "Without it there would have been no me, no this me" (Parker 2018, 49). A simple list of names convinces—persons, places, things, too, each a gnarl of inseparable strands. (I wonder what your list would be? What would contrapose my parents, Yvonne and Richard; my New Jersey and Nashville, Oregon and

Atlanta; my soccer balls, books, and LPs; my so many friends I didn't/don't deserve; the lovers I deserved even less and loved less well?)

One question (or two) is how we bear this weight, and what we bear thereby. Or so I find myself asking when Parker says, as if to remind us (and Emerson): "There is living, yes, but there is also the having lived" (Parker, 49). He is recalling, with pleasure, and some sense of loss, a place. Oregon. Its coast. Waldo Lake as well. And a time bound to a particular him (or times to hims), one beside a love he soon will wed. The reminder may be: don't forget to coil in our inevitable flight. Otherwise, you'll arrive without a sense of where or why, or rather, with an attenuated sense of both. Or worse still, in a paraphrase of Thoreau: beware arriving only to discover you had barely lived.

DO LOOK BACK

Some pasts remain, hovering. We needn't do much to recall them, and sometimes they butt in, regardless.

- Scarlet Fever. Twice. For the first I was seven, the second, eight. Same dream both times. A man in the distance is screaming. Running toward me. Our eye contact is unwavering, and with each stride it expands until his gaze absorbs me. Repeat. For days.
- A railroad trestle. Hungover. Below a crawl of earth that sometimes flows as water. I brought Dogen, believing I was on the verge of understanding him, not yet ready to find us both in that verging.
- "Fuck you," she said, our past in her mouth, soured and acidic. I had misled her in love. We were through. I had never heard her use that phrase before.
- A filbert orchard. Labor Day. Friends and family on creaky, white chairs atop the morning turf, listening to the wind and to Hilary and me, a promise trembling our lips.

The having-lived remains, but I approach it hoping not to repeat past failures and hoping to stay true to what remains current.

I may have missed Parker. Reading on, I wonder whether his reminder points as much to the present as to the past. He writes, lyrically, as if he were still beside Waldo Lake, "So here I am at lakeshore all alone eating a banana, listening to the water. Life no longer all in front of me but all around me, and from any number of perspectives that is what a person could go looking for and be satisfied to find, content to sit and gaze and remember and reflect and be patient, forever patient" (Parker 2018, 129).

This is a dizzying moment, the present of a recollection, hope displaced by patience, a kind of waiting without anticipation, more patient than agent. In another essay, Parker writes, by way of closing, "And we haven't yet learned how to sit still" (Parker, 179). A way of being there, less inert than resonating—it's almost musical, like the belly of a violin, varied according to its wood, shape, how dry it is.

Is it perverse to say I sometimes hope for such moments? Every now and then, say, perched on a trestle, I hope to fall into them. I hope that there and then some of what has been, what is, and whatever soon will be plays me.

LARGO

Nancy Snow argues that "we hope in and for the present in a deep sense," and that without it, "our lives would be largely bereft of meaning and lacking in positive affect" (Snow 2019, 17–18). More generally, she claims that "living in hope" makes it easier to find meaning in the here and now, even in the grip of a terminal illness. And that leads her to agree with Parker-Oliver that hope is a "belief that whatever happens will make sense" (17).

I find Snow's view somewhat at odds with my own, both substantively and methodologically. Because she wants to acknowledge hope among the terminally ill, she constructs an account that can include them among the potentially hopeful. The result is starkly attenuated, however, and evidence for why we should not theorize phenomena from extreme cases. When I think of people who are constitutionally hopeful, I think of people who want a good deal more than a world that makes sense. It does seem right to say that hope requires a world that makes sense, a claim she also affirms, but that is quite different from limiting hope to the belief that things will make sense (17). On my view, and now we are in the substantive aspects of my disagreement, hope disposes us toward situations as scenes of possibility; Snow refers to the "unsettled," whereas those in the grip of despair see foregone conclusions. Moreover, hope disposes us with the felt sense that things will go well. This may entail, among other things, happiness, pleasure, camaraderie, survival, growth, courage, honesty, even honor, and so also—and I certainly hope for this—a good death, all of which exceed the simple disclosure of sense. Anything one can recognize as happening must make a certain sense. But more importantly, hope seeks what we might call "sense plus," the event and the way of appearing that we want, say, death with dignity, death with controlled pain, death in the company of loved ones, or, as I would have it, death coupled with neither rage nor acquiescence but a wide-eyed anticipation.

I also find Snow's handling of the present a bit slippery. Before saying why, I think she is right to say that hope can name a way of being as well as a way of doing discrete things; one can be hopeful in more than one way. But living in hope does not simply attend to the present as opposed to the future. I say this because any "now" indicated must be a plurality of nows, as Hegel shows in "Sense-Certainty"—the now indicated and the now of the indicating. And this braid twists further in what James calls the specious present, which finds anticipation in every pulse of consciousness, what Snow refers to as an "attitude." Humans are proactively receptive. But the issue is not just the character of awareness. Any possibility is characterized in part as "not yet" or "to be determined." And so hope, directed toward that possibility, is expectant. In hope, I cannot separate the subjunctive from the indicative.

THERE MUST BE SOME MISUNDERSTANDING

Concerto in Black and Blue, by David Hammons, fills large gallery spaces left in the dark and illuminated by small blue lights given to those attending (and thereby coconstituting) the work. It constructs a place that allows participants their own blues in a scene doing at least double duty (darkness, blackness), with connotations of a bruising search for orientation in a world dimly lit. The fluidity of the scene allows it to be different things to different participants whose movements and negotiations nevertheless "ensemble," as a verb, or so they are directed by the title's use of "concerto," which calls to mind Bartok's Concerto for Orchestra in that it forgoes a discrete soloist in order to make more room for each instrument without abandoning the ensemble.

Hammons's work exposes the kind of sociality that flows through hope as we live it, evidencing the ambiguity that Beauvoir rightly aligns with a kind of solitude amid bonds, relations, and negotiations. It also, in establishing the site for that disclosure, opens questions concerning art's ability to rework the world, thereby disclosing the world upon which its intervention and so hope rests. The work thus stages the plight of hope even as it enacts it.

Traversing the site arranged by Hammons's installation, Fred Moten seems to mark yet resist the emptiness underwriting yet permeating Hammons's installation: "Understand this as a play of presences, not absences—or of presences held within a general absence that is, in fact, not there" (Moten 2017, 226). Typing and rereading Moten's line, a general absence comes into view even though it is not there, cannot be there if we think of being-there factually, as the play of a presence, say, the movement of a small blue light held by a hand in darkness. And it lingers as Moten riffs: "It's winter but it's Sunday and the fire's already been lit. The nothing that is not there appears, but only from its own perspective, to surround the nothing that is" (Moten, 226).

Moten's (r)essay of Hammons maintains multiple conversations. One concerns Stevens's "The Snow Man," particularly the "mind of winter," the mind of one "who listens in the snow, / And nothing himself, beholds / Nothing that is not there and the nothing that is" (Stevens 1971, 54). I am drawn to this series of nothings because Stevens is almost always on my mind and because I consider aspects of this ontology to be inescapable, whatever one hopes (Lysaker 1999a, 1999b, 2002). But there is more than one way to cast it, as Moten shows, and in a manner I would (r)essay to extend my efforts to locate this ontology within, without effacing, differential histories. Call this following after my hopes, twisting back as they turn toward.

In Stevens's poem, the mind of winter is decisively aesthetic rather than moral, at least on Stevens's terms. This mind is cold, and a longtime cold; it does not hear misery on the wind. Nor, in a bare place—some spot in North America (the speaker names pine, juniper, and spruce)—does the snow-mind consider what transpired to empty the expanses that so many of Stevens's poems traverse. The Huron, Mississauga, Iroquois, and Oneida all lived in what is now Connecticut. One could say, turning in a different but overlapping swath of historical violence, that the snow-mind refuses to write, feel, hope, and imagine in what Christina Sharpe figures as a *wake*, which would require the poem to "occupy and to be occupied by the continuous and changing *present* of slavery's as yet unresolved unfolding" (Sharpe 2016, 13–14; emphasis added).

Two absences then—a general absence, always there but not present, and, thinking now of Stevens, in Stevens, the unmarked fate of those buried in and erased from the scenes he continually reimagines as the shape of a general absence. And in marking both, thinking the former through the latter, Moten refuses to categorically separate the aesthetic and the moral (or to simply combine them). I say this because he refuses the snow-mind as a white mind (what I have until recently thought of, following Benjamin, as the mind of the victor). "Wallace Stevens is a wall, primordially white," Moten also writes, blindingly white, perhaps (Moten 2017, 226). And yet, Moten does not completely refuse the thought that Stevens poetizes: "The false ubiquity of absence, manifest as the proliferation of borders, must be radically and improperly misunderstood" (Moten, 227).

A misunderstanding arrogated by an imperative renders the impropriety of Moten's reading discerningly insistent. *My* bad, it writes along the white wall, underscoring a difference of hand that ripples across the generalized absence that must obtain if any borders or limits (any this and that, here and there, now and then, you or me) are to appear in their differences, and differentially over time. In *Concerto in Black and Blue*, the same room proliferates into many ensembles, a new work emerging with each circuit. "And the trick, of course," one I consider hopeful, "is this refusal of border under the constraint of border's constant imposition. *In* can't simply act as if *and's* segregation, however unreal, doesn't produce absolutely real effects" (Moten, 226).

CAGEAN INTERLUDE (WITH AND WITHOUT FEELING)

Find a piano.
Tap with fingers. Twelve times. Lid closed.
Open lid. Seven times, press keys slowly. Lids closed.
Open lid.
Cross hands.
Rap with knuckles. Seven times.
Press keys firmly twelve times. One
eye open.

Return to Moten's refusal of "border under the constraint of border's constant imposition." Move between its "must" and the energy of its phrasing as it moves toward its subject matter and toward you. This activity, in its insistence, pulses. It does not say, "Keep hope alive." It is alive in a kind of hope syntactically felt if not thematically asserted. I am thinking of its pulse against Stevens's purportedly blank ontology. Moten's refusal of border does not arise because he becomes "nothing himself," hence aesthetic, hence amoral. That is a snow job. Rather, almost inversely, Moten becomes something, someone who marks the demarcations and varied absences of our world, and revises what they could be while acknowledging what they have been. Heard as an inducement, his refusal—and its *must*—hovers between an invitation and a command to replay a general absence (neither here nor there) by (r)essaying some things that very much are. That's me too, I think, if also not me.

HOPE AND DESIRE

Desire cuts several figures. There is lack, which Robert Hass, in "Privilege of Being," figures as an intense distress that offends a creation full of itself, and which enchants "out of death for an hour or so" those hollowed out by eros (Hass 1989, 69). There also is an inability to leave well enough alone, which I find operative, if narrowed, in Adam Smith's suggestion that, by nature, humans truck, barter, and exchange (Smith 1981, 25). And there is an insistent need to enact some bourgeoning possibility, which Maggie Nelson, as if arguing with Hass, celebrates as the "pulsing of a pussy in serious need of fucking—a pulsing that communicates nothing less than the suckings and ejaculations of the heart" (Nelson 2009, 72). In each modality, and all seem on point, the not-yet is sought: something sweet, one more revision, another's lips, a full run and the abandon it enacts.

As the not-yet attenuates, so, too, desire—nothing to long for, no energy to vent into doing. Despair is not simply sadness, therefore. In its grip, we dwindle toward the inert. Not that desire's ebb always indicates despair. A studied indifference to the world of appearance, which Stoicism valorizes, exits the hope-despair continuum altogether. Contra Terry Eagleton, therefore, I do not take a "spirit of courageous resignation" to stand in opposition to hope (Eagleton 2017, 85). Yes, to be done with wanting is also to be done with hoping. But not all negations are opposites. The sweet, the sour, and the savory are all undone (rather than opposed) by the flavorless.

DESIRE AND HOPE

Hope seeks the better, anxious for its arrival. It is thus not free of desire. (Why should it be?) As it inclines us toward the future, hope induces action with something akin to eros in a broad sense—an affirmative, dispositional orientation that moves us toward an objective. This is what hope feels like: a pulse of energy. It not only animates the present with direction but confers a degree of proprioceptive "I can" that does not simply derive from evidence. (Hope is something other than confidence, therefore, although it might thicken it.)

INDISCRETIONS

Hope's vision is dreamlike—the actual lit with possibility, which wraps alternatives in a hazy allure. Not quite (because not yet) real, what is hoped for bears the contoured indefiniteness of the imagined.

For some, dreams unveil what reflection cannot or will not acknowledge. In their strange scenes, dreams can outsmart reflection and its ego adjustments. Benjamin and Leiris regard dreams as fuel for epistemic aspiration, indications of something larger than conscious inquiry can essay, as if the waking day were too prosaic, each person, place, and thing, each plot a discrete function in an accumulating equation rather than a fragmentary glimpse into wider circuits and currents.

My nights are less intriguing. Or my unconscious lacks their courage. Or, my wishful thinking is of the waking sort. But this turn toward dreams, this hope for dreams is dreamy in its own way. And it beckons toward a site where the adventitious is worth pursuing, tarrying with, husbanding. "Dream is not revelation," Leiris insists. "If a dream affords the dreamer some light on himself, it is not the person with closed eyes who makes the discovery but the person with open eyes, lucid enough to fit the thoughts together" (Leiris 1987, xi). This is how hopes move me—an inducement to continue down a refreshed and thereby refreshing line.

DESPITEFULNESS

Because hope ebbs and flows, comes and goes, and as it will, hope seems different than a reflective or propositional attitude concluding an inferential chain. "And therefore, I decided to be hopeful": not an impossible phrase, but an odd one.

But this is not to say that explicit stances have no bearing on hopefulness. Speaking of Black lives in general, Eddie Glaude has written, "For us, hope has always come with a heavy dose of realism. It couldn't be otherwise in a world such as ours, where the color of your skin closes off certain possibilities from the moment you draw your first breath" (Glaude 2016, 7). The lessons of experience underwrite hope. The innocent, the naive, the wise, the betrayed or disappointed—hope arcs differently in each. But hope never quite settles to the pulse of prudence. As Glaude sees it, hope persists despite the forces that chasten it.

Twenty years before Jackson's address, MLK also felt the need to keep hope alive. "King the exemplary dreamer," observes Cornel West, "was painfully coming closer to what both Malcolm X and W. E. B. Du Bois concluded before him—that America was a nightmare for the poor and the working-class black masses and that within America, oppressed black people would not win" (West 2018, 326). And so West wonders, perhaps to himself as well, "Was King's great rhetorical eloquence a desperate attempt to convince himself and others to hold on to a hope that was fading in the face of an avalanche of white backlash, class war from above, and imperial decay for without and within?" (West, 329). At times, what might yet be persists through a recursive dream, *Keep hope alive,* one stoked by the saying of it, the intake of breath, an occasional vibrato. And in less explicit moments as well—a blank rhythm, a hidden rhyme, the bob of a head getting ready to be ready.

This sense of hope surviving through an ongoing manner of performance, a way of keeping lively that feeds and is fed by hope (and no doubt other modes, say, stubbornness or anger), sets me alongside Joseph R. Winters, who imagines a melancholic hope that acknowledges a history of violence and inhabits it inventively.

On the one hand, he rightfully and creatively finds a point of noncontradictory overlap between hope and melancholy. The latter, taken as a "mode of attunement," enables one to find and tarry with, by witnessing, historical oppression, violence, and irretrievable loss—in short, tragedies (Winters 2016, 54). But that attunement and the acknowledgment it demands need not exhaust what history, or rather, certain histories might yet enable. The task is thus to live them in a manner that "signifies both a wound and an opening," and thereby "suggests that better horizons and possibilities might be enabled and opened by a heightened and more vulnerable awareness of the wounds and damages that mark our social worlds" (Winters, 251).

What is this manner? Before answering, allow me to share an observation by Katie Stockdale. Thinking about contexts where hopes arise in and through fearful situations, she states, "I also think that oppression can shape the character of people's hopes," and something like that is operating in Winters's text (Stockdale 2020, 122–23). Melancholy attunes him to historical currents that define, in part, what he hopes for—cessations, exits, but also contrasts and alternatives. Melancholy hope, like Stockdale's fearful hope, is not an admixture of opposites but an overall disposition, a valence that hope might assume.

Winters finds melancholy hope underwriting what he terms "literary jazz," working with multiple examples, including Ellison and Morrison. But rather than keep to the literary, I want to stay with those observations that also pertain to jazz as a musical performance, and because they capture some of what I have argued about hope's temporality, its recurrent inceptuality. Winters notes how Ellison's prose swings, taking that to be a "back and forth movement," which insures that "hope and possibility are always shaped by and determined by the way we remember and imagine the past" (Winters 2016, 87). But that is not all—in fact, the rub lies with whatever one does in the movement that swing establishes. When Winters also discusses Ellison's "awkward sense of time" and its relation to Armstrong as well as their performance of a certain kind of invisibility—living in breaks and cuts—I find a clear invocation of syncopation, playing ahead of or behind the beat, which is one of the ways in which Ellison (as cited by Winters) describes invisibility: "Sometimes you're ahead and sometimes behind. Instead of the swift and imperceptible flowing of time, you are aware of its nodes, those points where time stands still or from which it leaps ahead. And you slip into the breaks and look around" (Winters, 92–93; quoting *Invisible Man*).

Earlier I argued that hope tropes, and so intensifies possibilities. I would add, with the help of Winters, that in doing so it swings and syncopates, and this allows it to be melancholy—I would also add "honest"—without falling into despair.

DREAM #7

She steps outside, without fear.

WORLDLY HOPES

In my hands, hope refuses faculty psychology, which draws neat lines between the cognitive, conative, and affective, a trio recalling Plato's tripartite theory of the soul, although Plato cuts all from the same erotic cloth, thus avoiding a modular psychology. I thus wonder how my account relates to what Adrienne Martin terms the "orthodox definition of hope," which views hope as a combination of belief and desire (Martin 2014). I feel compelled to address the point because, as Blöser and Stahl report, a swath of literature over the last twenty years has debated whether the orthodox definition is sufficient or requires some addition (Blöser and Stahl 2020, 2).

One principal objection to the orthodox view is that two persons could have the same desire, say, to live, and the same belief, say, that they have a 1 percent chance of recovering from cancer, and yet one person could be hopeful about surviving and the other not, which suggests that hoping is not reducible to belief and desire. If it were, their disposition would be identical.

Before proceeding, a confession. Usages are orthodox for a range of users. I say this because if one works from the texts of Heidegger or Dewey or Bloch, it is unlikely that one would approach and assess hope as a compound of two, simpler states or dispositions, or pull hope out of the circuit of interactions that is being-in-the-world. I thus wonder whether one can neatly separate the desire from the probability calculation. Wanting something may lead me to see myself in the surviving group, as might felt obligations to dependents. And differently situated agents may interpret the probabilities differently. If I am a woman used to medical gaslighting, that 1 percent may look one way, whereas a history of entitlement may lead me to see myself among those left standing. That said, Martin's point really concerns the logical possibility. Imagine that all the attendant, contributing variables are equally present and the two still differ; one thinks, "one in a million" and lights up at the one, whereas another is undone by the million. I appreciate the counterexample, therefore, even if its logic presumes that its base terms are genuinely discrete, and that seems off, particularly in the matter of hope. Not that we should avoid terms like "belief" and "desire," but I cannot take them as ontological simples, and so I am not disposed to affirm or modify the orthodox definition.

And yet (and when isn't there an "and yet"?), I appreciate Andrew Chignell's suggestion that hope not only entails a probability assessment lit with desire but also a corresponding "disposition to focus on a desired outcome [in a specific way] as one whose possibility is unswamped by the salience of countervailing considerations" (Chignell 2023, 45). I favor the addition because it reminds us that hopes can and often do face countervailing considerations. I also think that "focus" resonates with my sense that hope intensifies scenes of possibilities, adding salience to various dimensions of a situation that are eclipsed by despair or obscured by stoic detachment. But I want to say more about the specific ways in which that focus operates, and more about that upon which it operates. Hope not only focuses upon the hoped-for but rotates it through anticipation and imaginative variation, hence its long association with daydreaming. If you want to, you could say this is what happens when cognition and desire mate; hope tropes in a manner that qualitatively expands the hoped-for. Second, hope not only discloses the hoped-for but also possible ways of addressing it. The hoper belongs to the future that hope anticipates, which allows hope to intensify inventiveness. Third, hope's futurity circulates through various scenes of realization and frustration, disposing us toward possible futures. It can thus fund deliberation even when it focuses upon the improbable.

This may seem a lot to pack into hope. But that seeming might be an effect of the modularity and subjectivism of the orthodox view. Every manner of self-finding (Heidegger's *Befindlichkeit*) is worldly, a dramatic scene of interaction. (A Deweyan would say that hope is a function of that scene.) Thought in this way, hope does more than focus on a discrete, desired possibility. It discloses a future possibility for the hoper, and in a manner that renders them more alert and poised for differences that might make a difference in outcome. Hope not only intensifies a hoped-for in my perceptual field, therefore, but a possibility (or range of possibilities) for my agency, and in a manner that intensifies my agency. This is what it means to say that "hope is a trope of the possible"; a possibility for us (to hope or not) transforms the character of what is possible for us.

IDLE HOPES ARE THE DEVIL'S PLAYTHINGS

Hope seems bound to action. Not only do I desire that for which I hope, but absent other desires that prove stronger, I also am committed to its realization, and to the point that I am prepared to contribute to its realization. I say this because should someone announce a hope—say, that a local school will survive diminishing enrollments—but remain passive in the face of clear chances to realize it, their sincerity would be questionable. Barring clear, mitigating circumstances, I would seriously doubt that they really hoped the school would survive. Not that they hoped it would fail. That goes too far. But hope is never listless, and so a hope that refuses to pursue its object is empty—less an erotic pursuit than a speculative, denuded gaze (if not an outright pose).

Put the matter in this way: hope seems absent if we remain passive in the face of clear chances to help realize the hoped-for—because Adrienne Martin has observed, rightly, that one can hope for certain outcomes and not really take steps to realize them (Martin 2014, 65–66). Her example is a primary election for a party to which one is opposed. One may hope that a certain candidate wins the primary and so stands for the general election, but may not campaign for that candidate or even vote for them. In fact, one cannot vote in that primary if one is not a member of the party in question, at least in the United States. But one can hope that the less noxious person wins. And that seems to allow hope to arise in a manner uncoupled from any concern for means to realize it. But should a chance arise to influence the likelihood of the hope-for-outcome—say, members of the rival party ask your opinion about the matter—and should you not take that chance, that suggests, I think, that one's hope is marginal at best, possibly even self-deceptive. Like all talk, hope cheapens when one refuses to walk it.

But it would be a mistake to think the presence of hope compels pursuit of the hoped-for outcome. We are a mixed bag, often wanting many things and even feeling conflicted about what we want. I might still hope that another will come to love me, but given the heartache caused by their not doing so, I might pull away, even avoid them, thus diminishing the likelihood that they would come to feel as I do. Does this mean I cease hoping they might reciprocate? Not necessarily. In fact, I might dream even more intensely that they will have a change of heart. But there might be things I also hope for, say, a family, and so I move on. Or maybe I just no longer can stand the recurring disappointment. In disposing us, hope nevertheless operates within a multifaceted erotic field.

HOPELESS CASES

Amid these provisional specifications—rather than categorical distinctions (call this [r]essaying the labor of the concept)—one might wish to mark the hopelessly hopeful, those who are so convinced their wishes will come true that they fail to do what is needed to help bring them about.

Terry Eagleton links a refusal to transfigure the present with optimism. "An optimist," he writes, is "someone who is bullish about life simply because he is an optimist. He anticipates congenial conclusions because that is the way it is with him" (Eagleton 2017, 2). On the far end of this type lies what he calls the optimalist, a kind of blinkered fool who genuinely believes that things will turn out for the best and greets whatever turns out as the best. Optimism orients us with less abandon, but even the optimist, Eagleton thinks, is full of "trust in the essential soundness of the present," which renders it conservative (Eagleton, 4).

Eagleton's distinction calls to mind (then) Senator Obama's book, *The Audacity of Hope*. The title comes, Obama writes, from a sermon by Rev. Jeremiah A. Wright Jr., but even while recalling this, he aligns it with a "relentless optimism in the face of hardship" buoyed by self-reliance and determination (Obama 2006, 356). In fact, in place of hope the book sometimes defers to optimism and confidence regarding the soundness of the American people and what they can politically redress, despite what Beltway politics conveys (Obama, 54, 149).

But to an extent, that fate—call it a willingness to play ball—is integral to hope. Hope conspires. It need not affirm the "essential soundness" of the past and present, but it does proceed as if untapped potentials remain for us to sound out and play. Eagleton's account thus has an air of stipulation. Its own hope seems to need an enemy, some idiot man-child against whom its longings shine. (I sometimes wonder: What do we gain when we castigate the thoughtless, and as a general type? Are we trying to recover them, either by provocation or instruction? Or is the address for another? Does the philosopher need the herd like a narrow humanism needs the animal?) However, I am compelled by an indirection in Eagleton's presentation: "Only if you view your situation as critical do you recognize the need to transform it" (Eagleton 2017, 5). Like art on Adorno's terms, hope articulates an "*it shall be different*," and pulls us toward it.

CAREFUL WHAT YOU PLAY FOR

But maybe playing ball is a prison sentence. Calvin Warren asks us to consider just this in his essay "Black Nihilism and the Politics of Hope." Initially he limits his critique to what he terms "the Political," associating it with the promise of an actualized equality for all, locating the promise in "The Declaration of Independence" (Warren 2015, 216). But that promise has not been kept. Nor can it be, he thinks, because the cultural logic underwriting "the Political" is anti-Black. To inflame Black hope, therefore, at least regarding "the Political," is to entice Black folks to pursue their own domination. Warren refuses: "Black nihilism resists emancipatory rhetoric that assumes it is possible to purge the Political of anti-Black violence and advances *political apostasy* as the only 'ethical' response to Black suffering" (Warren, 218).

Warren's claim is provocative. It not only rejects but castigates a view that many seem to hold, one articulated by Jenny Hansen, who writes, "Hope is a kind of temperament that serves as the condition for the possibility of envisioning profound political change" (Hansen 2008, 188). According to Warren, the hope that "the Political" might change profoundly is a condition contributing to the perpetuation of anti-Black violence. I have kept "the Political" in scare quotes because I am unsure how to delimit it. It could cover everything from electoral politics to judicial review to government-funded agencies to civic infrastructure. But my concern is less vagueness than the dialectic of enlightenment which, through the labor of the concept, renders a vast field immanent to itself, thus effacing differences that make a difference at the level of the conduct of life. (And to be sure, Horkheimer and Adorno fall prey to this dialectic as well, for example, with their notion of "the culture industry," even enlightenment itself.)

But for all that, one can still see vast grounds for deep skepticism about US political efforts, delimit them as we will, to rigorously and transformatively address anti-Black racism and violence. To believe that remains possible given business as usual is to fall prey to what Eddie Glaude has called, after Baldwin, "the lie," a "broad and powerful architecture of false assumptions by which the value gap is maintained" (Glaude 2020, 7). And while Warren and Glaude are in some ways vastly different, they agree that US history pronounces again and again that if Black lives matter at all, they matter less.

I have turned into Warren's visceral critique because it underscores that hope travels multiple terrains and conspires with multiple currents and agencies, some of which, possibly many of which, are dead set against the hoped-for ever coming to fruition. I also was and remain struck that Warren's essay begins by distinguishing a hope that moves within "the Political" from "hope as a spiritual concept—a concept that always escapes confinement within scientific discourse," because if we accept this distinction, "we can suggest that hope constitutes a 'spiritual currency' that we are given as an inheritance to invest in various aspects of existence" (Warren 2015, 219). I am not sure how proximate my essay is to this currency and inheritance; "spiritual" gives me pause, even when offered in scare quotes. Warren also later claims that anti-Blackness underlies the "categories that constitute the field of Ontology," which sets the scare quotes in bold, to put it mildly. But I do think the concept of "hope," thought through its myriad usages, involves currents that enable one to invest in various aspects of existence, which is to articulate my hope for "hope."

DESPERATE VIEWS CALL FOR DESPERATE MEASURES

Kant's name is often associated with "hope" in a kind of mention-without-use sort of way. Most likely this is because he believes that answering the question, "What may I hope?" is one of reason's chief interests. And anyone willing to philosophize about hope must agree, to some extent.

As Claudia Blöser shows, Kant addresses hope in a variety of texts and contexts, including the likelihood of our realizing the highest good, improving our pursuit of it, and seeing that good realized in (and as) an ethical community (Blöser 2020). In each case, she shows that, unlike wishing, hope requires rational grounds for hoping that any of these ends can and will be realized. Moreover, the hoper must find these grounds in the knowledge that one's own powers are insufficient to realize these ends, and that the existence and character of these grounds cannot be known in the way that we know objects of nature. For Kant, then, hope is a way in which finite beings orient themselves toward the future in their finitude. So far, so good. But I would be surprised if many found hope in how Kant accounts for these grounds.

On the one hand, a racist racialism courses through the nature in which Kant finds reason to hope that peace and the rule of law will spread and enlarge our rational capacities, at least at the level of the species. "Too weak for hard labor, too indifferent for diligent [labor], and incapable of any culture" is how Kant imagines native peoples. According to Kant, they are, "despite the proximity of example and ample encouragement—far below the Negro, who undoubtedly holds the lowest of all remaining levels that we have designated as racial differences" (Mikkelsen 2013, 186–87). Bleak. But even among those Kant finds adequately graced by reason, progress is an ironic result: "Individual men, and even entire peoples, give little thought to the fact while each according to his own ways pursues his own end—often at cross purposes with each other—they unconsciously proceed toward an unknown natural end, as if following a guiding thread; and they work to promote an end they would set little store by, even were they aware of it" (Kant 1983, 29). In fact, Kant suggests we should be thankful to "nature for the incompatibility, for the distasteful, competitive vanity, for the insatiable desire to possess and also to rule" that warps the wood from which nothing straight can be made (Kant, 32).

Here is Kant's argument. Venal, myopic pursuits of commercial wealth and political power nevertheless cultivate the rule of law and peace, if only to mitigate their most destructive effects, particularly war. And that, in turn, cultivates a capacity for autonomy, since the resulting laws are given from and to ourselves, or in the case of persons, and moving from war among peoples to strife among persons, duties are ventured and obeyed.

On this account, Kantian hope lies somewhere between a kind of despair (or grief) and a contentment afforded by a religious double consciousness that allows one to bear the slings and arrows of outrageous fortune. Or so I think when I read Kant's "Speculative Beginning of Human History": "Contentment with providence and with the course of human things as a whole, which do not progress from good to bad, but gradually develop from worse to better; and in this progress nature herself has given everyone a part to play that is both his own and well within his powers" (Kant, 59). And this, in turn, gives us courage to bear burdens and "not neglect our own obligations to contribute to the betterment of ourselves" (Kant, 58). (I call this a double consciousness, in Emerson's sense, because neither providence nor "human things as a whole" can clarify or direct particular interactions. To access them, one must enter the jet stream of the supposed a priori and then courageously return to the scrum.)

I have tried to imagine the longing, commitment, and energy Kant's position confers. What if I hoped in this manner? What would happen to my hope (and hopes)? I do not find much hope in a text that lands more comfortably in contentment and courage, and only after securing a ticket to providence. But I also think Kant's hope is underwritten by a view of nature too fantastic to countenance. In his "Idea for a Universal History with a Cosmopolitan Intent," he asks, "Is it truly rational to assume that nature is *purposive* in its parts but purposeless as a whole?" (Kant, 35). The question, at first glance compelling, proves less so when we attend to Kant's sense of the parts. The essay's first thesis states, "All of a creature's natural capacities are destined to develop completely and in conformity with their end" (Kant, 30). Really? Begin with prenatal developments that lead to death or the odd patterns of cell growth we call "cancer," or turn to congenital defects, some of which require a pluralism of human ends if we are to do better than trap people in the rhetoric of "disability."

But note, Kant does not really defend the claim that our capacities have clear ends destined for completion beyond a vague wave at "external and internal observation" (Kant, 30). What he does invoke is the specter of the accidental and adventitious, as if hope cannot persist in such a world: "If we stray from this fundamental principle, we no longer have a lawful but an aimlessly playing nature and hopeless chance takes the place of reason's guiding" (Kant, 30). But wait—the passage quoted earlier presents purposive parts as evidence for the purposiveness of the whole. But now that we are among the parts, evidence is slight, whereas the specter of an unordered whole does the heavy lifting. While not textbook circularity, the argument is far from exemplary. "Because of A, accept B." "Why should I accept A?" "Without A, we can't have B." But that is not the real problem. Kant secures hope by banishing the odd, the variant, and the unusual from nature, and by abandoning our embodied, empirical lives to *homo oeconomicus*, only to desperately imagine that eventually our propensity for awfulness can be corralled by a sense of duty and the rule of a law. Such a view does little to keep hope alive.

AS PLANNED?

Patrick Shade has written, "Hope shares much with wishing and planning" (Shade 2001, 54). He finds planning amid hope because, on his account, hope is bound to available means for the realization of its objective. And should those means be missing, Shade believes that something more like wishing is underway. This is too neat for me, and in two ways. Suppose I fall in love and hope another will love me, too. But not only do I not have any means in mind, I also am averse to the thought of finding the means to make them love me. Shade might suggest that by making my feelings known, say, by asking for a date, I am in the planning phase. But this says too much, I think. My goal in these instances is to let another know I am interested, not manufacture their love in return. With admitted trepidation, I leave the reply to them. Perhaps that just means my hope is really a wish on Shade's terms. Because I am averse to overwriting ordinary language in this instance, I will not concede the point. To speak of hope's extrafactuality is to stress both its departure from the grammar of prediction and its radical dependence on facticity, a dependence that proves more conspicuous in the absence of clear means, an absence underwriting the margin of our hopes. Hope may not reach toward the necessarily impossible, but it often stares down the "I'm not sure how or if it's even possible." And it bends with the road ahead.

But I do not want to overstate the disagreement. Shade argues that persistence sustains hope, and that includes patience, which "requires attention to actual conditions and to their pregnancy" (Shade, 81). This is what

I mean when I say that hope is bound to action, which falls into agreement with Margaret Urban Walker, who distinguishes hoping from wishful thinking by reminding us that hope readies us for, rather than takes the place of, action (Walker 2006, 53). To hope is to be poised to seize those moments in which our objective glimmers with realization. But that may require us to hold tight while the world stews.

GIVE US NOW OUR DAILY TREAD

"We cannot walk alone," King instructs (King 1986, 218). What links us, besides perhaps our arms? With many things in mind, including the charisma of just action, King appeals to *soul force*, as he also did in 1957 in a memo to Roland Smith and Daisy Bates, president of the Arkansas NAACP and advisor to the Little Rock Nine, which later appeared in the *Atlanta Daily World* (King 1986, 218; 1957). Soul force is a good name for hope, for its complexity and power.

THE MARGIN OF OUR HOPE

Early in *The Principle of Hope*, Ernst Bloch writes, "This book deals with nothing other than hoping beyond the day which has become" (Bloch 1986, 10). In hope we stretch into pursuit.

When Jesse Jackson implores the DNC to "keep hope alive," he is willing his audience into an open vision of a day beyond what has become. And when he warns against surrender, he is imploring his audience not to fold their plans and goals, even their dreams, into the political logic of his day. Hear his account of Michael Dukakis, whose 1988 campaign was confronted with the Willie Horton affair, which cynically marshaled, in the name of being tough on crime, a still-operative fear of unregulated (read policed, if not jailed) Black male agency. In his speech, Jackson praises Dukakis for not descending to demagoguery, and for "guiding his campaign out of the crowded field without appeal to the worst in us" (Jackson 1988). The worst? Dukakis campaigned in a manner that aspired to something beyond what had become the *realpolitik* of his day, a hope somewhat abandoned by Bill Clinton, whose 1992 campaign promised to "reform" welfare, which he eventually did under the aegis of "personal responsibility," thus resignifying structural, often racialized inequalities as personal moral failings.

In the 1960 presidential election, only 118,550 votes separated Kennedy and Nixon in the popular vote. And while Nixon took more states, Kennedy won the Electoral College. Looking back, Jackson locates Kennedy's victory in "the margin of our hope." Looking beyond the day that had become somehow won the day. I stress this because Darren Webb is right to worry that overly cheery discourses that imagine a hopeful future requiring little change may in fact be discourses of acquiescence, even subjection, say, to neoliberal economies of managed precarity and austerity (Webb 2019, 139–40). But hope always expresses a kind of discontent and so operates at the limits of the legible, and persists, transformatively. Recalling Beauvoir, I think it could be yet another name for our ambiguous facticity, less radiant than "freedom," but more ambiguous and fleshier, down to its slide between subject and object, the hope I feel and the hopes I have.

CONSPIRE OR RETIRE

"Do not seek to have everything that happens happen as you wish," Epictetus writes, "but wish for everything to happen as it actually does happen, and your life will be serene" (Epictetus 1928, 491). *Amor fati*—a love of fate that proactively binds will and desire to facticity, the actual as it transpires. Not that what happens needs our compliance. Epictetus, in keeping with Stoicism more generally, conceives of the whole in the hands of divinely wrought natural law, which allows one to "submit to everything that happens, and to follow it voluntarily, in the belief that it is being fulfilled by the highest intelligence" (Epictetus, 511–13). Submission or some contrary is thus the concern—say, the rage of frail deeds. Reaching beyond the day that has become, Epictetus counsels affirmation, come what may. Surprise is possible, disappointment unacceptable. One might avoid anticipation altogether, a self-effacing seeking to be present and only present, but that is not Epictetus's recommendation. In the passages I quote, reflection persists in the form of a wish and submission. "Come what may," sings the Stoic chorus beside every expectation and its fated assignations.

A part of me thinks: "How sad. From hope to surrender." Not that such a stance is unimaginable. Dealt a brutal hand (or guaranteed salvation), I, too, might release my might-yet to the might of a must and play it off as something else. But would I—would you—counsel anticipatory acquiescence if we were free from the grip of such pressures or promises?

"My formula for greatness in a human being is *amor fati*," Nietzsche proclaims, "that you do not want anything to be different, not forwards, not backwards, not for all eternity. Not just to tolerate necessity, still less conceal it—all idealism is hypocrisy toward necessity—but to *love* it" (Nietzsche 2005, 99). If anything, Nietzsche intensifies the counsel of Epictetus—do not just wish that it were so (which might crest in toleration), but love whatever transpires. Nietzsche also transforms the anticipated result: serenity gives way to greatness. But is seeking something different, wanting something else, always a flight, a denial, and thus less than great? A passage that opens book four of *The Gay Science* suggests that wanting otherwise is the failing: "I want to learn more and more how to see what is necessary in things as what is beautiful in them—thus I will be one of those who make things beautiful. *Amor fati*: let that be my love from now on! I do not want to wage war against ugliness. I do not want to accuse; I do not even want to accuse the accusers. Let *looking away* be my only negation. And all in all, and on the whole: someday I want only to be a Yes-sayer" (Nietzsche 2001, 157).

As in Epictetus, Nietzsche's stance bears some trace of the subject—or the personal, that scene of action that no one can do for us. Instead of accusing or denigrating those who resist what befalls them, Nietzsche offers a look away. (This allows him to try to elude the paradox of saying "yes" to those who say "no" and so say "no" and "yes" at the same time.) But a look away toward what, where, and when, and on what terms, particularly if we align the result with greatness or beauty? And are those evaluations captured by the look away? Or as seems more likely, are they distinct acts directed negatively toward wanting things to be different? A stage whisper accompanies the look away: "Those lives—not ugly, but also, not beautiful," or, more coyly, "Ah, the less than great." The questions press themselves because deliberate agency is always in two places at once and an embrace of fate puzzles like a self-effacing introduction.

But the deeper question is: What if possibility opens among what is necessary in things, and manifoldly? Is there only one way to look away?

Born when and where I was, and to whom, and among whom, "white male" named the part. A necessary part? Functionally, yes. I had no say. I was thrown into it, as Heidegger would have it. How, then, to proceed? Is conformity the only route? And even if I were inclined to conform, is there only one way to obey? Or is it not the case that even the most common paths fork? Even those who wish to be *real* men indicate, with the emphasis, the plurality they face, a point in keeping with Beauvoir's distinction between the subman and the serious man. Both conform, but only the latter is a true believer. In other words, even conformity faces the burden of how. (Imagine a comedy in which a group vigorously debates how to conform.) At least in these examples, necessity is fraught with possibility, and if that is right, amor fati is the flight, the refusal.

IN-POSSIBLE WORLDS

By riding and running ahead of desire, by heeding its own call rather than the operations of self-consciousness, by exceeding expectations, by proving irreducible to usage, hope seems extrafactual, fluidly situated. "Either we have hope within us or we don't," Václav Havel has written. "It is a dimension of the soul; it's not essentially dependent on some particular observation of the world or estimate of the situation" (Solnit 2016, 11). And yet, hope seems to make certain scenarios more likely even as it exceeds the grammar of "more likely." *Hope in the Dark: Untold Histories, Wild Possibilities*, by Rebecca Solnit, reminds us of various startling events: "Who, two decades ago, could have imagined a world in which the Soviet Union had vanished, and the Internet arrived?" Writing in 2004, she continues, "Who then dreamed that the political prisoner Nelson Mandela would become president of a transformed South Africa? Who foresaw the resurgence of the indigenous world of which the Zapatista uprising in Southern Mexico is only the most visible face?" (1). Solnit's examples aim to keep hope alive. "This book was written *for* something," she says (137). But they also show that hope often, even usually, remains bound to the actual-possible as its further realization. "South Africa" survives apartheid, and the "presidency" opens to Mandela. In a strict sense, hope seems less than utopian. Ecstatically circulating, it concerns the latent future in the present of an unfulfilled past.

IMAGINE THAT

Thoreau, aiming to live deliberately, attended to his diet. "Like many of my contemporaries, I had rarely for many years used animal food, or tea, or coffee, &c.; not so much because of any ill effects which I had traced to them, as because they were not agreeable to my imagination" (Thoreau 2008, 146). And in the paragraphs that follow, he repeatedly invokes the imagination where I would have expected to encounter conscience. "It is hard to provide and cook," he writes, "so simple and clean a diet as will not offend the imagination; but this, I think, is to be fed when we feed the body; they should both sit down at the same table" (Thoreau, 146).

Like hope, the imagination is extrafactual, devoted to what might or could be, or in this case, what could and should be. And we would have no conception of, or feel for, the future without its fantasies. In its forecasts, hope is thus woven with imagination, turning around the themes and variations of its "as if." And the imagination concretizes and intensifies when fueled by hope.

Wallace Stevens shadows many who turn to (and with) the imagination. And in that turning I am recalled to the "white wall" that Moten imagines Stevens to be. I take it that Stevens is not the kind of fence that makes good neighbors but a wall that keeps them out, perhaps one high enough to allow readers to forget there ever were neighbors (or certain kinds of neighbors). I say this, with the help of Marvin Campbell and Terrance Hayes, after rereading "Like Decorations in a Nigger Cemetery," a poem from 1935.

The poem is cryptic, and in more ways than one. But what startles is the aplomb with which Stevens drops the N-word, something he repeats in a letter referring to the poem (Campbell 2017, 177). As if that word were part of the plain sense of things—"N—." And my astonishment only intensifies when I realize that the poem gives no thought, no turn of the imagination toward what courses through that word. Nor does it give thought to who might in fact be buried in the graveyard whose adornments caught the author's eye and mind. Instead, each short stanza (there are fifty) is offered as a decoration for our mortality, as an instance of what poetry might accomplish and as a reminder of what it cannot. And therein rises the wall: poetry figured as blithely oblivious to the fate of Black lives, poetry as a wall that refuses to bring the fate of Black lives within its task, for example, saying the various ways in which different kinds of people qua kinds (and how fucked up is that?) are forced to consider and thus bear their mortality—as a generalized fate, as strange fruit, as a problem, on the ground. "Stay down," "Stop resisting," bang-bang-bang.

"No one living a snowed-in life / can sleep without a blindfold" (Hayes 2010, 57, lines 1–2). So begins "Snow for Wallace Stevens," a poem by Terrance Hayes. It imagines Stevens snowed in, blinded by a whiteness or electing not to see, possibly both. And it insists, I think, that one must have more than a mind of winter to decorate our graveyards, and I do mean *our*. But Hayes, turning out of the white cage, refuses to rest with that thought.

> Who is not more than his limitations?
> Who is not the blood in a barrel
> and the wine as well? I too, having lost faith
> in language, have placed my faith in language.
> Thus, I have a capacity for love without
> forgiveness . . .
> *(Hayes 2010, 57, lines 14–19)*

In "The Plain Sense of Things," Stevens insists that the absence of the imagination must itself be imagined. Hayes has done just that, and with something other than snow in this blank cold.

FOR AND AGAINST RIMBAUD

Life is elsewhere because of how it's here.

DREAM #24

Men learning from women, grateful and delighted. As they once did. Each of us.

MISPLACED PERSONS

The risks of hope are tied to its finitude. We do not know whether the hoped-for will happen. We do not fully know what the hoped-for will entail when it arrives, supposing it does. And the origins of our hope for it are somewhat opaque. It is thus reasonable to worry about false and foolish hopes, and I think we rightly blame the Pollyannaish; they have fallen prey to a stance that they could and should have avoided.

Margaret Urban Walker, arguing with Luc Bovens, defends hope against his worry that it risks devolving into mere wishful thinking. As noted, she argues that wishful thinking displaces agency whereas hope readies it, and manifoldly so, and thus hope does not pose inherent risks beyond the general problem that "emotions can get out of line" (Walker 2006, 52–53). Bovens is unduly suspicious of hope, she concludes. But hopes, precisely because they direct and so absorb agency, may do even more harm than wishful thinking so defined.

Imagine a group of people who hope for world peace and who, in their own way, strive for it, as Walker and I believe they must if their hope is genuine. But suppose that way is principally symbolic and hyperlocal. Belonging to a neighborhood association, they insist that it spend its time crafting declarations about US military actions and military actions by other states, and to the degree that other neighborhood projects are shelved or under-thought. World peace is the more important issue, they argue, and hoping it will come about, they set out to make a difference.

This example, partially fictional, reminds us that agency unfolds in a context of multiple options and so its exercise entails opportunity costs that may multiply when we pursue worthy hopes in irrational ways—"irrational" meaning in a manner that severely undermines other ends that we endorse or that are constitutive of the practice in question. (I presume that neighborhood associations should address neighborhood issues.) Or the ends themselves might be suspect—imagine a similar group taking over a neighborhood association to "make America great again," meaning whiter, if not brighter.

Enacting hope is fraught. The hopeful court disappointment, even flirt with despair. I am thus not baffled by the broad suspicion regarding *elpis* in the classical Mediterranean world, even if I do not share it. So I rather would not define hope in such a way that it avoids risks like "wishful think-ing" in a colloquial sense. Rather, the task lies in the conduct of life, with cultivating hopefulness, a way of being hopeful, that mitigates and thereby acknowledges such risks. To do so, I think we should, like Walker, treat be-ing hopeful as a "complex repertory of thought, feeling, and expression," what she refers to as a "patterned syndrome" (Walker, 48–49). But precisely because hope is such a braid of thoughts, wants, and affects bound to vari-ous actions, some brief, some unfolding over years, we should expect its various dimensions to slide into other possible ways of regarding ourselves, such as wishful thinking, patience, anxiety, etc. And it is by rendering those slides deliberate that the hopeful might protect themselves from fools' errands.

I HOPE YOU KNOW WHAT YOU'RE DOING

My position is odd. I think of hope as reason-responsive, to use Adrienne Martin's helpful phrase, but I am wary of bringing hope too far within the posits and prudence of practical reason (Martin 2014). Hope can carry us when reasons run out. That is its power and its risk. But let me work toward the thought.

Say I learn that a wealthy person is thinking of donating 500 million dollars to my university. I initially think and say, "I hope that gift comes through." And I start to imagine a world where it has come through and I offer my help to see that it does. But then I learn that the gift is designed to commence an expensive line of research and teaching that my university currently does not pursue, say nuclear physics. We have neither the build-ings nor the labs, and none of the faculty or the curriculum. Upon learning that information, the gift starts to look like a ball and chain that will draw resources away from other ventures, and for years to come. "Please no," I think, as my hope switches sides. Or suppose that the gift furthers some-thing dear to my heart with far fewer opportunity costs but comes with the stipulation that nonunion labor constructs the relevant structures. Again, "No thanks," as my hope turns coat.

The examples show, I think, that our hopes are or can be reason-responsive, and regarding ends or means, to the degree that distinction holds. Or, to put the emphasis elsewhere, hope is accountable to reply to a range of questions concerned with its moral worth, such as: Is the hoped-for good in the first place? And how valuable is the hoped-for? Is it integral to short-term aspirations or long-range goals, or does it also provide us with a sense of self, in the manner of what Blöser and Stahl term "fundamental hopes" because they constitute (at least in part) someone's moral identity and so orient their strivings, aversions, and deliberations (Blöser and Stahl 2017)? How improbable is its realization? What is the cost of failure? What opportunity costs accompany its pursuit, including fantasizing about its realization, getting ready to seize the opportunity should it arise, and laying down backup plans should it not? What is the cost of giving up? (As Blöser and Stahl note, abandoning fundamental hopes may require a change in one's basic self-concept, a phenomenon I witness among undergraduates every year.)

I pause at these questions (instead of providing principles for their resolution) because I doubt personal situations will prove sufficiently substitutable for principles to do their work. Moreover, I expect and accept that similarly situated people will respond differently. Hope beats out its own rhythm despite deliberation. So, after thinking things through, we might believe that things still can go our way, things we want, but we cease the full range of pursuits that characterize being hopeful in a nonattenuated sense. And we might even say, "I'm still hopeful X will happen"—say, that a beloved will reciprocate—"but I need to move on with my life." On my terms, hope comes in degrees and often dies a slow death. Or not. Sometimes hope is what allows us to persevere. Say we acknowledge the risks, costs, and uncertainties but go for broke. Our hope enables us to stare down the sheer unlikeliness of it all, even ignore it most of the time, and persevere despite pressure from friends and family and derision from frenemies.

While I have taken the language of reason-responsiveness from Adrienne Martin, my view is quite different from hers. First, she does not believe that desire is a "state we enter or revise for reasons: it is subrational" (Martin 2014, 37). This just seems false to me, as my donor example suggests. Learning the consequences of my desires often diminishes them, and in a form that Martin associates with practical reason per se: through consideration of rational-ends promotion. (Take this as another reason to resist the orthodox definition from the ground up.)

But there are more interesting differences between our views, and even a general agreement. Martin takes hope to be reason-responsive to the degree that "it is *possible* for the deliberator to revise the state as a result of her recognition of the reasons in favor of it" (Martin, 39). And something can be a reason if it can be a premise in such a deliberation, a view she adopts from Nishi Shah (Martin, 41). So far, so good. But how Martin imagines this playing out in hope strikes me as peculiar. She suggests that being hopeful not only involves an "attraction to the hoped-for outcome and a probability assignment between 0 and 1 to that outcome," but also "standing ready to offer a certain justificatory rationale for certain activities related to the outcome" (Martin, 69). In particular, hope takes one's attraction and the chance of success (no matter how slim) to count as reasons for doing the sort of things hopeful people do, which Martin presents as entertaining the outcome, anticipating with pleasure its realization, and "relying on it in one's plans," albeit without actively pursuing its realization, which she views as external to hope (Martin, 69).

I have already suggested that I consider Martin mistaken in severing hope from initial, even full-bodied pursuits of the hoped-for. Yes, there can be cases where we use "hope" to describe situations that do not involve such pursuits, but Martin claims to be describing hope in the fullest sense, and such situations are unusual, if not outliers (Martin, 62). But here my concern is less descriptive fidelity than how we should think of hope's reason-responsiveness. Martin's conception leaves us less able to account for our hopes.

If I am told, "I hope we'll be happy together," do I also hear, "I am licensed to imagine being happy together, to plan on being happy together, to take pleasure in thinking about that happiness?" Is someone thereby telling me, "I am licensed to do such things"? My point is not that Martin renders a prereflective activity in an overly reflexive manner. Rather, to my ear she misreads the expressive content of the speech-act, which conveys excitement, some anxiety, but little, if any, sense of authorization, particularly regarding the matters that Martin underscores. Let me repeat this point from another direction. When are we pressed about our hopes, and with regard to what? The most usual questions regarding the rationality of hope, from the classical Mediterranean onward, concern the actions it orients and the ends it affirms (Culbreth 2020). In other words, such questions concern people "setting the end of bringing about the hoped-for outcome," precisely what Martin denies is integral to hope (Martin, 64).

I confess, I have a poor feel for the kind of question to which Martin's hoper stands ready to reply. Suppose someone says, "But there's still hope!" Or, "Because I have hope." What are they justifying? What justificatory role does hope play in these locutions? "Why do you keep applying for that job?" "Because I have hope." Again, we find ourselves in the thick of the chase. What about: "Dude, she's not coming back." "But there is still hope!" That might seem closer to what Martin has in mind, but in this case, I think that opportunity costs are the principal concerns, not the flush and flicker of hopeful thoughts and fantasies, hence a follow up like: "You need to get on with your life." Not that one could not worry about the time and energy another spends in fantasizing and planning, but when those become issues, I imagine the worry is most likely either replacing action with fantasy or, again, opportunity costs. In short, Martin renders hope reason-responsive, but in response to questions that hope does not generally face. In fact, her account of desire as subrational makes it almost impossible to treat hope as reason-responsive in the manner most sought by its detractors and defenders.

In 2017, Pope Francis published *On Hope*, which accounts for what opens and preserves hope and the margin it traverses. God. Francis writes, "But let us never set conditions for God, and let us instead allow hope to conquer our fears. . . . He knows better than we do, and we must have faith because his ways and his thoughts are different than ours" (Pope Francis 2017, 57). We dare hope on this view because all that lies between the alpha and the omega has been wrought by the divine essence. Not that there is nothing for us to do. What has been wrought is a plan, and one that makes demands upon us such as love thy neighbor and do not despair. In fact, the sin that became sloth, namely, *acedia*, involved a weariness or distress (to recall John Cassian), which led one to abandon spiritual pursuits, to no longer persevere (to recall Evagrius, another desert father). Why might that be a sin? Despair pronounces God's plan unworkable, his demands unwarranted. Was that not, after all, Judas's true failing, namely, his suicide? Set no conditions on God. Nothing is impossible with Him, particularly forgiveness.

When hope runs through the plan of a *theos*, I find it hopeless. What is promised beyond today has already been worked out. "Christian hope," writes Francis, "is the expectation of something that has already been fulfilled; the door is there, and, I hope, to reach the door" (Pope Francis, 64). And this is why Francis can refer as often as he does to a kind of knowledge. "At the same time, however," he writes, "we know that we have already been able to contemplate and to have a foretaste of . . . signs of the Resurrection" (Pope Francis, 83).

As I think it, hope does not have recourse to this kind knowledge, even under the guise of faith. Stretched in hope's grip, we do not know. "Hope is an embrace of the unknown and the unknowable," Rebecca Solnit writes, "an alternative to the certainty of both optimists and pessimists" (Solnit 2016, xiv). And, or so I suggest, an alternative to the contemplative foretaste of faith.

I do not call theological hope "hopeless" because it fills me or anyone with sadness or despair. Nor am I claiming that religious hopes are hopeless in the sense that they will never be fulfilled. What Pope Francis proposes does not need hope to move it, propel it beyond the day that has become. In that sense, redemption is without hope, and so, too, Pope

Francis. He rests assured that redemption is at hand and has been at hand since the beginning. We might need hope to find that day. But the day itself, that radiant possibility, does not.

As I think it, as I feel it, hope dilates the future, and in its absence, the future less recedes—When is it not at a distance?—then closes, as if the sea and sky were rushing toward each other, extinguishing the sun.

GROVEL, GROVEL IN THE TOIL AND TROUBLE

The theological is variably legible across antiquity, although sometimes it manifests as just enough insight to know we're fucked, stretching toward heaven at the expense of itself. "Creatures of a day!" Pindar exclaims. "What is man? What is he not? / He is a dream of a shadow; yet when Zeus-sent / brightness comes / a brilliant light shines upon mankind and their life is sense" (Pindar 2007, lines 94–97). And no doubt this is why, as Andrew Culbreth shows, broad, ancient Mediterranean currents term hope (*elpis*) a fool's errand. Creatures of a day, we act in ignorance of the ends toward which we travel. Our hopes risk, therefore, affirming a prelude to an impending disaster. After reading lines from Semonides, Culbreth writes, "The attainment of good things is entirely up to Zeus, whose intentions are unknowable to us," and so hope, he continues, "may lead us to pursue illusory goals," even shameful ones, such that Pindar can speak of a "shameless hope" in the eleventh Nemean Ode and call us to "seek due measure of gains" (Culbreth 2020, 41, 47).

How might we seek what is in accord with our powers but not strive above our raising? As I see them, hope and theologically inflected dispositions unfold differentially at this very point. Pindar again: "But empty-headed boasting hurls one mortal down from / success, / and another, too little confident in his strength, / whose timid spirit drags him back by the hand / falls short of the glory he deserves" (Pindar 2007, lines 29–33). And further, with the most hopeless advice.

One should not fight against the god,
who now raises a man up and then again gives great glory to others.
But not even this thought cheers the minds of the envious,
who stretch the measuring line too tight
and so inflict a painful wound in their own heart
before they can achieve what they have devised in their minds.
It is best to accept the yoke on one's neck and bear it lightly;
truly, kicking against the goad makes for a slippery path.
(Pindar 2007, lines 88–95)

AFTER EMERSON

The arc of hope, like a burst of genius, is prehensile.

HELLO, CRUEL WORLD

How is it that we bear some of the things the world throws . . . less our way than at us? "Hope" seems one reply, or a part of a reply. We hope that something else awaits, something better. So, we endure. "Keep hope alive," so certain dreams keep alive, so we keep alive, or at least lively, getting after it, whatever *it* turns out to be.

Pride is sometimes seen as another resource for future aspiration. In its swell, pride insists that I am somebody. I count. I deserve something else, something more. Michael Eric Dyson has written, "Self-regard [later, it's self-love] is a key to both our psychic strength and our moral health" (Dyson 2006, 26 [62]). According to Dyson, pride both beats back the haters and inspires ongoing achievement. Pride, he suggests, is a "spur to excellence" (Dyson, 30).

Pride seems fueled by an accomplished past, individual or collective (no doubt both, like the course of our lives), rather than an expectant future. It also seems underwritten by the moral force of respect. Someone who is proud believes that he or she deserves or is at least worthy of something of value: recognition, honor, a shot at a great deed. Hope seems wilder in this regard, perhaps exceeding desert, particularly collective hope. And whereas hope tropes its past, pride uses it for leverage as it demands and leaps.

UNDERTOW

Although I am unsure whether I know the difference, at least in the thick of it, hope is normatively laced or leavened with a wish. That which it fingers without sight is something better. Not necessarily something saved or redeemed, let alone all things. Hope need not arrogate what the *theos* has purportedly settled. Several lines of partial development are possible objectives: more equality of opportunity, less ignorance, even new hopes. But hope is for the better. Its stretch seeks something against which the de facto falters.

I find this undercurrent in the terms that render my hopes concrete, such as friendship and democracy, happiness and justice, truth, too. Each invokes, should it appear, even approximately, what leaves the world better off than it otherwise would be, at least relative to the measure planted there.

But let me hasten to add that hope, in its occurrence, renders these terms concrete; it pulls them—and the betterment they mark—from an abstract grammar of universality (the ether of the *as such*) into scenes of possible realization. Normativity thickens as hope tropes.

BECOME WHO YOU ARE BECOMING

When I think of that me that I would like to meet (and whether I approximate the me I hoped to be), I imagine something like a physiognomy of action or bearing, what Emerson termed the conduct of life, all ways of rethinking "character." I find myself listening and responding, attuned by the questions, How and to what ends do I carry, endure, and, in some small part, help shape the world?

My conscience has settled here, which suggests that it was born, in part, in a hope for something like "my life." Said otherwise, the question and the phenomenon it in part institutes is bound to a hope for something, one part of which is a life articulately *mine*. Not every minute. Not every desire. Certainly not "my life as a whole," which remains a shadow of the God who wants me entirely accountable and brimming with praise. ("So needy, that Jehovah.") No, what is mine is a contour or set of contours, a way of moving toward nested destinations that will no doubt prove more complex and challenging upon arrival.

BEATITUDE

Blessed are the heteronomous. We, too, might change.

HARD OF HEARING

Hopes for oneself are hopes of reception and response, or rather, some braid of both, as with listening, a recurring hope of mine. To listen. Well.

Listening is a concentrated activity. And I reject the invocation of some passive "active"—the language is too active in its emphasis on the passive.

Listening is not a simple retreat into simple silence. It must risk being wrong about what it hears, and so venture forth, followed by something like "Did I hear you?" Not so much "Did I get you right?"—as if listening terminated in a kind of discursive possession. More a matter of "Are we here together?"—which requires interpretation but also a kind of hearing-over as one might look-over what one has done or think-over a plan.

Hoping to listen, listening with hope, each underwriting the other.

STARING INTO THE ECLIPSE

A nontheological current runs through Jonathan Lear's *Radical Hope*. In the context of the devastation that beset the Crow Nation, Lear wonders how anyone survives such a plight.

As Lear sees it, the Indigenous genocide shattered a lifeworld as well as lives, thus depriving the Crow of what Lear terms a "point of view," which I take to be a determinate orientation from which to plan, enact, and evaluate a life for oneself and in common. Unable to perform core rituals, and bereft of land and its coinhabitants, the Crow, Lear holds, found themselves in a world drained of significance. Plenty Coups, a Crow chief during the aftermath of the devastation, told Frank Linderman in 1928, "But when the buffalo went away the hearts of my people fell to the ground and they could not lift them up again. After this, nothing happened" (Lear 2006, 2).

The issue was not simply land, which lay in what is now southeastern Montana and northern Wyoming, even though it contracted dramatically across the nineteenth century. An 1825 treaty established over 33 million acres as Crow territory, but by 1905 it had dwindled to just about 2.5 million acres (Medicine Crow 1992, 3). Nor was the issue an increasing inability to move camp and hunt the land, although that wound cut deep. Linderman also recorded conversations with a medicine woman, Pretty Shield, who reports, "The white man began to fence the plains so that we could not travel. . . . We began to stay in one place, and to grow lazy and sicker all the time" (Linderman 1960, ix). But even before the 1825 treaty, other catastrophes had already struck. According to Frederick Hoxie, up to fourteen thousand Crow died from European-borne disease during the late eighteenth century, reducing the population to about 2,400 by 1805 (Hoxie 1995, 47, 131). And smallpox beset them between 1840 and 1850, reducing them further (Medicine Crow 1992, 14). "When a woman sees whole families wiped out," Pretty Shields says—and note, the Crow are matrilineal—"and cannot help, cannot even hope, her heart falls down and she wishes she could die" (Linderman 1960, 21). By the time the buffalo went away, the Crow were thus a profoundly diminished band.

I think it also matters that the losses and fate suffered by the Crow were inflicted by others as opposed to natural disaster. In the former, the storm not only hangs around but moves next door, a constant (and in this case, deeply untrustworthy) reminder. The Crow thus not only lost traditional sources of meaning making but suffered through numerous betrayals of what Frederick Hoxie has termed "immigration in reverse," which, in 1884, culminated in their relocation from the "foothills of the Beartooth range to the flatlands of the Bighorn and Little Bighorn valley," a move that "marked their confinement within the permanent boundaries of the modern reservation" (Hoxie 1995, 12, 15). With regard to land, motility, daily practice, and population, all under a thick awning of conniving oppression, their losses were immense. And it all happened incredibly quickly.

Another observation pertains. "The Crows of 1805," Hoxie writes, "were a dispersed community of hunters and their families who had few formal institutions to unify them. They spoke [but did not write] a common language, but they dispersed themselves across an immense, borderless landscape, and they had no centralized leadership" (Hoxie, 57). Around 1832, a quarrel among them established distinct bands, the Mountain and River Crow, and as late as 1868, there were efforts by the federal government to establish separate treaties with the River and Mountain Crow, with the former only joining the latter under duress and coercion (Hoxie 1995, 99). One should avoid, therefore, presuming that the Crow lost some prelapsarian feel for themselves and the world. They were a complex people organized around families of matrilineal descent, and they were of more than one mind regarding many things. Nor does Plenty Coup speak for *the* Crow. But this does not disqualify Lear's inferences from Plenty Coup's remarks. Not only does Pretty Shield echo Plenty Coups's remarks, but the lack of a centralized political life suggests that for the Crow everyday practices were even more orienting, and it is their loss that leads Lear to pose his central question.

How does one recover from losses (and violence) of this magnitude? Not: How does one return to what one had been? That is impossible. Rather: How does one go on? And who is one as one goes on, presuming one survives? Lear observes, "A culture does not tend to train the young to endure its own breakdown" (Lear 2006, 83). How could it? Such preparations also lie in ruins. Moreover, to the degree that virtues derive their general focus and authority from cultural traditions and the agents who enact them, one simply cannot rely on one's culture to see one through the wreck.

FROM THE WRECK

Pretty Shield, looking over her grandchildren, considering their future, admits to disorientation. They were growing up without instruction in Crow life, which left her unsure how to communicate with and so care for them. "I am trying to live a life that I do not understand," she says (Linderman 1960, 8).

At this juncture I appreciate the pull of theological hope, the promise of a peace that passeth all understanding. And I am hushed, if unconverted, when Cornel West tells Maya Angelou, "Whether black folk want to admit it or not, given all the imperfections, it has been in the name of Jesus that the folk have been most able to preserve a sense of spiritual sanity and mental health" (West 1997, 194).

But Lear turns to radical hope, which keeps to the shadows for a foretaste of arrival. It greets its day as a new day. It "anticipates," in Lear's words, "a good for which those who have the hope as yet lack the appropriate concepts with which to understand it" (Lear 2006, 103). Or, more bluntly: "It is committed to the bare idea that *something good will emerge*" (Lear, 94). Not that radical hope is sufficient to bring about or even pursue that newness. Previous virtues such as courage must somehow migrate and prove themselves in new, rougher terrain; courage allows one to face the future without any clear sense of even felt prospects, and after the battle has been utterly lost.

Lear thinks Plenty Coups needed courage of this sort to lead his people through defeat and radical loss. Does this make courage part of radical hope, or does courage take over when hope falters? Is courage the hope of the hopeless? Or, as Patrick Shade suggests, does hope play a role in "summoning the courage needed for its own realization" (Shade 2019, 54)? Hopelessness would seem to drag courage down with it, but it may be that courage also staves off despair. But one can put too fine a point on the provisional designations of a moral psychology (or what Lear terms "philosophical anthropology"). Said otherwise, I would resist the categorical drift of our distinctions toward something like another faculty psychology, as if "hope" or "courage" were distinct organs in an organic sensibility. The provisions stored here are hypotheses of a sort, but more as bases for action than borders on some map. Their essay awaits your assay. And then we should talk again.

But beyond courage, radical hope also relies on homelier virtues, the kind that allow communities to meet subsistence needs, to birth and raise children, to perform the kind of daily care work that seems missing in Lear's (possibly) hero-centric account. The Crow's "extensive and distinctive kinship system," which relied on large, matrilineal clans as opposed to nuclear families, seem to prove the point. According to Joseph Medicine Crow and Hoxie, these multiple, affectionate relations maintained a sense of being Crow through the most intense periods of disorientation, namely, from around 1885—after settlement—through the 1920s (Hoxie 1995, 169–71).

A general point is hovering, and it complements one reorienting social histories of oppression that think resistance, rebellion, and reconstruction from multiple networks of agency that often go missing in histories that center "iconic and invariably male figures," to borrow language from Aisha Finch (Finch 2015, 7). But my point is as much psychological as it is sociological. The roots of hope run deep into our ongoing conversations with one another and the world, conversations that seem to circulate beyond the reach of terms like "point of view" or worldview. Yes, that soil is somewhat opaque. But it suggests that hope is born of a dense weave wrought by more hands than Lear's account countenances.

IT'S NOT ALL WE NEED, BUT YOU NEED IT NONETHELESS

Conversing with Cornel West, Maya Angelou recalls the time when, as a child, she did not speak. The time was quite extensive. Throughout, her mother would comb her hair, as if brushing away the insults a young, mute, Black girl endured, and replacing it with the rhythms of affection, affirmation: "Mama don't care what these people say, Sister. You just keep on reading that poetry. You just keep on being a good girl. You're going to be somebody, Sister" (West 1997, 192). Looking back, much later in life, Angelou says, "I used to think, That poor, ignorant woman. But here I am. That's love" (West, 192).

OPENING MOVEMENT

Radical hope, because it is radical, is needy. Like all fires, it lives off intake—family, love, maybe even competence. A kind of hope flickers in proprioceptive feedback, its insistent if modest "I can," which marks an embodied-affective dimension of hope that Lear's overly (though not exclusively) cognitivist account underplays. I think of being ill, of that point when we begin to feel slightly abject. And how the return of some simple energy—say, to shower and dress—buoys us. Not that such sparks are solitary. Touch buoys as well—a hand on the shoulder, a hug, the full to-and-fro. And what, then, of jolts of sunshine and clear skies? My sense is that "I can" seems to rise with the barometer. Some days others pick us up, other days the sun shines in.

WHAT COMES AROUND MIGHT NEVER RETURN

Hope is a mark of our vulnerable and empowering dependency. It can awaken, be stirred, evaporate, or be crushed. Eyeing a photo of herself, age seven, Anne Sexton finds in the peeling image her own despair undermining what had been youth and promise. "I am aging without sound," she writes, "into darkness, darkness" (Sexton 1981, "Baby Picture," lines 16–17) The second darkness breaks my heart. The promises of the past have become early steps toward . . . well, nothing. Looking ahead, the speaker finds darkness, and beyond that, using whatever energy remains, energies devoted to the saying of it, more darkness. "Anne, / who were you?" asks the poem at the last. "Merely a kid keeping alive" (Sexton, lines 35–37).

WE GOTTA GET OUT OF THIS PLACE

I have been stressing the receptive dimensions of hope and tying them to its agential impact, resisting the grammatical habit to oppose reception and action. Thinking from Emerson's pun "the conduct of life," I take agency to entail a mode of response that works with (including against) what the world provides. I also have been underlining some of the ways in which hope is unmoved by reason's estimations and directives, its protestations too, even though it can be reason-responsive. And this has led me to wonder, perhaps you as well, how I distinguish hope from faith and whether, in fact, I do.

Hope trades in the demonstrably possible no matter how unlikely; the slightest probability opens a margin for hope. (I do not hope that my father, dead since 1991, will read and admire this book.) But faith can imagine and affirm what seems impossible—the second coming of a god-man of actual infinity or eternal life for the souls of those now living. And I use these examples because, like hope, they concern possibilities, which constitute hope's purview. Faith, however, also concerns settled matters that cannot be known in any a priori or a posteriori sense—say, the omnipresence of the divine essence or that such a being is an omniscient, omnipotent creator of this world but nevertheless omnibenevolent. Because faith can concern itself with matters that it regards as settled, it is less wedded to the finite, which gives it an aura of confidence, as we saw with Pope Francis. One even catches a whiff of this difference when someone says, "I have high hopes for her" rather than "I have faith in her." The former trembles where the latter glides.

Because faith can travel toward the impossible, it need not be reason-responsive, whereas hope should. Note, I am not claiming that faith cannot be reason-responsive. Rather, my claim is that we tend to take "that is a matter of faith" to explain, even justify affirming what seems, prima facie, beyond reason—say, that the King James Bible is the literal word of an almighty God. "With God all things are possible," I have been told, but never with the affective energy of a hope, which always bears the trace of doubt. Nor would I think of replying with arguments about the nature of translation or the editorial history of that text, from the Greek reception of what had been said in Aramaic to variations among the Greek texts used to compile the English to its reliance upon the Latin Vulgate for the final lines of the book of Revelation. Declarations of faith often decline, in advance, such discussions. They brim with what Adrienne Martin terms a meta-confidence, which she regards as "the mark of faith: the confidence that nothing she encounters can give her reason to stop hoping." Except that which slips from hope into something else, or at least something worth distinguishing more strongly. Hopes seem answerable in a way that faith is not, say, for their probability content, for the validity of their ends, and to the various questions I offered earlier to articulate what hope considers when it proceeds deliberately.

Circulating within the demonstrably possible, hope seems thereby bound to the finite and remains invested in human agencies while acknowledging their finitude. It even compels us, I think, to make whatever difference we can regarding its realization. Hope is thus always in us, in what we can be and can work to realize. Faith, however, can abandon the human in favor of superhuman (in the sense of "supernatural") powers. Think how odd it would sound for Christians to hope that their God can and will resurrect the dead. They might hope that they are deserving of such a fate, but that is a matter about which their conduct has some say. When it comes to what the divine can or will do, that is or should be termed a matter of faith.

Earlier I claimed that hope, oriented toward the better, has a troping character—it pushes its ends toward points of fuller realization or even qualitative change, as when we hope for a just world, a better tomorrow, or, more radically still, recalling the Crow, some unknown way to flourish. This is hope's commerce with dreams and its imaginative valences whose interactions with what has been opens onto somewhere and somewhat else. (And, therefore, I say I hope for hopes yet felt.) Does faith wield this kind of incalculable but palpable, transformative power? Like hope, it also steadies, even intensifies commitment, and it can inspire. And no doubt, on naturalized terms, it, too, fuels creativity—what did Bach not manage for the greater glory of his God? But on its own terms, thinking from the participant's perspective, I am genuinely uncertain whether faith tropes its object in the manner of hope. That seems an almost blasphemous thought, a move toward the divine decomposition I have recounted elsewhere, wherein faith in the divine so emboldens the faithful that they begin to imagine and pursue lives beyond theological orbits (Lysaker 2008, 107–17).

THEN AGAIN

But how definitive are the distinctions one can offer in a sea of usages? The line I draw between hope and faith reflects less a conceptual discovery than a semiotic intervention from and within a nontheological perfection-ism. I pause to stress this because I have encountered "faith" deployed in ways proximate to my sense of hope. In *The Darkened Light of Faith*, Melvin Rogers, drawing upon a Black Republican tradition, locates and scores a democratic faith. Based on a twofold conception of "the people" that brims with aspirational energy and factical as well as legal realism, each pursues a democratic future whose contours are disclosed (a) by critiques of its present occlusion under white supremacy, and (b) through the kind of community that its address both convenes and provisionally exemplifies. Said otherwise, Rogers argues that each author writes in a manner that exudes faith in some "we the people" that is more than a disingenuous invitation to some future body politic that will persist in disregarding the full value of Black lives.

What is this faith, and how does it align with the sense of hope I am developing? Interestingly, Rogers elected to speak of faith because for him, the word entails less confidence in the desired outcome than hope wields. "Both hope and faith share an attachment to something not present," he writes. "The source of the difference between the two is that hope marks levels of confidence in achieving what is desired, while faith is the expres-sion of a loving, even if difficult commitment precisely because there is no confidence to be had—at least based on some facts of the matter—in its realization" (Rogers, forthcoming).

Are our views compatible? We both think that faith begins to arise as one's probability assessment provides increasingly desperate odds, or, as in large scale dreams, as the very notion of a probability assessment sounds like a put-on. ("I put the likelihood of a more just America by 2040 at 18 percent.")

But Rogers's democratic faith eschews the religiosity of Douglass, King, and West, and so his text does not slide between faith and knowledge as one expects from a theologically moored orientation. And that closes the gap between our discussions, at least to my ear. In fact, where Rogers writes of faith, I would speak of hope to underscore that my reliance on orders beyond my ken is coupled with an acknowledgment of their finitude and all-too-human character.

But what of this line from King, delivered in Washington in 1963? "With this faith, we will be able to hew out of the mountain of despair a stone of hope" (King 1963). I see the sense (and feel the power) in this distinction. Hopeful investments in what the present affords might be insufficient to keep despair at bay. They may even invite it. But faith can hold the line at such tipping points. Even more so, it can fuel the imagination and so prompt dreams within which more strategic plans can arise, shorter steps along an unseen line. Rogers's distinction seems in step with King's, and I feel no strong need to revise it even though I am inclined to resist it, particularly given King's robust religiosity. For me, "faith" is principally a religious term that links the profane to the sacred. Hope unfolds without that verticality. But Rogers is right to suggest that the democratic faith he articulates lacks the kind of probability assessment common to most instances of hope. Each of us, therefore, is intervening by way of a revision that eschews prayer in favor of a different kind of offering—namely, our own examples, which, I hope, are legible.

ALL YOU NEED IS WHAT?

There was a time when none of this mattered. That time will never come again, though eventually, that also will not matter.

The indifference of the world prompts despair in those like Václav Havel, who require hope to rise from and gesture toward something transcendent, something "whose significance is not easily understood, is recorded in some way and adds to the memory of Being" (Havel 1997, 239). Or, said differently: "We cannot believe in the meaning of our own lives and cherish hope as a permanent state of mind if we are certain that our death means the end of everything" (Havel, 239). But why not? Or rather, "why not" after I insist that our death does not mean the death of everything, only those things, those determinate, singular things which bear our hopes?

I do not see why the romance of hope evaporates in our inevitable evanescence. What staging does hope need to move us? Because I cannot hope for another, I cannot answer on your behalf. But one can be the kind of answer that Havel finds impossible and so disclose a surprising significance.

TBA

Hope is a mark of our vulnerable, empowering dependency. The hoped-for, claims Anthony Steinbock, is "given as not in my control to bring it about" (Steinbock 2014, 167). I would agree, although it may not be totally beyond my control, either. Hope, in Erich Fromm's words, "means to be ready at every moment for that which is not yet born" (Fromm 1970, 22). And anticipating and being ready, like listening, are not particularly passive. Fromm again: "To hope is a state of being. It is an inner readiness, that of intense but not yet spent activity" (Fromm, 22). The deeper point, however, is that hope orients us toward a dependent future. No one hopes for what they can simply bring about.

But I do not want to dig too deep. Steinbock regards hope as intrinsically religious, by which he means a "kind of experience that lives from, however implicitly or broadly, the dimension of the Holy" (Steinbock 2014, 212). In his words, "It is in the religious dimension of experience that hope receives its fullest significance" (Steinbock, 170). This loses me, or maybe I just do not follow, or will not. Does hope prove more itself, more truly itself, the more it acknowledges its lack of control? Does hope become more itself when it terminates in an open regard for and embrace of the sacred? This is why I pause around the issue of control. If hope becomes more itself the more it sheds any sense of control, then the hope in question is in fact inhuman, meaning the hope behind this theory of hope is to abandon itself to something other than a human life. No thanks.

Steinbock also writes, "Hope is initiated as a way of taking up a situation and living through its meaning 'spontaneously'" (Steinbock, 165). Do we need to add some conception of the holy or the religious to find hope in this scene? If not, binding hope to the holy seems like adding something hoped for to the matter in question.

The spontaneity of hope marks its prereflective beginnings, which acknowledges that its current commences somewhere outside self-consciousness. And the thought that hope takes up a situation and lives through its meaning underscores its worldly dependency as well as its ecstatic character: of a situation while also surpassing it. Such events are sufficiently enabled by the shared alterity of this world held together and apart in a general absence. One thus does not need a dimension of the holy to account for hope.

But I fear I am being petulant. Bloch has said, "Only with the farewell to the closed, static concept of being does the real dimension of hope open" (Bloch 1986, 18). Could Steinbock and I meet in this line of thought? I prefer it for two reasons. Like Steinbock, Bloch underscores that hope breaks through what we think we know about what can and cannot be done. It rends the factical. But hope also makes possible the emergence of what exceeds what we think we know about what can and cannot be done. In our hopes, the factical rends itself. That is the marvel of finitude. Setting aside the holy, I could join Steinbock here: "Hope, we must insist, is evoked in the situation itself and emerges as part of its texture" (Steinbock 2014, 165).

HOPE FOR THE BEST?

Such an odd phrase. It seems to mean, "Let's hope that something other than the worst transpires." Sometimes we hope just to survive, we seek what is better than what the worst would be. (I take this to be a tick up from Sexton's "keeping alive.") Or some might hope for death, regarding survival, at least under foreseeable conditions, to be worse.

But could we hope for the best? Ernst Bloch delimits hope with the following: "The final will is to be truly present" (Bloch 1986, 16). I'm unsure how to hear this. What does one seek when one aspires to be truly present? Am I truly present when I am absorbed in the moment of my occurrence, either as a seamless unity or a synchronic symphony accompanied by an audience attending to just the occurrence, and nothing else? If so, this seems a variant of theological hope, at least on the side of the omega: just a present, fulfilled. I resist this in part because it loses the ecstatic temporality that seems integral to hope, for whom the present is a possible future modulating the past. And to will that loss is to choose the death of willing, either in death or a fulfilled, eternal life "where nothing really happens." (This is David Byrne, not Plenty Coups.)

But maybe being truly present is living ecstatically in the emergence of bounded possibilities. If so, "final" rings ironically in Bloch's remark, for living ecstatically only acknowledges the next, and as a node opening onto an elsewhere that will unfold as a matter requiring an interpretation and response. (It isn't just that willing introduces those for whom the truly present presents itself. As Dewey has shown, every end becomes a means to another.) But it seems wrong to even entertain this variant given Bloch's German, which speaks of the *letzte Wille*, which, as in a last will and testament, indicates the "final," as in the last of a series. And that seems to suggest that what, in the end, is being willed is a scene wherein we can forgo willing, and that kind of self-negation is what I am resisting in the name of hope.

Romantic hope would be my term for living ecstatically in, and thereby enabling, the emergence of bounded possibilities. The romance follows certain turnings in Emerson's "Experience" and "The Poet" and abandons the double consciousness that closes "Fate." It seeks the turn of genius into practical power by acknowledging that I am a fragment and this is a fragment of me, which reattaches me to a whole that flows through me and which I thereby conduct in ways that I do not and probably cannot fathom. But I conspire with them or conduct them whether I want to or not. My hope is thus to be a certain kind of conductor for uncertain yet glimpseable, unwritten futures.

With a greater emphasis on habit and available means, Patrick Shade has promoted a pragmatic conception of hope that affects a "conditioned transcendence" (Shade 2001, 17). The difference that makes a difference is in part a matter of degree—I am less convinced that "hope" can be brought so clearly under Dewey's "method of intelligence," and so I find it less bound to means and thus closer to wishes and dreams, to the ecstatic surges of what propels and orients primary as opposed to secondary experience. "Hope is not a mysterious force," Shade writes, "imbued with supernatural power which allows us to transcend any and every condition," and I agree with this refusal of the supernatural (Shade, 201). But hope, like the world that sustains and undermines it, is mysterious in its comings and goings, and sublimely so, and this leads me to emphasize its whimsical nature, which pragmatic emphases on habits, inquiry, and reconstruction seem to de-emphasize, or so I hear when Shade claims that a pragmatic account of hope "relies on our powers of intelligence and adaptability to find its [hope's] proper manifestation" (Shade, 201). Shade's account seems more oriented toward the project of realizing our hopes than the strange alchemy of their occurrence.

THERE IS NO ELSEWHERE

Mark Fisher has diagnosed a particular hopelessness, "capitalist realism," which he equates with the "widespread sense that not only is capitalism the only viable political and economic system, but also that it is now impossible even to imagine a coherent *alternative* to it" (Fisher 2009, 2). Not that this *real-apolitik* manifests chiefly as an explicit, propositional stance toward social life. Rather, it courses prereflectively. Concretely, it propels a kind of "depressive hedonia," which Fisher regards as an "inability to do anything else *except* pursue pleasure" (Fisher, 22). Where *The Man in the Gray Flannel Suit* (1956) confronted viewers with the workaholic, Fisher presents the debtor-addict who needs ongoing petty satisfactions to bury the meaningless churn of capitalist labor and consumption. And this need, in turn, becomes the target of emerging markets and the devices they peddle, and to the point that Fisher, (r)essaying Benjamin, writes of *pre-corporation*—the "pre-emptive formatting and shaping of desires, aspirations and hopes by capitalist culture" (Fisher, 9).

Capitalist realism is a kind of despair. It proceeds in the grip of the impossible and aspires, at best, to coping strategies which nevertheless remain in the grip of what the market prompts and supplies. Reading Fisher's book, I kept thinking of *Walden*, of Thoreau's belief that his neighbors, laboring under a mistake, lived lives of quiet desperation made even more desperate because "they honestly think there is no choice left" (Thoreau 2008, 9). But this similarity in affective tone should not obscure a profound difference in scope. What no longer alternates for Fisher are global world orders, whereas Thoreau has the course of a singular life in mind and its place in the cosmos. Beside *Walden*, Fisher's concerns therefore seem too narrow—the cosmos is eclipsed by the political—and too vast – the singular is dissolved into the political.

I pause with Thoreau because I worry about a hope bound (or a despair wrought) by the webs of a global political order. Is such a thing a genuine object of theoretical or practical reason? Can it be known and thereby acted upon? I do not doubt that human action impacts various nested relations on a global scale; global warming makes that evident. But is there a discernible object or objective that corresponds to what Fisher terms an "economic-political order"? Can it be brought sufficiently under a set of concepts such that one would know how to reconstruct the whole shebang? My point is not the Stoic conceit that the divine has the whole well in hand. In fact, Fisher seems closer to Stoicism than the romanticism I espouse insofar as his dream is draped around an epistemic-practical grip on the whole that has yet to prove possible or even seem probable. In fact, such versions of totality loom like shadows of God, their scope conceivable only from the view from everywhere. Moreover, such dreams, dashed or not, totalize the political in the manner made legible by Jean-Luc Nancy, thereby rendering lives, in their singularity, substitutable, their trials, illegible (Nancy 1991; Lysaker 1999a, 1999b). Pinning hopes on interactions so beyond our purview threatens to collapse the stages upon which hope enters, which is often from below.

TAKE 3

As I underwent it, the trial of existentialism involved learning to find meaning somewhere else than the stage built around the idea of God. If one keeps the stage and writes out God, meaninglessness awaits. Thus, while I agree with Akiba Lerner that there "continues to be little evidence to support the view that the hopes placed in solidarity and self-fashioning can substitute for the foundationalism promised in redemptive hope narratives that offered a sense of transcendence," I would argue for a change of venue upon which to stage that for which we hope (Lerner 2019, 87). Theological hopes dilate us beyond our grip.

COCONSPIRATORS

The independently invulnerable cannot be aided. A world unto themselves, they rise and sink alone. No touch, phone call, or institutional investment will make a difference.

In 1992, Zell Miller, then governor of Georgia, outlined the Hope Scholarship during his State of the State address. Through economic support, it promised to make the good of public education more publicly available. Mired as the initiative was in the reemergence of neoliberal education policy, and compromised as Miller's remarks were by his insistence that the scholarship was "not only for those who are minorities or from lower-income families," the scholarship both manifested and sparked social hope. And while it did not simply spring from the actual, it conspired with it nonetheless. Nontheological hope, radical or otherwise, takes its stand in the finite and factical. Hoping beyond the day which has become is nevertheless hope in—and therefore, for—what our day, yours and mine, might yet become.

KEEPING TIME

Historicism is ahistorical. The might of what has been is also subjunctive.

ARE WE DEVO?

Walter Benjamin profoundly distrusts "progress" and any politics that takes its bearings from the promise of the future. Progress, as a bearer of hope, he thinks, keeps us perpetually surprised that "such things"— fascism, mass death, contempt for the rule of law—remain possible. Moreover, as an objective, it breeds opportunism and a willingness to accept collateral damages en route to some temporary perch; the resulting *Leviathan* is more mass grave than a sword-wielding monarch of a body politic.

Hope, in orienting us toward the better, seems ineliminably tied to some conception of "progress," by which I mean I do not see how I can relinquish one and preserve the other. "Progress," a term of retrospection in some cases and prospection in others, carries some of the normative and temporal valences integral to hope. In hoping for the better, we aim toward what would count as progress given where we currently stand. (Thinking about diabetes, I hope we will have better treatment options by 2050.) Should our hopes be realized, we will look back at where we began and measure the distance with a term like "progress." (Still thinking about diabetes, it would be wonderful to say in 2050, "We've made a lot of progress since 2019," even in the knowledge that such advances came too late for many, and that health care is often undermined less by lack of knowledge than by a money-commodity-money logic.) And yes, hope might fixate on or long for a discontinuous future, seeking unforeseen ends, and so pursue some radical escape from this mess we're in, but that future would remain better and thus still constitute progress over what was left behind.

Admittedly, if one limits "progress" to incremental advances fully in line with extant expectations, the word remains in a calculative orbit. One might prefer to keep to the language of "better," therefore, and leave it at that. But "progress" reminds us that hope is temporally ecstatic, setting what might yet be in relation to what is and has been. I thus want a term that is intrinsically temporal and normatively comparative to capture hope's longings.

An essay by Samantha Vice gives me pause, however, at least regarding hope and something like pessimism. In a general way, she finds them compatible, as Winters finds hope and melancholy. But her regard is futural and so a bit more surprising. "My suggestion," she writes, "is that as long as pessimism remains on the whole general, directed toward 'human beings' rather than particular, identifiable people and behavior, it can avoid despair and thus be compatible with hope" (Vice 2020, 161). It would seem, then, that for Vice, as for me, hope concerns efforts that might progress, whereas Pessimism (the capitalization is hers) involves a more general orientation that sees a future without moral progress. But even with that compatibility, I worry, as I did with Mark Fisher, about dispositions whose object drifts into the ether. The Pessimism that Vice accepts denies that the "value we create and realize generally outweighs or 'counts for more' than the bad that we more reliably bring about" (Vice, 155). To be clear, I am not favoring optimism in such matters. Rather, I do not find myself in a position that enables me to address something like "the value created by human beings in general," and so weighing the matter quantitatively seems epistemically suspect. But I also worry about the creep of such dispositions. Beliefs regarding "human beings" open questions about each human being I meet. Yes, it would be fallacious to take a probability claim about a class to apply to each member, but it would be disingenuous not to wonder, in any case, whether those general views apply here and now. "So, ignore the negative?" No. But do not court the negative (or the positive) with abstractions that do not interact with agencies capable of conducting life, and deliberately so.

THE REAL PEOPLE WENT AWAY

"What is in question is not progress but Progress," Eagleton observes, taking the capitalized version to indicate a kind of fatalism, as if things were getting better all the time (Eagleton 2017, 7). But they are not, he insists, and many have and continue to suffer grievously in ways that could have been avoided. But Eagleton's principal aversion is to the trope of necessity, for which "Progress" is a stand-in: "The truth, however, is that catastro-

phe is not written into the march of history, any more than hope is. . . .
The contingency that can make for misfortune can also make for success"
(Eagleton, 132). And this marks Eagleton's departure from Benjamin: "Benjamin's philosophy of history, for all its spiritual wisdom, represents an
over-reaction to the idea of historical progress . . . Messianism of Benjamin's kind has too little faith in history" (Eagleton, 132–33). I confess, I
am unsure where this point lands. Does Benjamin have too little faith in
history or does his faith lie with a dimension of history often ignored by
Christian Euro-America—namely, the past and its claim on its heirs? Yes,
Benjamin finds catastrophe when he looks back (though not a necessary
catastrophe). But he also finds sacrifice, and so debt, a thought echoed by
Cornel West in this exhortation: "Never give up . . . because the folk who
came before who gave so much, they didn't do it for nothing. They didn't
do it for nothing" (West 1997, 33–34).

But wait. How did this become a matter of faith, Benjamin's or ours?
Eagleton's slide is telling. I, too, find invocations of necessity epistemically
hubristic and performatively paradoxical. Ours is a fate of the adventitious
and contingent. Neither simply nor dialectically does the whole come fully
into view even as we know, through the codependent relatedness of things,
that nothing stands alone. But determinism is not the only misstep one
can take regarding the notion of progress. Others concern which patterns/
orders/forms of becoming one takes to progress. I say this because Eagleton charges Benjamin with too little faith in history. But what is "history"
such that it bears or betrays our hopes? Unable to see that far ahead or
behind (or around me, for that matter), I neither hope for nor despair in
history. The mistake, I find, locates something like an actual or potential
subiectum, divine or human, intellectual or laboring, at the basis of this
world and its dynamic unfolding. And this allows one to imagine, through
faith or hope if not knowledge, that one might bring the whole under the
guidance and agency of whatever subject underwrites the full range of comings and goings that mark and exceed our condition. The view, a mode of
onto-theology, mishandles this world and its way of being differentially in
common. What concerns me here is how this determination, in its speculative reach, distracts and diffuses the power of hope. Hope conspires, but
when it relies on faux agencies, it seems to court despair or slide into faith.
Yes, hope follows certain desires when epistemic gaps open. But when it
fills those gaps with speculative fancies, it arrogates a fantasy.

The question before us is: If progress is integral to hope, what can prove
better off over time? History? Being? Or some fragmentary braid of actual-
ity and possibility, something like a practice (such as surgery), a relationship (such as friendship), a life (say mine and/or yours), or a community

(such as a city)? If my hopes drift into scenes arrogated by tropes that hide their internal differentiation (say, "humanity"), as well as their adventitiousness (both in what they name, again "the human," and in how they have come to name it, say by posing as "nothing themselves"), one enacts them histrionically. Like the war on terror, they generate a great deal of activity free of any sense of whether they are getting anywhere. Worse still, such hopes may drift back into an epic imaginary, where homogenizing tropes absorb our struggles at the expense of the progress that genuine differentiation enables.

When hope expands beyond what human agency can wrangle and shape, or when the adventitious presents as necessary, something inhuman stirs. To be clear, I am not suggesting that one is always mistaken to employ terms like "history," "being," "humanity," etc. Rather, my claim is that these are not the kind of things that progress, and so we should refuse them as bearers of hope or sources of despair.

As I find things, hope not only calls us to action, but limits itself to what one could conceivably pursue. Not that existing means to those ends or even those ends must be readily available or even knowable in some specific sense; that seems too practical to me. But to hope in a manner that tries to bottle the seas is more folly than I can praise.

Interlude

On Being Partial to the Truth

For the most part, we are not where we are, but in a false position.

HENRY DAVID THOREAU

OUTDOING OURSELVES

There are many things we do not know. We know this. We also know that we cannot know all that eludes our grasp. Our ignorance surrounds.

Situated, we lack a view from nowhere. We also lack the view from everywhere, which would be more impressive. But we know that we are somewhere, and we know some of where we are. You and I are partial.

Partiality offers its own vantage. It is certainly better than being nowhere. I am limited, not simply unwitting (although I can be). My moment, place, and capacities contract and focus my horizons. And I am mobile (as are all things, and in more than one way). And that multiplies vantages. So many windows in what is not a monad.

But this is stranger still. From our partiality, we cannot conclude what can and cannot be known about some particular person, place, thing, or event, including ourselves.

General and diffuse, Socratic ignorance opens onto an underspecified future.

MY LOVE IS LIKE A RED, RED ROSE IS
A ROSE IS A ROSE IS A ROSE

For many, epistemology helps declare winners and losers. It can identify and exclude the ill-formed, incoherent, and contradictory. But some losses are more than epistemic. Exclusions from inquiry, whether among the knowers or the known, entail injustice, possibly harm—orientation without representation, uninformed formulas. But this remains in the orbit of winners and losers, exposing limits in the former and pains in the latter. What about an epistemology of transformation? Thoreau writes of the love of the poet, and as a kind of knowledge. In love with its subject matter, it surpasses itself recurrently, singularizing. "You remind me of some other love" will close the book. "Tell me more about yourself" opens it.

"There is no science of the particular." Says "you," I want to say. But that is not whom I'm addressing. And does all knowledge aspire to science?

TO BE CONTINUED

Philosophy trades in insights rather than facts. It generalizes, but not by way of induction. It offers addressees a way of navigating the heteroglossia of social life. But on what authority? Or rather, what success criteria govern its offers? A grip on the significance of something true. Now for the hard part.

SO MUCH MORE TO HEAVEN AND EARTH
THAN HEAVEN AND EARTH

Hope orients, possibilizing the world, lightening it with what might be. And it does so (when it does, if it does) by seizing us with nested replays of what has been. Hope is homely.

"Where are *you* when you say that?" When I was a student, this was *the* question. It asked addressees to acknowledge their situatedness, to mark their part and how it parted us, thereby acknowledging difference.

I now hear the question of our situatedness through Emerson's query: "Where do we find ourselves?" Several replies come to mind, but one—admittedly multifaceted—has proven insistent. The questions find me in a finding disposed toward "you" in what I would call our world, the only world, the one *world*, or so I would use that word. You needn't. But if you multiply worlds, there is always the world in which one witnesses the multiplicity, marks the surfeit, argues over how best to describe it. There is one world in which worlds interact (well or not) or run in parallel. It is the relative of all that can be said to be relative to some other.

One world suffuses what hope imagines and transfigures. It is the world in which counting became possible among beings who had become actual, for a time. It is the world of *Erlebnis* and *Erfahrung*, a world of worldviews, where they arise, meet, fuse (in part), or talk past one another. It is a world of objects and their domains—organism, atom, quanta, the inorganic, etc.

It is the world of schemes (paradigms, webs of inquiry, vocabularies, stand-points, etc.) and their limits.

One cannot fall from this world, nor will it come like a kingdom. It is the world of exile and homecoming, longing and nostalgia, the world of gene-alogists, metaphysicians, and skeptics, too, of all romances, true or false. It is the world in which we might doubt its and our existence. It is the world in which another's strangeness provokes: "What world are you from?"

NEITHER HERE NOR THERE

Whatever exists shares sites wherein differences—quantitative, qualita-tive—occur. But such a world does not appear as one among many. Its difference is different, which is why, like Wallace Stevens, one might speak of a general absence, a there that is not there beside some hill in Tennes-see. But by running between every "where" it nevertheless underwrites an expanse of coursing relations: jar, hill, wisp of cloud, picnicking lovers. To be this or any "thing" is to be differentiated from some something, to unfold in a shared alterity, together and apart, always among other things that too are among. The truly one would be the only one and thus none. It could not be anywhere or any when, or even "one," for that matter. To be one is to be among some. *There* (which it could not offer), you and I would have no one to talk to, nothing to talk about, not even *moksha* from *maya* or the mind-blowing encompass of *Brahman*. (*Om* would have no syllables.)

Ours is the one world in which a god might appear, either as an unimagi-nable potency or as the filament of a startled imagination wandering at its edge. Or more than one god. Polytheism is no more believable, but it has an honesty about it, one that pantheism and monotheism lack. Wind above water, one sun rising, or a child born blue, gods enter stage left.

There is one world. Across the slightest sum of these littered expanses, the human emerged, an ever more curious phenomenon. And along con-tinuous, nonidentical reaches, the human will fade through an exposition en route to somewhat else. This is where we find ourselves, in a world of deeds and relations, things and persons, words and ecologies, weather and institutions. Every venture flashes or is dashed in its corners and joints. Whatever turns on a stem or axis or dime twists and turns here.

AGAIN, BUT LIKE YOU MEAN IT

Words no less than things are worldly. Metaphors bear source domains even as they allow us to stay on top of things or fall behind the times. Speech is breath, and so wind, and so atmospheric pressures reflecting variations in temperature, thus blurring earth and air at an elemental level. Trees have fallen into the weaves of paper, and regarding ink, so much flows from the tip, a mixture of parts like pigments and dyes, solvents, resins, and lubricants, each of which leads even further afield until the book of nature unveils nature in the book, and not just as a self-secluding, withdrawing ground. Beings bear their dependencies far more openly. (Are they debts? With whom, measured how? One should beware of thinking of the cosmos as a bank.)

Words also belong to phrases and sentences, to assertions, justifications, questions, and insults—that is, to deeds no less in common than trees, hands, the stratosphere, or microbes. The trial of slapping words onto things is the dream of a lonely man. The mindful do more than course between sign and signified. Triadic in nature, words function through reference to referents and offers to addresses, and always in determined settings. Not that we interpret or respond to speech-acts in the same ways. We know we do not, but that is because we utter and mutter across one world.

ETCHINGS

The finite is bound. This is neither an axiom nor a stipulation, but a common usage repeated to suggest something more general but nevertheless finite, even relative to all that "finite" says.

"Such as?"

One sense of "finite" concerns what is completely determinable by thought. But that sense of thought is not itself finite, whereas my sense is.

Usages are a mark of philosophy's finitude, as when I insist (and I do) that whatever is finite is *some*-thing among other things, a part apart that does not exist through itself but through something other. The finite is thus always in relation and so subject to influence, for better or for worse (or indifferently so, as it is for most). And there are numerous ways to be finite: a point, a line, a square, one hour, a term for an elected office, a human life, humanity, a planet, a star . . . name it, you got it.

MONO NO AWARE

Death (like birth) is a facet of finitude—at least ours. We come to be and pass away. We might wring our hands about when life begins but it does, we do. And while death criteria may be difficult to pinpoint, our energy refuses to be conserved, and precisely because of our dynamism.

As Beauvoir suggests, living and dying are an ambiguous braid. We can die because we live, and every living day brings us closer to our death. Moreover, to greater and lesser degrees, we live in the face of death. The days themselves die. Not that they disappear altogether. But the possibilities of a day give way, never to return. And we feel that, say, in the fast fuse of a blossoming cherry or the recurring memory of a failure, fuck up, or fumble.

IT TAKES THREE TO TANGLE

We do not exist through ourselves. Nothing does. Substance tropes the finite toward its disappearance, gobbling up the crumbs.

TANGLED WEBS AND TANGLED WEAVERS

It is strange that a lyric poem can undo you in a quandary—who is reading, what is happening, now, here, if those words make sense anymore?

MY SECRET IDENTITY IS

The room is empty,
And the window is open
(Simic 1989)

I discovered Simic when a friend, Rebecca Szekely, gave me *Unending Blues* in 1990. Better still, she sent it to a former address, which I discovered when I returned to collect, unsuccessfully, something I had left behind. There are near hits as well as near misses, and this hit is still with me in the space where the period should have closed the poem that closes *The World Doesn't End*.

But the point made by this absence of a point is far more expansive than an open-ended diachronic link, although it is that. All answers to the question "Who am I?" are unfolding, relentlessly. But also, we breathe and so live in an atmosphere, a compendium of gases (foremost nitrogen, then oxygen, then argon, carbon dioxide, and various trace gases) that circulate in layers in response to fluctuating temperatures. The troposphere accounts for 80 percent of that froth, with four other layers making up the difference, the last, the exosphere, a liminal zone, neither quite that of earth or space, but somehow both as well. We move and surf what gravity allows, even if we resist it or manage the velocity to break its local grip.

We eat what we do not grow (even if we farmed it). We speak what we did not author.

We are also creatures of transport. But who laid the roads and tracks or paved the tarmac? There are answers, but our names and the name "humanity" does not complete them. What accounts for the histories of all that we call fuel? How much and how many meet in a lump of coal?

And then there is all we need from one another, and not just as infants or procreators: love, help, recognition, praise, sex, teammates, coworkers, parents, fellow citizens, friends, strangers too, even enemies in a certain way, or at least the ability to know them.

Finitude names our belonging together, our inseparable yet differentiated being together. Everything we do nests in the weave of something else. Don't you love it?

UNMOVED

Variously, even before the "West" named itself as such, or some who lived there proclaimed it such, perfection has been associated with what (purportedly) exists through itself, even as a law unto itself. To be one's own cause, for many, that is where bragging rights lie, even dignity.

To my ear, "autonomy" secretes self-loathing. It disparages the wonder of our manifold relations, the reverberating strands we traverse, which thicken and diminish asynchronously. Look around: the rise of a mountain, the gestation of a cicada, the ten-day life of the male mosquito, our sun firing for ten billion years until . . .

Can you count all that has left its mark on you, orienting and reorienting your days? To whom and to what do you owe not only your life but the cast of your character, the intricate lace of your lungs, your temperament, the nutrition that fueled your development, your words and grammar, your go-to justifications, the curve of your jaw . . . the list continues. Heteronomy is less a second skin than the layers of any skin, voice, or gait. It does not delimit what is already there but generates what emerges, including us. I will not celebrate its negation.

PLAY WITHIN A PLAY

An essayist composes ludes. Something underway—whether found or imagined—is played with or on (the Latin *ludus*). But unlike *Vernunft*, the essayistic imagination seeks the conditioned, revels in it. And so, the standard prefixes (pre-, inter-, post-) are affronts; the interval demands its own currency.

THE ERROR OF OUR WAYS

Philosophy's native realm is error. It is born there, and error is where it lives. And should it die, and I presume it can and will, philosophy will feel more at home in the company of failure than success.

INCITATION

Philosophical specialization proceeds at the expense of wisdom, and eventually, its love.

TRIPPED INTO BEING ME

Learning is a humbling affair; one was either mistaken or ignorant. Surprise is also bound to mistakes. What seizes our attention exposes our ignorance or some misstep—how cold the water is, how hot the dancing lights, how differently a book reads thirty years later. Even experience is something like a child of error. Were our anticipations always right, I doubt we would notice, and I doubt that anything like "noticing"—one name for one movement between anticipation and occurrence—would ever have evolved.

Where would we be without error? I doubt we would be in-the-world as we are. To be clear, my point is not Heidegger's when he argues in *Being and Time* that we are ensnared in the everyday, and thus forgetful of our being's strange grounding in possibility, or, in a related argument from "On the Essence of Truth," that our absorption in the world of beings renders us forgetful of the clearing event that enables us to be there amid beings (Heidegger 1962, 1993). I have something more prosaic in mind. Were our relations mostly adequate, the character of our being would be quite different. We might hover like Rilke's angels, *fruhe Gegluckte*, "early successes," *Gelenke des Lichtes*, "joints of light," mirroring the rushing world.

But not to worry. The earliest scenes of instruction envelop us in error. As awareness dawns, the world expands around our tiny mouths. Return to childhood haunts—the woods behind the house, the swampy stream to its left. If you are like me, you'll be startled. They seem so petite whereas once they were too vast to survey: dandelion and skunk cabbage, bullfrog and toad, chipmunk, white-tailed deer, though variously, depending upon the season, which was itself a marvel—spring peepers despite the lingering snow. Not that such a site has been exhausted. That would just be another error. Even keeping to the deceiving glow of universals, the scenes are rich beyond our ken: *pseudacris crucifer, symplocarpus foetidus*, pine and birch in spring and fall, ground water buried deep but seeping, granite and shale in Ossining, possibly from *assunung*, meaning "place of stones" in a Lenape dialectic of Algonquin called Munsee, spoken by those also called Munsee, though several names swirl around the land I have in mind, such as Wappinger and Kitchawanks (Grumet 2013, 117).

"We can never surprise nature in a corner," Emerson writes, "never find the end of a thread; never tell where to set the first stone" (Emerson 1971, 124). Nature not only likes to hide. It also shows itself variously across a vast, changing yet woven complexity, synchronous in certain ways, asynchronous in others—rock and water, soil accruing, nurse logs and ferns, but also persons and people, which in my corner of Ossining, New York, involves migrations, invasions, microbes, and murder. Our recurring introduction to the world is awash in this surfeit, and so, over time, anticipation and presumption twist noticing into a desire to know.

SWING AND A MISS

An eventual inadequacy awaits philosophical ventures. Even its most illustrious practitioners warrant correction. In fact, the greater the figure, the more powerful the counterstroke: Aristotle to Plato, Spinoza to Descartes, Hegel to Kant. Not that the squabbles are unresolvable. Aristotle demonstrates convincingly that ethical deliberation is insufficiently oriented by definitions of the good *überhaupt*. Spinoza rightly argues that the search for truth criteria opens onto an infinite regress. And Hegel was right to historicize the patterns of knowing (and doing) that propel natural consciousness. Nothing convinces for very long, and many exquisite moments are born in the realization and demonstration of another's shortcoming.

PITHY AFTERTHOUGHT

Socratic ignorance can prove a humblebrag. Own up, but don't overdo (or overrun) it.

FOR SO MANY REASONS

Any word that would be the last word on what can be cannot be.

NOTHING REALLY MATTERS

Delivered in 1929, Heidegger's "What is Metaphysics?" is a broadside against Hegel, who holds that negation is the activity of a subject, a dialectic replay of the *subiectum*, hence neither a simple substratum nor some detached awareness that knows it: "This living substance is being, which is in truth *subject*, or, what is the same, is in truth actual only in so far as it is the movement of positing itself, or is the mediation of its self-othering with itself. This substance is, as subject, pure negativity" (Hegel 1977, 10). To be clear, such a subject is neither you nor me nor some aggregate we, but *Geist*, the self-othering, self-recovering cosmos for which we have front row seats, meaning we can recognize it as such and our own place (and practice) therein—me and you looking at you and me looking at everything, including me and you, looking.

But what allows spirit to think and posit (*setzen*) itself in word and deed? What opens that scene, arranges that stage, and so enables that activity? "Negativity" is also Heidegger's response, at least in 1929, but freed from the activity of subjects who presuppose an open, differentiated world whose simplicity might be negated (the first, self-othering negation) and then negated again (the second, self-recovering negation). But to say that condition of possibility per se, Heidegger must rely on locutions even stranger than Hegel's—the nothing itself nothings or nihilates, *das Nichts selbst nichten* (Heidegger 1993, 103).

As I read him, Jean-Luc Nancy intensifies Heidegger's turnout of Hegel, rethinking nothing as the finite being-in-common of existence, what I have presented as the one world. I have already glossed the thought by presenting finitude as the fundamental relatedness of things, which claims that existences have their character through otherness, and vice versa, such that existence is a matter of shared alterity or differential relatedness. And across the board, that is, not just for I's and you's, but I's and its, and its and its.

Nancy's advance is grammatical, locating the drama of ontology amid beings, in their finite unfolding, what he once termed their *compearance* (Nancy 1991). I call the move grammatical because it redirects our attention, like a shift in case. Nancy's ontology orients us toward other beings (whatever else an existent appears with) rather than (a) some *subiectum*— mind, matter, god—that manifests itself through the fireworks, or (b) some ontologically differentiated Being (or the nothing) mysteriously opening the show. In other words, Nancy's ontology locates us, or rather, helps us find ourselves in the one, finite world, and without rendering it a site of diminished occurrence: "*Finitude* does not mean that we are noninfinite— like small, insignificant beings within a grand, universal, and continuous being—but it means that we are *infinitely* finite, infinitely exposed to the otherness of our own 'being' (or that being is in us exposed to its own otherness)" (Nancy 1993, 155).

Nancy opens a common fate. "We begin and we end without beginning and ending," he writes, "without having a beginning and an end that is *ours* but having (or being) them only as others, and through others" (Nancy, 155–56). But this is not to account for all that befalls us, thereby leaving us singular in a manner that converts every occurrence into an allegory of a never-ending story. Tarrying with the grammar of compearance grants facticity citizen's rights in ontology. If we are not best understood as the appearance of some *subiectum* manifesting through us—how modish— then whatever we are, in our compearance, characterizes our existence. And this allows for wildly (and terribly) asymmetrical fates, including (a) those shackled to other existences with whom they compear, and, for the story always has at least one other side, (b) those whose conduct, wittingly or not, smiths the bondage of others.

Imagine you and me in common, a differentiated braid. Or don't. We still are. Now race us, differentially, keeping to the United States (although we need not). And now read Fred Moten (again): "*In* can't simply act as if *and's* segregation, however unreal, doesn't produce absolutely real effects" (Moten 2017, 226). There is one world of compearance. Its finitude is vast and, in many ways, glorious. But those points at which shared alterity reverberates can nevertheless prove asymmetrical, and in ways brimming with error, ignorance, and violence born of hate.

CITIES IN SPEECH

The world I have in mind and that occasions mind is not constructed by individuals or some group of people. Socializing the Kantian synthesis is even less convincing than the original's empirico-transcendental polka. I thus resist María Lugones's use of "world" to denote various constructions such as a "traditional Hispano construction of northern New Mexican life," which she contrasts with a "racist, ethnocentric money-centered Anglo construction of northern New Mexican life" (Lugones 2003, 88). Because she can observe these differences, move between them, and because they interact, I find it unhelpful to designate each a world unto itself.

But I know what she means. I nod in agreement when she insists, "In describing my sense of 'world,' I am offering a description of experience, something that is true to experience even if it is ontologically problematic" (Lugones, 89). Sense of self—say, of one's confidence, capabilities, or relative safety—varies with shifts in social locations, sometimes dramatically, sometimes subtly. Positionality is ontologically real for dependent, relational beings. To account for the emergence and recognition of those differences as well as interactions among them, including the traveling that Lugones advocates, I prefer language that is ontologically less problematic.

My concern is the inverse of Mariana Ortega's, which wants to account for the "oneness or continuity of the multiplicitous self" that travels between worlds and experiences itself as in-between them (Ortega 2016, 78). With a hermeneutic of emendation, Ortega allows texts by Lugones, Anzaldúa, and Heidegger (principally *Being and Time*) to complement and correct one another, leading to the claim that "multiplicitous selves . . . are being-between-worlds and being-in-worlds in different ways" (Ortega, 68). I agree that we are multiplicitous, and I've built a complementary case, although I would distinguish continuity (which we have) from unity (which we do not) (Lysaker and Lysaker 2005; Lysaker and Lysaker 2017, 2021). But I want to free "world" from the subject-dependent orientation still operative in *Being and Time*. The being-in-common of what is does not result from the hermeneutic projects of *Dasein*, which remain responsive and so always dependent and derivative. We can account for differences in lived experience without confusing ontological gestures. And we need reference to one world to account for our account of those differences.

IT'S A SMALL WORLD AFTER ALL

Markus Gabriel would have me drop the term "world" for "fields of sense," which I can appreciate, having also regarded "sense," or *Sinn*, as a characteristic, differentiated way of appearing and thus as a primitive term for existence (Gabriel 2015; Lysaker 2002). "Sense" names the character with which a phenomenon appears amid others. And I am doubly pleased by his reliance on "field," which metaphorically transposes an agricultural term (possibly a domestic one, if the Old English *flōr* underwrites it). But let me hasten to point out that "sense" is just a more settled metaphor, coming from the Anglo-French *sen*, *sens*, concerning "sensation, feeling, mechanism of perception, meaning," which comes from the Latin *sensus*, from *sentire*, "to perceive, feel." And even those terms may echo the Old High German *sinnan*, meaning "to go, strive," as well as the Old English *sith*, "journey." Whatever exists journeys in a field of sense.

Why favor "fields of sense" over "world"? Gabriel claims that "world" "always suggests a closed totality"—more particularly, a domain that includes all objects and all domains of objects, from those assessed by physics to nation-states to memories to the ideality of a sign standing for series of things such as "memories," "nation-states," or "physicists" (Gabriel 2015, 65). But such a phenomenon cannot exist because it would need a context in which to appear, which in turn would mark an outside to its would-be, all-encompassing scope. "The world does not exist," Gabriel concludes. "If the world were to exist, it would have to appear in a field of sense, but that is impossible" (Gabriel, 78).

Gabriel's argument reminds me of Heidegger's self-critical observation regarding epochs (Heidegger 1962). At certain points in Heidegger's corpus the sense of beings appears bound to historical epochs—the *ens creatum* of the Middle Ages, modernity's object of representation or valuation, the fungible potentiality of energy in the age of technology, etc. But epochs have their own origins, their own journey, as it were, and that sets them within a site of differential appearing that they in some sense share by way of compearing within it. Epochality is not the last word on originary sense, therefore. But then, neither is "fields of sense." Each has its own manner of compearing alongside others and the phenomena they render conspicuous (which is not to say "construct"). I am thus unsure what decides a dispute at this point. Any term will transpose an extant sign onto what, strictly speaking, is no-thing and yet not otherworldly, that is, not independent of the surfeit of what appears as a this, that, who, it, what have you (and whatnot). And it is precisely that strange weave of things and no-thing, of time and space, that leads me to favor the word "world" to name the shared, differential site of compearance. The world is not a thing within the world, but neither is it otherworldly. Rather, it indicates that whatever appears compears and so does not stand alone; it is worldly.

"But that is to take 'world' metaphorically." True, like "field." And its particular metaphoricity may be a strength. No term that draws an analogue to some-thing is quite apposite in this context. How, then, to refer to a "dimension" of existence that is neither substance nor mode, neither sign nor signified, and certainly not a spatiotemporal object or some law governing its operations? Nor is it the activity of an agent. And yet it is part and parcel of the character of each insofar as they appear—or rather, compear.

I welcome the play of metaphor in ontology, its give and take back, as it were, because I find the core of Gabriel's dismissal of "world" perplexing. "World" does not always or even usually refer to a closed totality. It invokes a bounded, distinct range of nested and interacting phenomena, but rarely if ever is a world closed, at least in English. The earth is a world within a solar system, warmed by the sun and tugged by the moon, which is why H. G. Wells was able to imagine a "war of the worlds." Culturally speaking, we refer to the world of people X with the presumption that it emerged from predecessors, existed among others, and gave way to scions. And even then, we know it for a shorthand that proposes more unity than exists. The academic world is such a phenomenon. It is distinct enough to refer to but far from univocal, let alone closed, hence its distinction from the "real world" awaiting its graduates (and paying most of its bills, including faculty salaries). And while we do say, in English, that someone lives in their own world, the usage drips irony. Finally, the etymology of the English "world" refers us to the Old English *wer* and *eald*, indicating the age of man in contrast, one presumes, with times dominated by the presence of other forces and creatures. In short, "world" rarely names a closed totality; it remains open at its fringes. And that is also why I favor the term. It allows me to gather what compears without invoking the otherworldly or inverting the worldly, and it does so without pretending to conceptually bind that anarchic surfeit.

EQUAL TEMPERAMENT

Think of philosophical concepts and sentences as musical scores—instructions for generating thoughts that find their way to others or fade from use. You won't know unless you try.

EPHEMERA

Keeping it real loses its way through the distinction on which it relies.

The particular is the universal's poor relation.

The accident shows its quality when substance is found among the casualties.

LEARNING OUTCOMES

Rorty's insistence that vocabularies are not truth-functional is less compelling than it once seemed (Rorty 1989). As he understands them, vocabularies (e.g., Newtonian mechanics, quantum theory, psychoanalysis), can only be tested in a circular manner—namely, by presupposing their own domain of objects (say, a world of wave and particle, or the unconscious and its sublimations). And he concludes that vocabularies are invented or evolved rather than discovered, and that such inventions or fictions enable the kind of discoveries that can be hammered out in ways that are true or false—namely, at the level of sentences.

I once affirmed this thought (Lysaker 1996). It now seems unconvincing. Vocabularies do not arise independently of discoveries, and so the truth (and falsity) of various discoveries is part of the mortar that holds together a vocabulary's outer and inner walls. (Newton did not awake one morning to Newtonian mechanics, and Saul opened his eyes as Paul in the thick of a messianic, theistic context.) And that is no less true if we drop "invention" in favor of cultural evolution. The process of epistemic change remains bound to discoveries and their contestation—an anomaly is a discovery, after all, and one communicated by way of a finite set of truth claims (as opposed to an entirely new paradigm). It is thus not the case that paradigms die all at once. Instead, they die in part because they receive multiple small cuts delivered by truth-functional blades. Secondly, and more importantly, vocabularies must prove phenomenologically fit if one is going to enact them. Rorty often invokes psychoanalysis as the kind of invention that could fuel self-creation rather than self-discovery, although discoveries become possible once we accept the invention. But is it just a matter of accepting the vocabulary (or not) without reference to experience's epistemic valence?

Imagine a continuum marked by two extremes. One involves an apprehension that leaves nothing unanticipated, including the logic and character of anticipation—call it complete, absolute knowledge. At the other, nothing that has been anticipated occurs, and the basic structures of anticipation operate unconsciously—call this absolute ignorance. How would you respond to a vocabulary that approached absolute ignorance? Not just that you kept misinterpreting your dreams. There never were any "dreams" to interpret, and so the invitation to do so found nothing to address. Not that you found the "death instinct" odd, but desire itself was . . . what now? Rorty's pragmatism invites us to accept and reject vocabularies depending on our interests. But a vocabulary approaching absolute error would prove unable to further any interest or include a term as felicitous (if vague) as "interest" or "vocabulary."

Not that Rorty's error is wholesale. If anything, it works well enough to run counter to the point he wants to make. Rorty's distinction between sentence and vocabulary has some traction—that is, it brings us into a working relationship with some swath of our experience, say, disciplinary habits and broad social conventions. And it helps me think about different approaches to similar phenomena, something I might miss if I kept to the level of sentences.

"Is the concept 'vocabulary' somehow literal, therefore, or a natural kind?" No. In Rorty's work, "vocabulary" is clearly a metaphor. But metaphors can be apposite or not, or better still, more or less apposite. My claim is that "vocabulary," as deployed by Rorty, is somewhat apposite to the phenomena in question—that is, it rings "true."

I no longer believe, therefore, that one can altogether detach vocabularies (or paradigms, or webs of inquiry, or epochs of being, or discursive regimes, or patterns of inquiry) from epistemic considerations. Nor do I think that philosophy can take refuge in discourses indifferent to truth. Their value to us is bound in part to the traction they provide, which is what I always took James to mean when he claimed that the true is "only the expedient ['in the long run and on the whole'] in our way of thinking," meaning it secures our footing (James 1978, 106). And while the modifier "only" is hasty, one could hear it this way. We grant certain claims the status of "truth" because they fit the scene in which they are uttered. That is what we mean when we say of some remark that it is "true." "To agree in the widest sense with a reality," James writes, "can only mean to be guided either straight up to it or into its surroundings, or to be put into such working touch with it as to handle either it or something connected with it better than if we disagreed. Better either intellectually or practically" (James, 102). But today's working touch is tomorrow's clumsy grasp, and so even what merits the approbation "true" must remain open to reassessment: "The truth of an idea is not a stagnant property inherent in it. Truth happens to an idea. It becomes true, is made true by events. Its verity is in fact an event, a process" (James, 97). Rather than simply valorizing expediency, therefore, James's "only the expedient" keeps us on our toes.

WAS IT GOOD FOR YOU?

Binding philosophy to something like the desire to know, and linking knowledge to truth as accord, does not settle the question of the value of truth, nor abandon care of the self for know thyself. Addressing sexual phenomena, one might, like Foucault, wonder whether discourses of pleasure (the *ars erotica*) are preferable to those that address sexuality only to know it (the *scientia sexualis*). But, even in denying truth a seat among the greater goods, it remains a value. No discourse of pleasure can operate outside epistemic considerations without dissolving into an unordered collection of painful directives.

FADE TO WHITE

Convention T was Tarski's effort to capture how "true" operates in relation to sentences (Tarski 1983). "Snow is white" is true if and only if *snow is white*. "True" applies when there is agreement or accord between an assertion and the affairs to which the sentence refers. Not that Convention T explains what "accord" means, or whether any other conditions must also obtain for there to be accord between assertions and states of affairs. In fact, Tarski's approach seems more anthropological than epistemological. His theory verges on ethnography. Find people using the word "true" to describe sentences (or suitable translations of "true") and you will find accord between what is asserted and what is found.

IT TAKES A VILLAGE

Coherence theories ask us to pursue a holism that is less ambitious than Hegel's. Focusing upon the moment of evaluation, they argue that "is true" requires more than accord between an assertion and the affairs to which it refers. The assertion also must prove consistent with some other beliefs that one also affirms. The point is not just that coherence informs practices of justification, but that one needs coherence to say, with confidence, "is true." According to Brand Blanshard, for whom Euclidian geometry approximated the ideal, coherence is achieved when "every proposition would be entailed by the others jointly and even singly" and the whole ensemble could account for every situation (Kirkham 1992, 106). (The proviso is crucial: a belief could cohere and still be false if other beliefs are also false.)

Coherence theories are dissatisfying. If all states of affairs are accounted for, why the need for coherence? Also, to the degree the ideal is just that—an ideal—we are left, as Richard Kirkham suggests, with coherent but incompatible rivals (Kirkham 1992). But coherence theories rightly force us to complicate what funds evaluations that result in judgments such as "is true" or "is false." We don't simply compare the assertion with its referent. We also compare the assertion with other assertions. This is not to say that reality is mind-dependent, and I confess, I find that issue ontological and, in this context, distracting; accord of the sort captured by Convention T can be had (or lost) in either case. The pertinent issue is that "true" and "false" belong to a practice that considers how a given assertion relates to more than isolated states of affairs—namely, its relations to other assertions already deemed "true" or "false" also count. On the side of the knower, therefore, "truth" unfolds in dramas whose complexity exceeds what Convention T stages.

BE REAL

Honesty revolves around truth telling, although the affairs concern our beliefs, feelings, and deeds. Self-presentations also can be true or false, and if they are intentionally the latter, they are lies. Not that we are transparent to ourselves. But we have sufficient self-awareness to lie or tell the truth, and in either case, Convention T and its relation of accord are in play. The honest person states what is the case as far as they know and so satisfies the convention or doesn't.

The prototypical truth-claim calls to mind a judgment about objects and events, about what was, is, or will be the case. But truth also orders certain relations between different subjects and between subjects and themselves, underwriting a chief virtue of intersubjectivity, possibly even dignity. "At least be honest with yourself," she said, with disgust.

I THINK THE WORLD OF US

Norms mediate our relations. Or let Foucault spin the Hegelian top: norms institute *us* in relation. You say, "Paper burns at 451 degrees Fahrenheit." I reply, "Is that true?" And so opens a scene, including: (a) a speaker, (b) an assertion, (c) a referent, (d) addressees, (e) some preestablished scene wherein speakers make assertions about things to others, (f) possible evidence, (g) an evaluator, and (h) an evaluation on the order of "true" and some contrast term like "false" or "error" or "lie." And that is just the beginning, a string of paper dolls. The synchronic field I am marking is also diachronically suffused. Each variable conducts a history, and at many points one finds *savoir* for the known. And always a *mis en scéne*. Among the deeds, at the beginning, was the world.

REALLY?

Theories of truth, particularly semantic theories, often focus on utterances like "That's true." The question is: What is thereby conveyed? But this may be too narrow a scene for the nature of truth to manifest. If nothing had fallen into question, if there weren't doubts, or better still, disagreement, why find words for good beliefs? We say "true" when it might be otherwise. The idea of truth is thus a response (among other possibilities) to more than conditions of accord—in the least, uncertainty (hence error) and disagreement.

"So?" Coming to terms with a concept like truth requires us to acknowledge possible error and disagreement, which in turn acknowledges a kind of sociality wherein those possibilities arise. The sociality in question does not simply lie with the fact that assertions imply addressees or that speakers, as concrete others to one another, also speak from the standpoint of a generalized other. Rather, an interest in truth further exposes us to one another, coordinates us in a certain way. We become answerable, and in a manner that we must learn.

NOT SO FAST, FREDDY

Inventions require discoveries. Discoveries worth making are inventive. A fiction outside a world of facts would be unreadable. What would you be reading, and what would have led you to read that rather than burn, hurl, or eat it? Even errors are not completely out of touch. They get right being the kind of thing that can be wrong.

KNOCK ON WOOD

"Truth" marks a point at which you and I, in company, pivot to pause and order ourselves in response to the world. Not that such a point is simple. To be true can mean to be loyal (a true friend), to be stable and reliable (may your sword be true), to accurately describe or predict something (paper burns at 451 degrees Fahrenheit), to be legitimate (a true heir), to be symmetrical (the bicycle's wheels were true), to be fully realized (my dream came true), etc. The etymology of "truth" is also variegated and suggests multiple, metaphorical migrations—Middle English *trewe*, from Old English *trēowe*, faithful; akin to Old High German *gi-triuwi*, faithful, Old Irish *derb*, sure, and probably to Sanskvrit *dāruṇa*, hard, and *dāru*, wood.

TRUE THAT

"That's true" also signals agreement with an assertion, which exposes the performativity operating in the idea of truth. In fact, "that's true" can be a pro-sentence for an assertion the way that "he" is a pronoun for John Lysaker. We sometimes use "discovery" in this way, as a shorthand for what was discovered.

And yet, we sign on in these ways because we think the assertion in question accords with what it designates. (If snow isn't white but I signal agreement with your claim that it is by saying "that's true," I've done so mistakenly.) Not that those who champion the performative have not discovered something in their readings of "that's true." But what they have discovered rides piggyback on truth's assertoric sense.

FOLLOW THE LEADER

Some time ago, when I lived in Nashville, a curious server saw me reading and writing and asked what I was doing. "Qualifying exams," I replied, and then clumsily described the task. "Epistemology," I continued, using the notion of truth as a paradigmatic, epistemological concern. "Jesus is the truth," she replied, and wondered if that could be the basis for an answer on my exam. I knew what an anthropological account would say, but I was less certain how to reply philosophically. What does it mean for a being (a divine being, admittedly) to be the truth? Is this to say that as the really real, Jesus (the trinity, more thoroughly), is the whole to which my mortal truth claims aspire, and not just in word but deed as well? Is this what follows from identifying the *logos* with Jesus? If so, truth would not principally be a relation of accord but that with which one comes into accord (or not). And that seems to introduce an unhelpful ambiguity into our proceedings, albeit a common one that riddles *logos* as well. The idea of "knowing the truth" also emphasizes the far side of Convention T as opposed to the relation itself—the truth is that which we want to know, snow, in its whiteness.

But that reading of my server's remark is too one-sided. The idea that Jesus is the truth comes from John 14:6: "I am the way, and the truth, and the life. No one comes to the Father but by me" (May and Metzger 1962, 1308). This softens the ambiguity, I think, and again sets the notion of accord at the heart of what "truth" calls to mind. Jesus's astounding assertion is that he, as the way to the father, is in accord with the father, and thus, if we wish to be in accord with the father, we must be in accord with him. To be a true Christian is to be Christlike.

KEEPING IT REAL

"True": the word itself is a mobile army of metaphors. As Derrida observes, reading Nietzsche: "Indeed, there is no such thing as truth itself. But only a surfeit of it. Even if it should be for me, about me, truth is plural" (Derrida 1979, 103). One can hear this in several ways. "Truth" and its variants establish multiple relations between persons and themselves and others, or the world more generally. Which is a different point than one concerning the iterability of "truth." One holds that truth, like being, is said in many ways; the other, that "true" must be said many times if it is to have any currency. There may also be a third point: the truth of anything may be manifold. Can you say everything that is true of your smile?

KNOW WHAT I MEAN?

The more you understand, the less you know.

NOTHING TO SEE HERE?

Beholding the mobility of truth prompts the question, Does the assertoric sense of true explain anything? The negative intuition thinks that Convention T only explains that one is authorized to say "is true" when an assertion accords with an affair. It does not explain what accord entails, and thus it does not empower inquiry by indicating some special trait that true beliefs bear. When we try to determine what is true, the view continues, justification does the heavy lifting. What prompts the approbation "that's true" is evidence compiled on behalf of the assertion, not our perception of some special truth-state borne by the assertion or running between assertions and the world.

I agree that having a good theory of truth will not help us locate true beliefs in a sack of false ones. But I also think it reasonable to ask whether there is a difference between "is justified" and "is true." We can readily imagine an assertion being justified—in fact, being the best assertion around—but later proving false. It seems "is justified" is not the same as "is true."

Pascal Engel poses this question to Richard Rorty (Rorty and Engel 2007). Rorty denies that his view is based on an "accurate analysis of the concepts of justification and truth as they are currently employed" (Rorty and Engel, 2007, 41). Instead, he is proposing a revision in order to run our normative projects more productively. As a reply, this seems to be a vintage *Rorty shrug*, a gesture whereby he refuses to acknowledge a burden that his interlocutor believes he bears. But more can be said on Rorty's behalf. Why, in a normative project, defer to tradition, which here operates through semantically fueled intuitions? Or, said less rhetorically, an "accurate analysis of the concepts of justification and truth as they are currently employed" does not yield results that wield conclusive authority over knowledge-seeking practices. They might, but more needs to be said than "This is how we've always done things" regarding truth.

But Engel's question persists. Should we distinguish "is true" from "is justified"? "No," Rorty thinks. He is unable to make useful sense of "accord"—my term, via Heidegger. (Rorty favors correspondence.) Moreover, Rorty believes that our knowledge-oriented practices are "better off when we take ourselves to be responsible to others rather than nonhuman entities such as *truth* or *reality*" (Rorty and Engel, 40). The thought is that justification keeps us oriented toward one another—those we are trying to persuade or be persuaded by—whereas "truth" directs us toward a world that cannot, on its own, settle disputes.

Rorty's position is difficult to evaluate. What indicates that we are "better off"? And who are "we"? This seems like burden shifting. The normative question that "true" was to solve seems to have been outsourced to "better off." I think we can make some progress on the matter if we consider what an addressee wants from someone venturing truth claims. If you tell me something and I ask, "But is it true?" is my principal concern that you have your reasons, or am I asking, "Will this bring me into working accord with the world?" The latter seems the more telling interest. Many people have *their reasons*. That is a minimal criterion for membership in a community of inquiry. But once that is met, and when I specify that the issue is truth, I want to know whether the reasons or justifications are good ones.

One criterion for good justification involves relevance. The justification must address the matter at hand. You claim that I am not at home. Your reasons are paper burns at 451 degrees Fahrenheit, Washington was the first president of the United States, and heliotropism is false. These are bad reasons. They have no bearing on whether I am at home; they are out of touch with that phenomenon altogether. Each could be true or false and I might still be at home (or not). I am concluding, therefore, that justification faces a demand for relevance that tethers justifying ourselves to a working notion of truth as accord. To be relevant, a justification must bear on whether a given assertion accords with what is asserted.

If I am right about justification and accord, I think we can see why it seems so easy to distinguish "is true" from "is justified." The latter aims at the former but can fall short. And that gives us two reasons to be interested in the distinction. Truth as accord is something justification aims to demonstrate in assertoric speech-acts. Second, justifications can be persuasive and establish consensus and still fall short; keeping "is true" distinct from "is justified" keeps that possibility on our minds.

"But wait," Rorty will interject—this renders our epistemic responsibilities oriented toward "nonhuman entities such as *truth* or *reality*" rather than each other. I don't think so. In fact, truth keeps us honest in our responsibilities to each other. We fulfill our responsibilities to one another in assertoric matters by limiting *true that* to cases where we believe that Convention T has been satisfied, cases where accord has been found between what we assert and the world.

TRUTHS AND SOCIAL FACTS

"Radiation sickness occurs when high-energy radiation damages or destroys certain cells in your body" (Mayo Clinic 2021). Presume this is true: radiation sickness occurs when high-energy radiation damages or destroys certain cells in your body. To be clear, this sentence involves stand-ins for more complex matters. "Radiation sickness" is associated with a range of bodily events such as nausea and vomiting, diarrhea, headache, fever, dizziness and disorientation, weakness and fatigue, hair loss, bloody vomit and stools from internal bleeding, infections, and low blood pressure. In the case of radiation sickness, those events can be explained by the damage to or destruction of certain cells, such as those in the lining of an intestinal tract (including the stomach), or the blood cell–producing cells of bone marrow. And that damage can, in turn, be explained by exposure to high levels of radiation. The sentence thus names a relation among several states of affairs, and when it correctly aligns them (and thereby us), it proves true. But to what degree? After all, "exposure to high levels of radiation" is shorthand for other events including atomic weapons and industrial accidents. "Radiation sickness" is thus a social fact even as it is a physiological one; that is, social actions are among its causes, actions not always apparent in the concept "radiation sickness." And we will need to locate other social facts to explain why a given set of people suffer from radiation, such as a group from the Marshall Islands, particularly the Bikini Atoll, where hydrogen bombs were tested in March of 1954.

When I find social facts within states of affairs like radiation sickness, or X suffers from radiation sickness, or X died from radiation sickness, I feel dissatisfied with an approach to truth that stops at semantic satisfaction. That isn't the whole story, I want to say; something less than the truth is being uttered. (And this leads me to double down on my investment in the distinction between "is true" and "is justified.")

My dissatisfaction resonates with Max Horkheimer's "On the Concept of Truth." "The truth is a moment of correct practice," he writes. "But whoever identifies it directly with success passes over history and makes himself an apologist for the reality dominant at a given time. Misunderstanding the irremovable difference between concept and reality, he reverts to idealism, spiritualism, and mysticism" (Horkheimer 1995, 200). The problem is not that mind stuff cannot grasp matter stuff, or that subjects inevitably introduce bias and so cannot be objective. (Those already are concerns for traditional theory.) Rather, a concept—better still, a judgment—discriminates and so proves partial. In other words, one can know the conditions under which "radiation sickness" is true and not truly know what radiation sickness is. This is not to say that Convention T fails to capture the conditions of semantic satisfaction for "is true" from a third-person, anthropological point of view. But from an epistemic point of view, those conditions fail to acknowledge their partiality and so prove epistemically insufficient.

WHODUNIT?

Skepticism arrests the concept and winds up imprisoned.

PLATONISM IN REVERSE

The truth will make fools of us all, which is the beauty of it, the goodness, too.

THE TRUE ROMANCE

I have been inching toward the thought that truth, one inception of our answerability and an outgrowth of the desire to know, disposes us toward self-surpassing accounts of whatever a claim purports, a thought I also find in: "I know better than to claim any completeness for my picture. I am a fragment, and this is a fragment of me" (Emerson 1983, 47). Emerson is claiming to have a certain kind of knowledge of his own partiality and thus of the whole to which he belongs. I have been recounting the kind of knowledge this is and how it is enriched by a certain approach to concepts and activities that constellate as "truth."

The point is not just Emersonian, however. I don't want to rest with any account of radiation sickness that avoids social facts. I thus remain interested in truth with a capital "T," the kind Hegel seems to have in mind when he claims, "Das Wahre is das Ganze." And it was just this line I had in mind when I sketched the scene of what might be involved when we relate to the world and ourselves through ideas of truth. A kind of whole arranges itself, and I think something like the truth of truth lies with this whole.

But I also had Foucault on my mind, as I noted, and how he might take the next line of Hegel's *Phenomenology*: "Das Ganze aber ist nur das durch sich Entwicklung sich vollendende Wesen" (Hegel 1977, 11). I imagine Foucault could accept: "The whole, however, is only the essence that accomplishes itself through its development," which softens *sich vollendende*, which carries connotations of perfection and completion. But maybe even "accomplish" is too teleological, and so one might drop the root *vollenden* for something like *vormehren*, to propagate. On this reading, development entails the generative diversification apparent in the etymology of "true."

But note, this Foucaultian turn remains within the effort to tell the truth about truth. Quite a contortion. All along I have tried to avoid reifying my partiality. But in remaining true to the task at hand, I have found a plurality to "truth" that cannot be brought under a singular usage, which returns me to: "There is no such thing as truth itself. But only a surfeit of it. Even if it should be for me, about me, truth is plural."

I regard this lat-longitudinal movement between parts and an ungraspable, dynamic, differentiating whole to be one of the principal activities of romanticism, one that can affirm claims from James and Horkheimer and not be blackmailed into choosing between Nancy or Emerson or siding, exclusively, with either Cavell or Derrida. It also finds itself in proximity to Joseph Winters's melancholic, syncopating hope and Fred Moten's (r)essay of Wallace Stevens. In particular, and to quote Moten, it shifts into a "kind of philosophical writing enacted and reenacted in the annular rememberment and dismemberment of community," although "not in the name of an originary creativity or a grounded and telic liberty, but of a free which is to say anarchic and atelic, generativity" (Moten 2003, 45–46).

Romanticism, once unleashed, is also hungry for a historical recounting as promiscuous as the thought (or the task, or tasks) just enumerated. But this would require us to saunter across languages and times, continents and vast global divides (North/South, East/West), marking but not halting at the color line(s) coursing therein. And to be clear, this is not to simply line up ethno-national romanticisms. Crack one open and you will find currents flowing from elsewhere. All agree that Coleridge is a window through which German winds blow. But open *Walden* and you will find traces of Vedic philosophy easily as thick and strong as the Stoic elements long (and recurringly) noted. And one can find lines from Emerson not only fronting the 1902 edition of Rilke's *Auguste Rodin* but—with shifting enthusiasm—across the writings of José Marti as well as closing the opening chapter of Anna Julia Cooper's *A Voice from the South*. And that is just to read with the grain.

Romanticism unleashed can even return to Convention T and serenely predicate whiteness of snow, thereby pocketing truth with a lowercase "t." I invoke the lower case because such truths are partial, and acknowledging that should prompt a kind of restlessness that wonders about "snow," about colors as well, even predication, even about whether anything is well understood through the substance-accident pairing that Kant sets as an a priori category of the understanding. To think romanticism from romanticism is to fragment whatever we have taken it to be and, in turn, to open it toward what it might yet become.

THE TRUE IS THE HOLE

When Heidegger sets his sights on the phenomenon of truth, he finds . . . well, what he usually finds. All who find accord (or discord) between an assertion and some situation must also find themselves given over to a world in which that relation, true or false, appears or is disclosed. That is, in the event of truth, one finds another event: the disclosure of beings. And Heidegger regards this other event as the essence of truth, its *Wesen*; it is integral to how being true (acknowledging the manifold ways in which this is possible) comes to pass. And when he accounts for how a scene of disclosure opens, he does so in accord with a logic that eschews analogues with the various ways in which beings come to pass—creation, causality, the modal expression of a substance, the representation including the self-presentation of a subject, even the fungible expression of formless energy.

Habermas is impatient with Heidegger at just this point (Habermas 1984). Because originary truth occurs irrespective of whether the eventual judgment is true or false (so much for snow), what Heidegger terms the essence of truth has no epistemic import, at least at the level of assertoric truth and falsity. But Heidegger's goal is not to conceptualize the operations of the empirical sciences. In fact, that is just what he refuses to do in "What is Metaphysics?" Instead, his goal is to consider the full range of human being-in-the-world from the standpoint of being, thereby doing justice to our full breadth, possibility, and limits. And this is where it gets interesting. Habermas wants to limit "truth" to assertoric speech-acts governed by the evolving standards of empirical inquiry, acts he distinguishes from moral judgments oriented toward rightness and aesthetic judgments concerned with the authenticity of expressive (or dramaturgical) acts. But do these three modes of action exhaust human being-in-the-world? Not if we must determine the domain to which a given phenomenon belongs. A dog approaches. Do we orient ourselves to it through truth, rightness (our own as well as its), authenticity (again, ours but also its), or all three? If we must ask, and we do (rightness, for example, only arises among beings with moral standing), we find ourselves in a scene of disclosure (or exposure) prior to Habermas's threefold account of social action.

I think we should refuse Habermas's impatience with Heidegger on truth. "Truth as disclosure" seeks its own accord even as it thinks past the accord of assertions and states of affairs. Pursuing self-knowledge, enacting a technology of the self-in-common, it aims to bring us into accord with the basic occurrence of our being, and in a manner that cannot be brought under the exclusive domain of the empirical sciences. In fact, it marks a site from which we might reconsider empirical science as a domain of inquiry. I say this in part because originary truth, marked as a no-place of emergence (the *Enstehungsherd*), helps Foucault in "Nietzsche, Genealogy, History" turn the Hegelian *Entwicklung* into Nietzsche's *Enstehung* (emergence) and *Herkunft* (descent), and in a manner freed of linear necessity or identity (Foucault 1984a). Heidegger's conception of originary truth, set into the plurality of human practices and their various normative efforts, thus throws into stark relief Habermas's efforts to colonize the language of truth within the instrumentality of the empirical sciences (suitably reconstructed by a theory of action). Mistakenly, Habermas proceeds as if those sciences were a rationalization of the language of truth rather than one among its descendants.

ORBITS AND OBITS

Megan Craig has helped me wonder about romanticism in the context of what Gianni Vattimo has termed *pensiero debole*. "Weak thought" aims to be edifying in relation to various histories of interpretation (thus inhabiting a de facto, unresolved pluralism of perspectives) as opposed to demonstrations of the *really real* or the categorically inevitable (thus assuming a de jure, monological stance).

Romanticism and weak thought meet, I think, in an acknowledgment of finitude. Vattimo's sense of edification gives me pause, however. It revolves around a de facto metaphysics of the interpretive horizons that, when enacted, produce a truth that is ultimately rhetorical. Vattimo seems to espouse such a view when he bids farewell to truth by positing truth as a "question of interpretation, of the application of paradigms that, in turn, are not objective [since no one verifies or falsifies them except on the basis of other paradigms] but a matter of social sharing" (Vattimo 2011, xxxiv).

Vattimo is right to socialize truth claims (and to contextualize truth claims within inquiry as opposed to an act of pure apprehension, discursive or otherwise), but binding truth claims to paradigms is, if anything, not weak enough. I say this because concepts like *paradigm* and *worldview* seem like linguistically outsourced theaters of the mind that self-execute idealities in univocal ways. Moreover, they presumably account for most if not all of a person's beliefs relative to some pattern of inquiry, as well as the measures by which such beliefs are evaluated and endorsed (or not). Or, even more robustly, they name a set of coordinated dispositions that account for the whole of an agent's lived experience. But who has or lives through such a profoundly woven web of disposition?

If we keep to empirical inquiry under conditions of normal science, we find novel applications, significant disagreements about what a data set indicates, and rival theories. In other words, even within a paradigm one inquirer's truth is another's hasty generalization, and one group's theory is another's dead end. Whatever truth is supposedly being made, therefore, is also false, and so appeals to interpretive horizons or paradigms are insufficient to account for whatever comes to stand as "true" for however long it stands.

Now step into the notion of a worldview, a more personal source for the generation of truth in a rhetorical sense. Consider your attractions, from foods to climates to facial structures and body types. Do they form an integrated perspective of attractions, one that predicts the rise of each inclination? Consider your aversions to a similar range of phenomena, including disgust reactions to rotting fish and human feces not of your own making. Again, do they form an integrated perspective, and one that replicates your attractions? My point is that such orientations, given their breadth and enacted flexibility and creativity, neither derive from a single source nor are systemically integrated over time. And that only becomes more evident when we multiply domains of concern: how we negotiate tensions among family, our various beliefs about friends, acquaintances, and colleagues, how we relate to our fellow citizens and to foreign nationals, and then across the various scenarios I've already mentioned. Beside this multiplicity, both in its dynamism and emergent novelties, the notion of a paradigm seems like a flash of conceptual art. It may have its place in the history of science, but paradigms oversimplify the weeds of social-psychology and agency writ large, even in the empirical sciences. In fact, it now seems like an outsourced soul-atomism, some longed-for center to explain what reflection cannot quite grasp, beginning with ourselves.

DOING ONE'S PART

Ever on the fly, romanticism defends the concrete with lustrous abstractions. Over the course of its conversations, each and all are required to take a turn.

CYA

Max Horkheimer finds an intriguing dialectic linking dogmatism and relativism. Relativism, Horkheimer suggests, delimits the validity of judgments to particular perspectives by indexing claims to various modes of subjectivity, from individuals to culturally evolved and transmitted worldviews. On this view, knowledge claims are valid from within a given perspective but not across perspectives. In an apparent contrast, dogmatism maintains commitments because of an "impulse to blind faith, to absolute submission, which has always been linked with relativism as its opposite" (Horkheimer 1995, 114). Its opposite? The two converge as they strive to fulfill a Kantian dream: to think (and think from) the unconditioned. While dogmas are unreservedly true and authoritative, so, too, are worldviews, albeit without the self-correcting energies that a concern for truth helps generate. Yes, the perspective or worldview may be historical, but stay within its folds and one enjoys de facto validity in the sense that one's perspective cannot be called into question, at least not on the basis of a question like: But is it true?

I am not advocating a neopositivist turn. Romanticism leads to a loving epistemology of the fragment, which acknowledges partiality and singularity. But I am resisting what I regard as a reification of that partiality, and I am resisting it by maintaining a commitment to truth as a meaningful epistemic concept, and by setting epistemic standpoints and perspectives within the same dynamic, relation-ontology into which ecological thought sets its objects of inquiry.

STAND IN THE PLACE WHERE YOU LIVE

If I were to develop this thought of partiality into a more robust epistemology, I would no doubt land amid standpoint epistemologies and face the task of which paths to follow through what has become a region unto itself, albeit one that borders on early critical theory and classical pragmatism. Let me begin to wave in that direction, if only to give you a sense of a few thoughts underwriting my sense of what I am doing (and from where) when I generalize about hope, trust, and forgiveness.

In thinking my partiality, I tend to follow Linda Alcoff and speak of "interpretive horizons," taking "horizon" to name a "complex (meaning internally heterogeneous) set of presuppositions and perceptual orientations, some of which are manifest as a kind of tacit presence in the body" (Alcoff 2006, 113). And, following arguments I have offered elsewhere, I would pluralize those horizons within people as well as among them. One moves through the world in multiple ways, and without an enduring subject of attention or agency (Lysaker 2017). Whether worlds collide or not, we do, inside and out.

I also would follow Alcoff and numerous others in correlating interpretive horizons with social identities or, perhaps better still, positionality, given that each identity can be positioned in multiple ways through the interanimating intersection of identity variables. (The stress in "positionality" seems common to, if differently voiced in, a historical multiplicity that includes Nietzsche's nonatomistic psychology, Bahktin's dialogism, pragmatism's transactional metaphysics and functionalist psychology, Foucault's nonjuridical histories of power, Mariana Ortega's thought of the in-between, and Patricia Hill Collins's intersectional insistence on the irreducible operations of phenomena like race, class, and gender.)

In positioning interpretive horizons, I hasten to note, like Alcoff, that such correlations do not "rely on a uniformity of opinion within an identity group but on a claim about what aspects of reality are more or less easily accessible to an identity group" (Alcoff, 126). Said otherwise, and relying on Collins's rejoinder to a paper by Susan Hekman: "The notion of a standpoint refers to groups having shared histories based on their shared location in relations of power—standpoints arise neither from crowds of individuals nor from groups analytically created by scholars or bureaucrats" (Harding 2004, 248). Thought in this manner, interpretive horizons do a double duty. On the one hand, they indicate a social position wherein social power circulates, and they indicate that one needs multiple social positions to track social life's differential operations. One could call this the expressive function of the concept "interpretive horizon." On the other hand, those positioned in these numerous ways remain knowers and doers within such operations, and so they have claims on (and about) what befalls them. One could call this the concept's interpretive function (which may also express social facts about various ways of knowing). But rather than simply individuating the interpretive function (which the term "standpoint" seems to do), one should distribute it across the ongoing conversations that in part prompt, even solicit, and often provide replies to whatever interpretations emerge. The gain here is that any interpretation must make its way in a community of inquirers, and whatever knowledge is thereby achieved distinguishes itself through its ability to account for itself in a context of potential, even likely disagreement. (But note to selves: do not hold forth on places one has not traveled.)

Privileging conversation over mind as the social location of an interpretive horizon accords nicely with Nancy Hartsock's insistence, shared by Kathi Weeks, that a standpoint or an interpretive horizon is an achievement rather than a given, and one that could be empowered by epistemologies that acknowledge the fundamentally situated character of inferences and the conversations in which they circulate (Harding, 245). And while that opens as many questions as it seems to answer, it suggests one thing I want to underscore. If an interpretive horizon is an achievement, it is also a task. And that calls for something like a perfectionist epistemology wherein the task of becoming a knower is part and parcel of the task of being human. Said otherwise, how one knows (which is integral to how one converses) becomes part of one's answer to the question "Who are you and for what do you stand?"

CHARITY BEGINS AT HOME

"But what happens when disagreements arise among those with differing interpretive horizons?" Plenty, and differentially so. Also, do not forget that disagreements arise within conversations and not simply between isolated clusters of propositions, let alone discrete judgments.

Responding to Kripke's account of Wittgenstein, Cavell observes that if we follow a chain of justification and hit bedrock, such that our spade is turned, we certainly can appeal to a convention in the hope that the yea's will have it (presuming that is our side). But that is not all we can do (Cavell 1990, 64–100; 2005, 192–212). We might go home and try again tomorrow. Conventions move differently after a good night's rest. Or, moving from loggerheads to cooperation, we might agree not to try to win the argument within the terms at hand but to collectively generate an advance. Or we might start by asking each other to assume the rival point of view and defend it for the time being. Also, we could seek out a third interlocutor. Or, like the Dewey John Stuhr has championed, we might open genetic inquiries into our orienting concepts to see whether their presumptions maintain intuitive force in the wake of their historicization (Stuhr 1997). And in every scenario, we might try to be more generous, or patient, or imaginative, knowing that agreements and disagreements arise out of more than a clash or mesh of propositions. A turned spade does not close the story.

I also want to pause before the presumption that disagreements are likely to hit bedrock. Often? Regarding most of what anyone takes to be "true"? I pause here because this thought—call it the endgame of incommensurability—disposes us toward one another in our answerability. I worry that anticipating incommensurability pursues self-preservation more than it enacts epistemic humility. I cannot argue that we will never find spades turning in our hands. But with what force have they rolled our wrists? I have never encountered an internally consistent, riddle-proof defense of any ambitious position, even in the absence of rivals presenting incompatible claims. Perhaps we might complement the principle of charity by not only giving the best account we can of our rivals, but also by seeking, proactively, insistently, better accounts of ourselves.

Trust

He that despiseth small things will perish by little and little.

RALPH WALDO EMERSON

TRUST FALLS

In the summer of 2019, I met with a group of prisoners. All men, they lived at Atlanta's Metro Reentry Facility. All had been "inside" for an extended period, some for over forty years, but most for less. I do not know their crimes and did not think it my business to ask. But I knew that many had freedom on the horizon—some imminent, others in a few years, some maybe, just maybe.

For five weeks, twice a week, two hours at a time, we talked philosophy. We were there for college credit and to see where philosophy could take us. I found the time intense, charged, and occasionally rapturous. It brought me back to something I believe but, until recently, felt with diminishing zeal—philosophy is an intimate affair.

But not always. It can be hard to find each other in philosophy. And I was unsure what would be possible at Metro Reentry. Not that I had specific doubts. I had few particular beliefs about the men I would meet or what would happen when we read and discussed texts from Plato, Descartes, Peirce, Epictetus, Aristotle, Beauvoir, and Du Bois. And my lack of anticipation (fueled and kept open by the fullness of hope) was intentional. Such presumptions would limit, I felt, even undermine our ability to find each other, or some part of each other that could generate a space of honest speech.

In the third week, virtue was the topic, specifically courage. We were reading Aristotle and letting it sound us out. I know that sounds dramatic. But by then the men were electric, and it was palpable. A week earlier,

Dr. Sarah Higinbotham had visited. Along with Bill Taft, she is the co-founder of Common Good Atlanta, which administers the course and others like it at several area prisons. The men called Sarah "the big cheese," and I traveled on her coattails whether she was there or not. She and Bill have carefully and lovingly crafted spaces for learning behind all those walls, checkpoints, and barbed wire. All I had to do was help us find each other in the assigned pages. On the day of Sarah's visit, as time was running out, the men were playfully distraught. We were just getting into Aristotle—the nature of action, the good, and *eudaimonia*, the flourishing/happiness that confers value on life's length and breadth. When it became clear that only a few minutes remained, an audible "no way" rippled, and it was sincere and cheering. Afterward, Sarah told one of the men that she found the discussion thrilling if somewhat unusual. As a professor of literature, she usually worked from plots. The student replied, gesturing in a circle, starting with me: he's the plot, we're the plot.

If you know Aristotle, you might also shiver. Regardless, I hope you can see the insight and appreciate its depth. We are the plots of any genuine philosophical discussion. We are the believers and doubters of epistemology, the judged and judgers of ethics, the who amid the whats of metaphysics. And those men, who honored me and philosophy every week, recognized that and rose to the occasion, taking me with them.

I asked the men whether and how courage might move from the battlefield into other domains of life. At some point, one suggested I needed courage to enter the prison and engage them. I am still not sure if he believed this or if this was a test of sorts, or a bit of both, as if the current we were generating was too good to be true. Regardless, I understood the point, at least on its face. The unknown breeds fear, particularly in a context layered with threat, real and imagined, and here there were prisoners, guards, stigmatizing tales of degenerate villainy, and many people who had done bad, even terrible things. In such scenes, courage allows one to endure fear to realize something of value, something good. At Metro, his argument went, he and his classmates could be a source of fear, at least for those on the "outside" who might presume that the incarcerated are inherently untrustworthy, mere con artists and thugs. But even as I acknowledged his correct extension of the concept, I felt stigma haunting the exchange, and stigma is what we had to outwit if we were to remain the plot. So, echoing Socrates (we had read the *Apology*), I said I never felt afraid because I knew I did not know them, and I trusted myself to meet them where we found each other. I added that I found a kind of courage in their willingness to continually open themselves to me and to philosophy more broadly, to see themselves, their character as the true stakes of our discussion.

While our discussion centered on courage, my thoughts migrated toward trust. It was trust rather than battle that, over time, issued from their courage. And trust was what we needed if philosophy was going to recast how we found ourselves and so recast the selves we found. To think outside the denigrating fantasies of the carceral state, I needed to earn their trust and trust them in turns and returns of intensification. If we were to step into the indeterminate future that philosophy foments, I also needed to trust myself, that I could be there.

TO BE HONEST . . .

Some voices we do not trust. Someone's manner may give us pause. "He's full of shit," we say, thinking, "Even he doesn't believe what he's saying." And that makes the exchange pointless. Not that we could not consider the point, but to do so, we would have to read (or listen) past the address; do both jobs. Others try to win arguments just to win them. Again, one could push past the bluster, but that is my point. Fruitful dialogue presumes honesty, and its absence wears and tears at interlocutors and the productivity of the exchange.

Aligned issues arise even when overt dissimulation is not in play. Some prompt distrust through laxity. Their lack of even trying to get it right puts us off. Harry Frankfurt considers such a case (Frankfurt 2005, 29–34). Fania Pascal was at Cambridge during the 1930s. She taught Russian to Wittgenstein and Francis Skinner. After she had her tonsils removed, Wittgenstein called to ask how she was faring. "I feel just like a dog that has been run over," she replied. He replied, with evident disgust, "You don't know what a dog that has been run over feels like" (Rhees 1984, 28–29).

It is perilous to read anecdotes, and Frankfurt acknowledges that we must presume a great deal to do so. But he presumes because the vignette leads him to an interesting observation. Imagining his way into Wittgenstein's reaction, he writes, "Her fault is not that she fails to get things right"—namely, by analogizing her pain to that of a dog's, which she does not know—"but that she is not even trying" (Frankfurt 2005, 32). We sometimes distrust voices that evidence a lack of care or even honesty, as in "an honest day's work," as Frankfurt notes. But there is also trying too hard, forcing a matter. Is it true that Pascal's analogy does not even try to get things right? Simply venturing a metaphor is a try, and anyone who has a dog and imagines it run over, hence unable to lie down, eat, or even sleep without pain, will likely find common ground. Not very precise, but not a complete miss either. Frankfurt acknowledges that the analogy at least conveys feeling bad, but he stops there. I think it says more than that. Being run over will likely prevent a dog from doing the basic things that make a dog happy, and that kind of misery is more than a matter of feeling poor. The analogy directs us toward a kind of shared deprivation of core goods—neither can pursue the activities that constitute their well-being. One might insist that because we cannot access the minds of nonhuman animals, Wittgenstein's impatience was warranted. But that returns the gripe to error, and the charge is insufficient care.

As read by Frankfurt, Wittgenstein's remark seems to run afoul of the same principle it presumably employs. Not that he fails to grasp the analogy. Rather, he rushes to judgment, based on any number of presumptions, none flattering. (Pascal recalls, more than once, Wittgenstein's dislike of intellectual women.)

Sloppy work is not the only form of dishonest work, therefore. Rash work (with a taste of righteousness) is another. It may also evidence a lack of trust. Pascal's analogy is brief, hence opaque. If I trust you to be thoughtful, to have done honest work, I'll incline toward richer receptions. If I think you intellectually untrustworthy (or just unworthy), I will start at the bottom.

IN OED WE TRUST

"Trust" is a well-traveled word. In 1645, J. Howell distinguished, "Eywitnesses of those things which others receive but in trust" (OED 2022). And in the same year, J. Wells declared, "Let that God . . . be my trust, who purposes such love" (OED). A few ticks earlier, in 1475, we also find: "Be ware of weyn confidens of mercy; Offend not a prince on trust of hys fauour" (OED).

In these remarks, "trust" names an orientation toward others—a prince, God, those purporting to be eyewitnesses. Trust, moving between one and another, perhaps several persons, is one of the ways we can relate to others—with trust, trustingly. Hearing from eyewitnesses, one wonders how to respond. Working for another, an opportunity presents itself. It is lucrative but risky. Can we trust our overseers to appreciate the circumstances if we go for it and fail?

The historical usages I have sampled suggest that trust arises with the feeling of (or in acknowledgment of) dependence. To trust is to depend, whether the trustee is God, some official, or an eyewitness. A fourth usage from 1712 renders this explicit: "I am in a Trust relating to this Lady's Fortune" (OED). The nominal form is broadly telling. A trust joins two people in a relation of dependence in which the trustor is dependent on the judgment and actions of the trustee.

These senses remain current. Things are still held "in trust," and those who oversee it are "trustees." We entrust ourselves as well as things to others. Many are told, sometimes by US license plates, that the state trusts God. We have trusted friends. And "they have earned my trust" is a phrase that acknowledges, with comfort, the vulnerability of such situations. Trust is thus a disposition, an orientation that positions the trustor within the orbit of the trustee, leaving the former in the hands of another.

For centuries, then, trust has maintained a basic character. I would need comparative linguistics, however, to venture thoughts beyond what an English survey affords. And even among the English, my examples belong to modernity or the foreground of its emergence. But such a terrain is more than vast enough to warrant an experiment with usages, senses, and implied structures.

KEEPING FAITH

Trust is kin to true, at least etymologically. In English, both descended through the Old English *trēowe*, meaning faithful. The link is reliability, perhaps. My trusty bow shoots straight and true. A trusted friend, like a true friend, is reliable. And carpenters true up beams to make sure they can carry their loads. But "faithful" may not need explication through reliability. When I trust another, I expect them to be faithful to me. Perhaps "faithful" clarifies the kind of reliability trust expects.

Trust is also kin to true through honesty. "Trust is a presumption of meaningful communication," Trudy Govier writes. "We must believe that the other says what he means and means what he says" (Govier 1998, 8). The honest person tells the truth, at least as far as they grasp it, and the trustworthy are truthful. I would be hard-pressed to trust someone I thought dishonest. Relying on them feels like betting on a weak hand.

TOO CLEVER FOR OUR OWN GOOD

Links between true and trust (and honesty and trust) interest and caution me. Terms for what we value often intersect. Moral vocabularies are often more distinct than ethical life. A good life has parts, but their character is fluid. Perhaps trust is an effort to true our relationships, as one might true the wheels of a bike. And one facet of that praxis involves honesty—with ourselves and with one another.

FINDING OUR BEARINGS

Trust is a possibility, one bound to distrust, suspicion, and fear. The manifold nature of trust unfurls relations in scenes of varying character and intensity: friends, acquaintances, colleagues, strangers, neighbors, family, eyewitnesses, various professions, the state and its nodes, the media, a particular corporation, and so forth. To be disposed through trust is to move through a historically evolving figure whose lines of thought involve continua rather than discrete terms. Trust is positioned and positions us in a field of possibilities. Ethical life is never paved brick by brick.

AS FAR AS I CAN THROW HIM

Trust's various contraries and the continua they open also suggest that trust is not an on/off phenomenon. Over the years, my trust in Hilary, my wife, has spread across our life. There are limits, however. She does not trust me with the laundry, as my weak attention to detail is a liability. And there are things I know to do if I want them done sooner than later. Not that these are trouble spots. If anything, owning up to limits (and acknowledging them) keeps things real and limits frustration. It might even render each of us more trustworthy. The point instead is that trust is almost always—maybe just—a matter of degree.

DREAM #12

Light as snow, trust accumulates when rewarded, brightening the day.

THE TRUSTING SORT

Many argue that trust is integral to life as we live it. Annette Baier, who made trust a topic for professional philosophy, writes, "We inhabit a climate of trust, as we inhabit an atmosphere and notice it as we notice air, only when it becomes scarce or polluted" (Baier 1995, 98). Inventory your most important relations and weigh the trusts involved. Trust is essential to what is most important in my life: my wife, my friends, my family, my pets. If I were to lose trust in any of these contexts, the character (and value) of those relations would diminish precipitously, and so would my sense of well-being. In fact, loss of trust, at least in these contexts, would leave me isolated, vulnerable. And because much of what I hope for is strung across this set, collapsing trusts threaten despair.

I also want to and luckily do trust most of my neighbors farther than I can throw them. If something seems out of order (an alarm, an odd odor, an event affecting traffic on our street), they will not look the other way but will call me or intervene. And trust certainly enriches the workplace; trusted colleagues are far preferable to their contraries. One spends less time worrying about what might happen and more time imagining, with excitement, what could be.

Professional relationships also can involve significant trust: doctor, dentist, tax accountant. In each case, at least after engaging them, I trust them to do honest work, which, as my representative, involves more than dialing it in. To a degree, they are looking out for me.

We might trust public defenders to work for their clients, and trust judges, overworked as they are, to try each case on its merits. With an ambiguity to which we'll return, we might also say we "expect" that of them, as when, disappointed, we say, "I expected more from you." And while I do not trust elected officials, the reason why is because they maintain the emerging picture. My interests mean little to them, and my general interest, one that presumably binds the polity, appears to mean even less—namely, that they safeguard the rule of law and represent the polity, not just those who voted for them.

Other publics also might involve trust, or could. Every day I rely on reports about matters unseen, particularly from news agencies. What did X say? What did Y do? What did Z save, destroy, help, or harm? Can I trust what the media says? Not just that they have not lied, but that they've done due diligence and shown sufficient care to get after the truth.

Note also that Howell, writing in 1645, must trust himself. Personal experience is an epistemic minefield, haunted by error and deception. Can we trust what the eye witnesses, even when it's our own?

Baier's metaphor is apposite, therefore. Like an atmosphere, trust envelops sites that really count. It is a well-traveled word because so much of life opens scenes for and rewards trust, while ruin haunts its betrayal.

AN UNSURPASSABLE HORIZON

Liberalism may not be the last word on who we, any "we," might be, politically speaking. It would be sad if that were the last aspiration. But whatever you see just over the most distant hill, the travails of trust will be there should you arrive—which you will not, if you have no one to trust along the way.

FOR GOODNESS' SAKE

There is something sad, even ugly about a world in which no one trusts anyone else. Not that I blame the suspicious. There are many cases where distrust is deserved, even among strangers. The general currents of US social life remain ill-disposed toward Black life, and misogyny persists. It behooves many to live with their guard up. But most believe that such conditions call for redress, which suggests that most would agree that a life without trust is a diminished one, meaning less than it could be, less than we aspire to be. As with friends, it is unlikely that someone would elect a life without trust over one with it. There may be exceptions (and there probably are for creatures whose existence precedes essence), but lives that are capable of and enjoy trust are preferable to those riddled by suspicion and betrayal.

Turning from quality of life to quality of character, an incapacity to trust or be trustworthy when warranted seems like a failing in the sense that such incapacities leave one less praiseworthy as a person, less admirable, even pitiable if one becomes so through little fault of one's own. Imagine someone profoundly betrayed and unable to recover. "They never really got over it," we'd say, with sympathy. Or imagine someone temperamentally suspicious to the point of not really trusting anyone. Intimacy with others would be compromised and ease of mind would contract.

The broad desirability of trust suggests that it carries similarly broad, ethical valences. It is a good, one we realize where we can. Consequently, those concerned with a good life should have something to say about trust. Its realization requires trust, at least in part, and trust, like friendship, seems integral to its character. Those who are unable to trust or be trustworthy when warranted seem less than they otherwise could be. And when we imagine futures for children, ours or otherwise, we hope that they will be capable of trust and trustworthy as well.

BE REAL

Honesty never fails to impress, except itself.

GET A GRIP

My task is not to find minimal conditions for "trust." I am not a taxonomist's attaché. The essayist is always, in part, an ethicist surveying a topic, pursuing something representative to tell (and show). Yes, one essays

words with referents, and in a manner that would be true in the sense of
faithful. But the goal is to empower addressees to better realize the values
therein. As Aristotle has it, the task of ethics is to become better, and to
seek and employ a degree of precision that furthers the task. An ethical
approach to trust thus favors middle and maximal examples; they better
orient us. And trust, at base, is just that: an orientation, a disposition, one
we want to cultivate in an exemplary fashion. I add this because one might
be naive or a dupe, or unduly suspicious. And such fates undermine us.

STRONG BOXES AND SOUNDING BOARDS

Imagine a trusted advisor. When I must make a difficult decision, one with
appreciable implications (for my marriage, my friendships, my family, my
job, my social-political projects, etc.), I do not simply consult experts, or
only them. I need more than technical know-how. I turn to those I trust.
But what precisely do I trust in such cases? Not just that they will keep
my confidence, although it is interesting that trust aligns with images of
holding and guarding, as if it were a safe of sorts. I also seek the counsel
of someone who can grasp the situation, examine options, and keep me in
mind. They are sensitive to my particularities, to paraphrase Nancy Potter's
account of the trustworthy (Potter 2002, 28). Trusted advisors do not simply
say what they would do in my place, though I may ask them to answer in
this way. They assume my point of view and deliberate from my perch. And
if they cannot, I may rely on them, find them useful, but they will not be
a trusted advisor. Not that I would therefore distrust them, but my trust
expands in the presence of someone who can see it my way.

"So, you want someone who will agree with you?" Fair, and clarifying,
but no. Someone who has your back against your current wishes is someone
you can really trust. Instead of "my point of view," I should have said, "in
accord with my better interests," which is to acknowledge that my point
of view is conflicted at times, even self-deceived, and hopefully launched
within a learning curve. A trusted advisor may reorient us by negating a
current disposition.

SLOW LEAKS AND SUDDEN IMPLOSIONS

Trust secures, like mortar. And when it crumbles, the walls come tumbling
down. Moreover, every step of trust is haunted, conceptually, by betrayal.
I do not think I have been "betrayed," which carries a blunt force connota-
tion. I have had rivals who wished me ill, and the occasional enemy plot-

ting. But they were known variables, and none ever blossomed allegorically, twisting me into paranoia. At worst I have learned to think as my enemies think. But that's just prudence, a certain casualty of aging.

But the thought is not foreign. One fall evening, crossing the street, chatting and carefree, a friend and I were struck by a car. She was thrown to the side while I, upended, rolled across the hood. Quite a scene. Miraculously unhurt except for cuts across my scalp from where my head greeted the windshield, I ran to my friend, who was woozy on the ground. The car had come from almost nowhere, having pulled a U-turn on a cross street to shoot up ours. After the accident, crossing the street brought anxieties reserved for skilled labor. Something I had presumed safe now seemed a source of peril. But nothing like my ability to trust was impacted. No other dependent or vulnerable activity became more so in its wake. No doubts threatened other activities, such as driving. And in a few weeks, I crossed the street as I always had. If anything changed, it was how my friend and I trusted one another. Having come through the wreck together, we were tighter.

Qualitatively and quantitatively, the reach of betrayal exceeds what I underwent. But the scenes are proximate. A safe spot in the horizon proves false, and the resulting tear runs. Imagine that they were good. They were right for each other. A long future had been imagined. She had made plans. But all that was predicated on something untrue. He was a cheat, with a shadow life. Or was hers the shadow life? She could no longer tell, and many of her relations trembled in the tumult. All faces became two. Who had known or suspected but said nothing? Who else kept secrets? Who else rang true but lived falsely? Most friendships persevered, some even deepened, but renewal was required. Eventually, there were others—new friends and lovers, new plans. But doubts gnawed at every line.

A THOUSAND PENNIES FOR YOUR THOUGHTS

The Basic Trust Game, or just the Trust Game, is often used in experimental settings. One set of subjects (A-subjects) is given ten dollars each. They may keep the money or send some or all of it to someone in a second group (B-subjects). All the money sent to B-subjects will be tripled. They may keep it all or give some back to their corresponding A-subject. Both parties know the setup, but they don't know each other or anything about each other. Importantly, the game is played once. There are no future transactions that the initial decisions can influence.

In 2011, Johnson and Mislin performed a meta-analysis of one hundred and sixty-two experimental uses of the game involving almost twenty-four thousand individuals in thirty-five countries. While objections to the Trust Game have been lodged, it "remains a popular choice among trust researchers" (Johnson and Mislin 2011, 866). The Trust Game is popular because it confounds a prevalent intuition: "Standard assumptions on rationality and selfishness predict senders pass no money to receivers and subsequently no money will be returned. Despite this, replications of the trust game have consistently supported the finding that individuals are willing to send and return positive amounts" (Johnson and Mislin, 871). For example, one test, which used a variation known as the "investment game," reported that thirty of thirty-two A-subjects sent an average of $5.16 to B-subjects, although other experiments found fewer A-subjects sharing the wealth (Berg et al. 1995, 123; Johnson and Mislin, 871). Nevertheless, as Paul Faulkner reports, "A key experimental result is that people, with some interesting qualifications, do by and large cooperate in the *Trust Game* even though it is played as a one-off game under conditions of ignorance" (Faulkner and Simpson 2017, 111).

As an experiment, the Trust Game poses many questions. What happens when the amounts involved are increased or decreased? What happens when the subjects are well-off or poor? What if they know each other and/or are known by the experimenters? What happens when the game continues for a few turns, and giving and returning become part of a calculative process? And should we assume that all A-subjects give money with the expectation of return? But there is a prior question. When participants act under these conditions, is trust being enacted, and in some basic way? Are the deliberations of the A-subjects and B-subjects paradigmatic for trusting? Paul Faulkner takes the Trust Game to offer a reliable path into questions surrounding the nature of trust. Because we often don't know if those we trust are trustworthy, we must decide who to trust and on what basis. The anonymous and one-off character of the Trust Game underscores this, and so it seems to highlight a question facing all who trust, thereby pointing toward "a problem of the rationality of reliance broadly—a problem of the rationality of cooperation" (Faulkner and Simpson, 110).

Faulkner believes that the Trust Game raises three questions that concretize "the problem of trust." Let me limit the issue to A-subjects, who are wondering whether to share any or all of their initial ten bucks. In deciding what to do, A-subjects must rely on B-subjects in the knowledge that B-subjects may keep the dough. Second, A-subjects know this is a one-time or short-lived relation and so they cannot count on B-subjects to act in a manner that will produce mutual benefits over time. Third, A-subjects do not know what motivates B-subjects in particular, and more importantly, they "recognize a general motivation to be unreliable" (Faulkner and Simpson 2017, 111). (Faulkner takes the third condition as a single one, but I think it blurs two, categorically distinct issues: what we know about others as individuals, and general expectations about groups, including humans in general. I will speak, therefore, of conditions iii-A and iii-B, respectively.)

Does the Trust Game disclose trust's basic operations? Condition iii-A is absent for most wondering whether to trust another. Most people usually know something about the people they trust or distrust. Even in the company of strangers, we respond to eye contact (or its absence), tone of voice, and posture. Also, variables of identity inform who people trust and how people respond to being trusted. In other words, trust works under conditions of working knowledge, even if generated on the fly. Condition iii-B is even odder, therefore. How many proceed without relying on some general, presumably reliable thoughts about the class of people involved? If most in fact do, then the Trust Game in its basic form tries to preclude them from doing something integral to trust. More telling is that the Trust Game institutes conditions of anonymity. Skepticism haunts those who trust. Such is the plight of finite actors. But most who trust or distrust do so based on admittedly fallible knowledge about (a) specific actors alongside (b) general beliefs, deemed reliable, about people in general (or some class of people). My objection may be deeper than this, however. When we trust another, we have a feel for their motivations—namely, that they can act with our interest in mind, as Faulkner himself suggests. In other words, trust is inherently intersubjective. But the Trust Game renders B-subjects inscrutable to A-subjects, particularly under the conditions that Faulkner articulates, leaving them with nothing in which to place their trust. Instead, they must guess or predict what the other will do. But this is closer to gambling, as Hawley indirectly suggests when she refers to the "trusting-gamble" of A-subjects as opposed to the "rich trust" she associates with friends and family (Hawley 2012, 36, 42). I want to break the hyphen. Gambling is one thing; trusting, another.

KNOWN QUALITIES

"I hope Len will come through." Such a sentiment seems quite different than "You can trust Jena. She'll come through." The latter claims to know something about Jena and so relies on her, whereas the former lacks the feel for what Len will do when left to his own devices. But hope underwrites a kind of reliance nonetheless, though it is different than reliance wrought by trust. Trust knows more, or thinks it does.

BOWS AND BLADES

"Machinery can be relied on, but only agents, natural or artificial, can be trusted" (Jones 1996, 14). Karen Jones's claim, which I accept, runs afoul of ordinary language. We have trusty cars. Also, theorists like Niklas Luhmann seem to equate "trust"—the German is *Zutrauen*—with fallible belief (Luhmann 2017). This may be because *Zutrauen* also means "confidence," and so it extends to beliefs about objects like the floor, a bridge, or the road. But such usages seem overly broad, and if we perpetuate them, we'll need a different term to capture trusting one another (and ourselves). Jones's distinction is philosophically useful, therefore; it preserves something. The trust we value most involves more than a prediction about the weight-bearing capacities of a bridge, for example. Trust relies upon the agency of another, which includes their actions and the deliberations that inform them. Imagine a cheesy spy flick. Our hero is suspended over a shark tank. Upon exiting, the villain says, "I trust you not to escape." The irony works because the agency of the supposed hero has, presumably, been nullified.

Distinguishing trust from reliance further opens the intersubjective scene which the Trust Game obscures. Even more so than your attitudes toward me (like, dislike, attracted, repulsed), I need to access and evaluate your agency when faced with doubts about whether to trust you. I need a sense of what you'll do and why (should my dependence upon you require your reply). This becomes even clearer when one sees how the dependence and vulnerability integral to trust morphs into power when we trust well. My house is safer beside trusted neighbors, my deliberations enriched by trusted advisors. The trustee's agency extends my own. Not that a trustee is a tool. I trust another's agency, which includes their deliberations and commitment as well as their deeds. Trust (as opposed to mere reliance) thus makes a kind of joint agency possible. Jones captures this in a later essay. Thinking about the phrase "I was counting on you," she writes, "The potential for making such a complaint is the hallmark of a case where we assume we have a genuine 'we' rather than a mere convergence of agency" (Faulkner and Simpson 2017, 92).

But Jones may want my account to be more modest than it is. Elsewhere she suggests that we "are often content to trust without knowing much about the psychology of the one-trusted, supposing merely that they have psychological traits sufficient to get the job done" (Jones 2004, 4). I am not sure we disagree, although many people who trust or distrust based on generalizations about persons or classes of persons often think they know a great deal. But if we do disagree, it lies with my insistence that trust operates intersubjectively. When that is absent, we have reliance.

SEEMED A GOOD IDEA AT THE TIME

Trust acknowledges vulnerability by affirming it. It celebrates heteronomy, opting for what we can do only as we. Not that it is free of anxiety. It is not; trust is haunted by an epistemic gap, as Onora O'Neill has noted (O'Neill 2002, 6). I trust in in part because I do not know. Karen Jones tries to capture this by suggesting that those who trust are optimistic that the trusted will look after them (Jones 1996). I think she is right to underscore that trust, while irreducible to prediction, nevertheless has a predictive element. But I also want to underscore, in line with Stephen Darwall, that trust's orientation toward the future, its expectation, is ethically charged (Faulkner and Simpson 2017, 36). If you asked me to look after your fish, and I did so with due care, but it died anyway, how would you respond? If the situation were reversed, I might feel sad, but I would not feel let down, let alone betrayed. In short, I would not think you broke my trust. Now, if you did a half-assed job, I would feel let down; I expected more from you. And that would leave you less trustworthy in my eyes, presuming there were not mitigating circumstances. In other words, when I trust you, my disposition toward you is charged with ethical significance; it is "robustly moral," to invoke Alisa Carse's phrase (Carse 2010).

Suppose my scaled friends died because you were incompetent. Imagine that, in the absence of clear instructions, you overfed them. You did everything else right, and carefully, but you did not know that fish ration portions poorly. They gobbled down whatever grub you gave so you gave them more. Reverse roles again; would you feel betrayed in this case? I would not. I probably would not ask you to fish-sit again, and I'd expect some contrition on your part. But your incompetence would not be sufficient to break my trust.

From various angles I am trying to elaborate the good that courses through trust, why we praise its occurrence, lament its loss, and excoriate betrayal. Trust exemplifies shared agency oriented by competent goodwill. While no doubt valuable in multiple cases, trust also bears a general significance that is more than merely utopian. When fulfilled, trust points toward a way of being that shines more brightly than strategic alliance. While maybe not our best, trust shows us at our better.

PEOPLE ARE STRANGE WHEN YOU'RE A STRANGER

"I just don't trust them." I have felt this, and in a way I couldn't shake. Where trust underwrites, distrust undermines, contracting sociality. Unleashed, distrust exhausts and threatens isolation. "Cover your ass" becomes a governing maxim, and you wonder what moves beneath the caps and heads of hair outside your window. But the trusted are there with us even when they are not.

GETTING HERE FROM THERE

Because we are social beings, and from the ground up, it is tempting to render distrust a privation. It depends on where we look, and when. Perhaps we begin life full of it only to see it attenuated by experience. Or maybe desire and need propel us, and trust emerges down the line when doubt and deliberation become possible. I prefer the latter, and so resist thinking about trust in a manner that elides the epistemic gaps it must cross or makes light of how our vulnerability intensifies when we trust. In trust, we let our guard down. Its beauty is inseparable from its danger.

POKER FACE

I find "trust" a narrower concept than many. When I come to a four-way stop, I would not say that I trust the other drivers to wait their turn. I do not. In fact, in line with defensive driving, I distrust them. Moreover, I remain alert for signs that they are about to do something stupid. But driving is just too convenient and sometimes necessary, so I gamble.

Bad behavior prompts reactions like blame, censure, retaliation, and forgiveness. Say a stranger local to the area gives me bad directions. But I, too, am local, and they are bad enough for me to realize what is happening. "Nice try, asshole"; that is, I censure him. But not in the name of trust betrayed. I neither trusted nor distrusted him. I take this not only to be a possible situation, but a common one.

I am confident about many beliefs that I have not vindicated through anything approaching disciplined inquiry. I thus agree with Heidi Grasswick, who claims that the "human condition is one of deep epistemic dependence" (Dormandy 2020, 161). And Elizabeth Fricker concurs with greater specificity. "The wealth of one's epistemic superabundance," she writes, "is bought at the price of one's huge epistemic dependence on the word of others—one's past and ongoing accepting reliance on testimony, primary and extended" (Dormandy, 64–65). But, and this is not to object to anything Grasswick or Fricker says, believing someone (or some text) is not the same as trusting them (or it). Often, I simply believe what I read like I believe someone who tells me what time it is after checking their watch. If someone says something unusual or unbelievable, trust may become a possibility. But often it does not. Dependence is ubiquitous. Trust, less so.

I think it a mistake to imagine that trust operates wherever social actors willingly depend on one another or cooperate, as Lahno seems to suggest (Faulkner and Simpson 2017, 131). Often, we simply rely or gamble, as when we believe that incentive and disincentive structures lead people to behave predictably enough to act accordingly. And in those cases, we willingly incur the risk of incompetent or ill treatment. I order a coffee. Do I trust the person to give me what I ordered? Not really. But in this case, I do not distrust them either. In most cases, I have no reason to trust or distrust them; my expectation is predictive. Suppose they serve me a vanilla mocha instead of a coffee. Yuck. I return it and they say, "Oh, we're out of coffee." Do I feel as if my trust were violated? No. I may be irritated, and if I am already cranky, I might say, "At least do your job." I also might think the server lazy, and that would have its own ethical current, but it would be different than what trust conducts. But what if there was more coffee and the server just did not like the look of me? I still would not feel let down or betrayed. (Would you?) Such exchanges involve thinly convergent agencies, as Jones has it, not the "we" that trust commences.

HOLDING PATTERNS

I want to distinguish distrust from skepticism even though they have similar effects: contracted sociality. The skeptic, the bigot as well, are moved by abstractions, by class-based dispositions that circulate above the currents of intersubjectivity. Distrust as I think it remains bound to those currents—something about you is off. Not that third- and second-person dispositions are unrelated. Everyone is oriented in part by generalized views about classes of people, and some of those views make trusting easier, more difficult, or even impossible, perhaps with good reason. Many are regarded (and/or disregarded) through categories that efface them in their singularity, which forces them to interact based on class-based predictions. They thus bear their world by way of gambles, at least where conditions of categorical violence rule—white supremacy, rape culture, total subsumption under capital. The very possibility of trust or distrust is thus borne differently by people positioned differently, if it even arises. Distrust is not the only cause of social distance.

MICROCLIMATES

The narrowness of my conception of trust runs counter to Karen Jones's notion of basal security, which she regards as a kind of meta-trust regarding dependency relations (Jones 2004). Following Baier's Heideggerian observation that we tend to notice trust relations when they break, Jones is led to theorize basal security from the aftershocks of traumas, which often lead people to declare, "My trust in the world was shattered" (Jones, 13).

I have zero interest in disputing the phenomenon that Jones identifies. My earlier account of betrayal foreshadows just these possibilities. A loss or betrayal or assault can ripple through life to the point that our vulnerabilities are thrown into unbearable relief. And I do think the result has a "meta" quality insofar, as Jones observes, it overdetermines a whole set of possibilities irrespective of the risk assessment warranted by those possibilities. Like Cartesian doubt, basal insecurity does not proceed case by case but addresses classes.

But I do not find basal security to be a species of trust, and I do not think such concerns are merely semantic, as Jones suggests they could be after posing this very question (Jones, 13). First, traumas might generate broad, even global senses of vulnerability without there having been a preexisting global sense of security. One can thus acknowledge the former without positing the latter, claiming instead that, pre-trauma, the person in question just did not think about all the ways in which, simply by existing as beings-in-the-world, we are exposed to harm. And that seems more plausible to me, particularly because trust, when it occurs, is a determinate orientation rather than the simple absence of distrust. (I thus do not share Baier's belief that we usually notice trust when it is let down. Trust has a felt character that smooths over gaps opened by doubt and uncertainty.) And if that is correct, there might not be some preexisting felt relation in need of repair post-trauma. Rather, the task would entail displacing the presence and intensity of the newly emerged basal insecurity, and this might require different kinds of work in different cases—going outside, seeing strangers, seeing family, meeting friends, feeling attracted to someone, etc. In other words, if no single lever will effectively redress all these scenes of vulnerability, the difference that makes a difference is clinical as well as theoretical.

A second thought also inclines me to resist treating basal insecurity as a form of distrust. In many cases, basal insecurity seems to cover more than cases of trust. Depending on its source, basal insecurity might cover dependencies like traveling by plane or along an interstate, or living in a high rise. To the degree this is true, it suggests that the concern is not the discretionary power of others to whom we have entrusted something, but our vulnerability in all reliance relations, not just trusting ones. True, people do speak of global losses of trust post-trauma, but as Jones herself observes, people also use trust to cover all reliance relations, and to a degree that she finds insufficiently restrictive (Jones, 4). Her deferral to ordinary language in this case thus seems like a case of special pleading.

A third concern is tied to the nature of distrust, which, like trust, is intersubjective on my view. I distrust when my nose twitches. Something about *this* situation seems off. General beliefs may come into play, but they are prompted by the case at hand. But basal distrust exits the specific and absorbs it. Its broader reach thus gives it the character of skepticism, which also helps explain its reach across multiple reliance relations and its resistance to counterexamples. It does not concern the particular, but the general vulnerability that is part of all dependence relations. It is thus uninterested in success stories because they can never prove that disaster is not around the corner.

Does this mean that trust is not an atmosphere? I think it is, but only in localized ways, some of which are operative in an ongoing manner. In other words, there is an atmosphere of trust for many, but it consists of microclimates tied to friends, family, neighbors, coworkers, etc., within more global fields of dependence. Now, if we are the type of person who refuses purely transactional relations, even when the principal is exchange, we may have enough of a feel for the people in our lives to trust (or distrust) them. But that is not the rule. In fact, on my view, trust relations are more of an achievement than a default, to use a term from Margaret Walker (Walker 2006, 85).

Walker thinks of trust relations (or "zones of trust") as reliance upon others in the context of mutually grasped, normative expectations. But any practice entails normative expectations, and those are mutually grasped by all who understand them. And that misses the individuating expectations of trust, which does more than expect people to do their jobs—which I do, even when I think people are shifty or I am too distracted to give their bearing a read. At least in contemporary societies underwritten by global exchange and abstract, positive law, reliance, rather than trust, links social actors. Something more can arise, however. We do not need to treat people like bridges, but most of the time, many do.

And that brings me to a final concern regarding basal security and its relation to trust. What is special about trust is the incipient "we" that it helps generate, the exception it introduces into business as usual. I thus want to preserve its intersubjective character and the kind of particularizing goodwill it requires when the trustworthy exercise discretionary agency.

In trust, one has the back of another. But in complex, differentiated societies, we gamble more than we trust. Their sheer scale demands this, and commodified exchange relations incline people to see their advantage in a manner that is independent of, if not at the expense of, another's. This does not mean that I reluctantly rely on others in contemporary capitalist societies. But calling that kind of collaboration "trust" romances it in a manner that rings false, and to the point of ideology. Let the basally secure beware.

THE TENTH AMENDMENT

Covet if you must. But thou shall be trustworthy.

WILL WE ALL GO DOWN TOGETHER?

Baier's "Trust and Anti-Trust" (1986) aligns trust with goodwill and competence, which maps nicely onto questions of agency—its why and what. Those I trust mean well by me and are competent to do me well should the occasion arise. "When I trust another," she writes, "I depend on her good will toward me" (Baier 1995, 99). And: "Trust, I have claimed, is reliance on others' competence and willingness to look after, rather than harm, things one cares about which are entrusted to their care" (Baier, 128).

Most accept that trust involves a positive assessment of the trusted's competence. Some mean well but cannot deliver. This is clearest in professional scenarios. My physician, tax accountant, and electrician need to know what's what if they are to empower my agency. (Interestingly, the competence requirement resonates with "trust" when applied to things and machines. They get the job done.)

Many doubt trust requires goodwill, however. Suppose I neither wish you well nor am out to get you. How does that orient you? If I were faced with such a scenario, your disposition might not preclude my trusting you, but it would negatively impact the degree to which I do trust you. And if I know you well, say as a colleague, and remain unsure of your regard, I would be reluctant to trust you. When I am among those I know, such uncertainty will manifest as a degree of suspicion. I might cooperate, but I would cover my ass in ways that indicate a lack of trust.

Like Baier, I think goodwill is presumed in the trusted, and I think this presumption gives trust a kind of utopian energy. As I enact and receive it, trust conveys a "look after me" plea, and that initiates a relation that expects more than absence of malice. I trust your agency—that is, your competence and a positive disposition toward me that informs your deliberations and commitment. Trust is different than giving someone the benefit of the doubt. The latter is a neutral stance: innocent until proven guilty. But that lacks the affirmative nature of trust, which feels that another is committed to me in some manner and will come through if tested.

SHORELINES

Trust, as I have imagined it, seems a neighbor to friendship. But I am unsure. It does not require (or preclude) the kind of love named by the Greek *philein*, that nonfeverish, heartfelt concern for the welfare of another that favors them above strangers, associates, sometimes even family. Also, my friends form a much smaller set than those I trust. But the "we" that trust initiates might be a step in that direction. It exemplifies a life where people look after each other, and competently. But maybe this says too much.

We are moving into murky waters, and I do not expect to discover the proper uses, the clear and distinct uses, of a term like "trust." Ordinary language is too diverse to prove authoritative, and yet our analysis relies on usages, given that we are unable to intuit the true meaning of trust. I thus proceed by way of examples that favor an emphasis, and so my offers move between the descriptive and prescriptive, remaining provisional, and not just in relation to their object—or so I hope. Ethical agents face one another when their terms slip and slide.

STRANGERS AS FICTIONS

Imagine the following: I am at an airport, and I would like to leave my bags while I hit the restroom. I consider my neighbors and wonder: Can I trust one or all of them to look after my stuff, presuming they are willing? Do I trust them not only to keep their hands off my things but to wait until I return? And should someone else show too much interest in my bags, do I trust them to intervene? My evaluation concerns several variables, including the bag's contents, how long I expect to be gone, my ability to communicate with these people, how sketchy the overall scene seems, and so forth. But suppose that everything (or enough) lines up. I ask them to look after my things, they agree, and I walk away trusting them and expecting my bags (them, too) to be there when I return.

Strangers, by definition, do not know me. It would be odd, therefore, if they immediately favored me with friendship, and equally odd if I presumed that they did. But might I not presume goodwill? We often expect something like common human decency, which I take to be a low-level form of goodwill. (And some are friendly in a more general way, meaning they are dispositionally beneficent.) If someone's grocery bag breaks and their items tumble out, I will help pick them up. We hold doors for people hustling in from the rain. I see someone huddled against a wall at night and I ask if they are alright. This is not the person-specific favor and goodwill that friendship exhibits, but it does involve looking out for others, and often in cases where we neither know them nor expect to see them again.

IS IT ALWAYS ABOUT YOU?

"Wait—I thought you said that trust cannot arise in conditions where another is opaque to me." That is my view. So if I trust my fellow travelers, I trust something about their orientation toward me. But what? Justifications for our trust may offer some clues. These strike me as typical: "They had an honest face." "I had a good feeling about them." And because of this, I favor the view that trust attributes some level of goodwill to the trusted, taking goodwill to run a continuum from common decency to incipient friendship. But is that operative in the "honest face" reply? Maybe it just means we expect them to keep their word. Their loyalty is impersonal; it lies with the norm, not us.

Back to strangers. My detour through the coffee shop shows that a failure to act in accord with a norm need not result in the feelings of betrayal that usually arise when someone violates our trust. And I take that to indicate that trust most likely was not operative in those exchanges. I think this also suggests that trusting someone expects more than action in accord with a norm. But before I explore that possibility, let us not lose sight of the honest face, which led me to leave a bag with a stranger.

Am I wrong to think that an honest face indicates a kind of goodwill? I very well could be. It could be a predatory ploy. But whatever the trait, sometimes I take it to indicate something like goodwill. Perhaps not toward me in particular, but toward anyone, including me, to whom such a person commits. There are many ways for a will to prove good. Sometimes inclination carries the day. Obligations open another route, to accept, for the moment, Kant's world of wills. To presume goodwill in another is to presume that my welfare matters to them, meaning it will be a positive variable in their deliberations. How it comes to matter is not the decisive issue. (My trust does not hinge on another's metaethics, in other words.) An honest face reassures me that someone is unlikely to steal from me and that they will look after my bags, particularly once they say they will. I leave thinking: in this modest way, they have my back.

You might be thinking, "When people are moved to act by their allegiance to a norm, the norm orients them rather than the person with whom they are allied. Think of fair people. We do not worry whether they like us or not. They are fair, and that is why I trust them. Justice is blind." On this view, how the trusted regards those who trust them is irrelevant. What is decisive is the norm in question, not their regard for me.

I think Baier has exposed the limits of this account. Imagining an administrative structure of oversight, she writes, "At each of these levels the one in whom trust is placed is not merely a rule applier but a decision maker" (Baier 1995, 137). And: "To trust is to let another think about and take action to protect and advance some thing the truster cares about, to let the trusted *care for* what one cares about" (Baier, 138). After you commit to a norm (keep your word, be honest, treat your neighbor as yourself) you still must apply it. And that requires judgment, if only to ascertain whether a given case falls under the norm in question. ("Yes, I said I would look after that guy's bags, but that was thirty minutes ago and I need to board my plane. I didn't sign up for this.") But more than that, many cases—most, in my administrative experience—involve nuances that require reflection and deliberation. Snowflakes are not the only differential phenomena, and justice requires more than treating like cases alike. It also insists: do not render the unlike alike. One thing distinguishing the bureaucratic functionary from the trustworthy overseer is an ability to address cases on their own terms. Would you trust an overseer with a poor feel for particularity? I would not. And precisely because I would think, "I don't count here." I would not presume ill will. But the absence of goodwill would orient me away from trust and toward prediction. Nancy Potter says this well: "We can predict good treatment on other grounds than an attitude of goodwill toward us . . . but it is not likely to be trust at a very deep level if the good treatment is based on a commitment to universal principles *and* accompanied by an indifference to feelings for others or an impersonal and impartial stance" (Potter 2002, 6).

Baier's point also concerns contractual relations. Suppose I hire a plumber to install a faucet, move a garbage disposal, and, on their recommendation, install new piping to relocate the P trap. Yes, I expect them to do the agreed-upon work. But if I expect more than competence, I expect more, don't I? I also expect them only to recommend work that I need. Is it necessary to relocate the P trap? Suppose they recommend it, I agree, and they do an excellent job, but I later discover that its previous location was more than adequate. In that case, something like my trust was broken. I trusted them not only to do what they said they would, but also to work in ways that my situation required; no more, no less. Baier makes the point regarding the postal service: "We trust the mail carrier to deliver and not tamper with the mail, and to some extent, we trust his discretion in interpreting what 'tampering' covers" (Baier 1995, 104).

Because agency requires discretion or judgment, Baier configures trust in terms of goodwill (and competence). When the situation calls for an unscripted response, we expect goodwill from those we trust. Whether they come by that through sentiment, principle, or both is immaterial. What counts is that we count when the trusted must decide what to do. Not that we expect the rule-oriented among us to bend in our favor, although many do expect preferential treatment from those they trust. Regardless, all who trust expect something more than a generic assessment of their situation. Trust expects honest work, and honest work avoids clichés.

THE CAT'S MEOW

I trust my cat Freya. Less so Jack, but with him, it is a matter of competence. He is not careful enough with his claws when we play. Not that he strikes out suddenly, like Baier's kitty, who leaves her with the hope that play doesn't roughen (Baier 2010, 195). But Jack does not seem to grasp that "claw beats skin" in a game of paw, hand, and claw. I thus distrust him and remain alert. But I hold both without fear and nuzzle them as they nuzzle me, and I let Freya's claws make biscuits in my beard. And while they occasionally miss the mark, moving across my neck or lips, I trust her not to suddenly scratch me, and to adjust her paws if her claws should catch. In such scenarios, she is careful with me, and I am careful with her. And should she want to get down, she wiggles—not quite a squirm—and I set her down. No fuss. No sudden fury.

Our cats trust us, me and Hilary. Returning to the house, they enter without hesitating and greet us, usually with a squeak or a chirp. But if we have a visitor, particularly more than one, they enter cautiously, sometimes not at all, at least in Jack's case. And they enter silently, unsure of the situation. We have earned their trust and they have earned ours. We have held them ever since they were tiny, and we don't fuck with them—just play in ways that bring them delight. Both often gaze intently into our eyes, and we gaze back. "But how do you know that they trust you?" I do not. But so it is with trust.

CARE TO JOIN ME?

"Invitation to trust" is a term of art. Authors use it to describe situations when another assures us they can be trusted, say with a nod, by giving us directions, or with an explicit promise. The assurance indicates that they are trustworthy regarding some specified tasks, and it places them under an obligation to come through. On this view, an invitation to trust establishes something like a contract.

I want to run this in the other direction. When someone trusts another, they invite them into the kind of ethical community that trust helps generate by turning us into agents of another's well-being, and in a manner that exceeds the specifications of contracts, even convention. In saying this, I am following Baier's observation that trust positions us within the discretionary care of another, at their disposal. I also think this is compatible with Hinchman's claim that betrayal is a "failure to engage your needs in the way that you're trusting her to engage them," although it pulls the intuition away from Kantian concerns over specified obligations into the phronetic exercise of something like care (Faulkner and Simpson 2017, 51). I think this also rings true to Darwall's suggestion (in line with Baier) that trust not only renders us vulnerable but also enables a creative, even proactive cooperation that otherwise would elude us (Faulkner and Simpson, 35–50).

Thinking an "invitation to trust" along this line clarifies, I think, some of the disappointment that occurs in the wake of broken trusts. Beyond the specifics, a basic, social invitation has been refused. The trusted turned out not to be the kind of person we had hoped they would be. Trust anticipates that another might enlarge one's ethical community by being someone who looks out for others, and not in some general way, but where they live.

WILL THE CIRCLE STAY UNBROKEN?

The "we" of trust is not really a circle of friends. Friendship expects more. The goodwill that trust requires need not involve affection, and friendship begins and persists in the often-mysterious fact that we prefer the company of some. That is why friendship is a species of love. Trust has a broader orbit. Haunted by an epistemic gap, trust imagines the trusted to be dispositionally beneficent, and that is its utopian character; it aspires to organize our world of mutual dependence with a kind of goodness that looks after people and in a manner that does more than simply follow the rules. In fact, drawn from unscripted currents, the incipient "we" of trust falls outside two cardinal sites of ethical life: the formal rules of morality and the mores of convention. Not that trust is unimpacted by either. When someone makes a promise or signs a contract, that may expand my trust, although I will have to find the performance convincing. If we stand in conventional proximity to one another (neighbor, acquaintance, colleague), that may influence whether and how I trust you but not guarantee that I will. Trust relations thus seem irreducible to paradigmatic ethical alliances:

family, friendship, contracts, conventional roles. Read as an image of human relationality, trust images an incipient "we" charged with possibilities that exceed our scripted futures. Like hope, it is—or can be—a wellspring for the better. And therefore betrayal signals more than a particular disappointment. If the trusted do not come through, the relationship is harmed, and the resulting disappointment includes a sense of isolation. Loneliness haunts Caesar's *Et tu, Brute*.

SALTIMBANQUES

Adrift in a history of barbarism—which continues to accumulate—Walter Benjamin saw something else sparking in the capacities of those who endured it.

> Class struggle, which for a historian schooled in Marx is always in evidence, is a fight for the crude and material things without which no refined and spiritual things could exist. But these latter things . . . are not present as a vision of spoils that fall to the victor. They are alive . . . as confidence, courage, humor, cunning, and fortitude, and have effects that reach far back into the past. . . . As flowers turn toward the sun, what has been strives to turn—by dint of a secret heliotropism—toward that sun which is rising in the sky of history. (Benjamin 2003, 390)

I find something similar in trust, which becomes even more important among the vulnerable or transgressive. Trust is directed toward competencies, our manifold *savoir*, and so its incipient "we" is born amid agency, its currents concretely utopian. Yes, they are partially nowhere relative to standing convention and explicit moral rules. But they remain here, among you and me and what we can do. Trust enlarges agency because it begins and terminates beneath the more abstract patterns that often orient it.

FROM US TO THEM

My focus has been (and will remain) trust as an interpersonal occurrence. That is not its only modality, however. People also trust in institutions, even brands, and some trust in nations and families. Or not. Never trust a Hatfield.

Because I think trust requires a degree of intersubjective availability, I pause when trust is extended to groups, whether formalized (say, a corporation) or not (like a family). In either case, it depends on who you meet. I do not have any way to access a group's disposition toward me, if it even has one. I find the US Postal Service incredibly reliable at processing and delivering mail, but I do not really trust or distrust the USPS. I do trust my carrier, David Bohman. He is not only competent, but in a general way, and regarding my mail, he looks out for me. (Actually, I trust him beyond this, but that is not germane here.) My trust in David is not abstract. I am happy to post letters from home but not from work. There is no one I distrust at work, but those handling the mail there seem a bit careless and so I think it an unnecessary gamble given the alternatives. And that difference informs, in part, my general sense of group trust. Group trust is often determined in individuated scenes, and when those are absent, reliability is closer to what is at stake.

But sometimes individuated scenes are available. AT&T has a history of deception. If someone told me, "I switched carriers because I don't trust AT&T," I would understand them. From 2009 to 2015 or so, solicitors selling AT&T recurringly told me that AT&T would give me access to optic fiber cables, which provide better Internet access. But that was false. And I knew it, having researched the matter when I moved to Atlanta in 2009. Those cables were not in my neighborhood and there were no plans to lay them there. Because the lie was repeated by more than one salesman (who all were young men) I grew to distrust AT&T, and because of dishonesty as opposed to unreliable service. Not that I presumed ill will toward me. But I knew I meant nothing to them beyond a shot at a sale. And so, I wrote off AT&T. "AT&T as a whole?" No. I did not distrust their installers or their IT division or their HR department. And when a friend took a job with AT&T, she did not fall under suspicion. My distrust was directed at the marketing and sales division of AT&T and based on a generalization from a handful of encounters.

Group trust can approximate the logic of intersubjective trust. From a handful of encounters, we generalize about a group like we do about a person's character from a handful of actions. If you do not pay me back a few times, I will not trust you to do so in the future. I might even think, "Don't trust them with money." But I might still trust you to pick me up if you say you will, and I might also trust you to look after my pets while I am away.

FROM THEM TO US

Prestige can be and often is a variable in intersubjective scenarios. If I have a good feeling about a doctor, my trust is likely to expand if they work at a prestigious clinic or hospital. And if they do not, my trust might waver a bit regarding their competence. Trust thus moves from individuated scenes to social entities. The general character of those entities, to the degree they have one, also are variables in intersubjective trust, and self-trust too. As a young scholar, I felt authorized when the University of Oregon hired me, particularly after two years of failed job searches. Hiring me as a junior professor entailed a recognition that checked my growing self-doubt.

I DIDN'T SIGN UP FOR THIS

Trust is conditional. This becomes apparent when someone fails to come through but we neither feel betrayed nor are moved to resentment, as when, in an unforeseen manner, a situation exceeds another's competence. Suppose I have been asked (or I volunteer) to look in on a friend's dog, Nellie, while my friend travels. Once a day I walk Nellie, returning in the evening to refresh her food and water and let her out back. Sadly, the neighbor uses a pesticide that has poisoned a stream running through several properties, including my friend's. Nellie often drinks from the stream. One evening she seems a bit off, but not unusually so. I suppose Nellie merely misses her family. But when I arrive the next day, she is seriously ailing. I rush her to the vet, but I am too late. Nellie dies. If I had brought her in the night before, something could have been done. But I was unable to recognize the signs. I just didn't have the training and knew nothing of the pesticide. I'm devastated and have to make an awful phone call. My friend is devastated as well. But they do not feel betrayed. No one knew about the poison and neither of us, just stopping by, would have recognized the symptoms as symptoms. My friend thus saves their wrath for the neighbor.

Because trust reaches into the unscripted, it should prepare for extenuating circumstances. Some may exceed our competence whereas others may negate our ability to safeguard what has been entrusted. I might be injured and thus unable to come by. And the injury may be severe enough (imagine a short-term coma) such that days pass before I can alert the owner or find a replacement. We can also imagine cases where counterdemands arise that lead the trusted to turn their attentions elsewhere. Imagine my child is the one poisoned while playing in a stream. Recognizing that something is very wrong, I spend forty-eight very anxious hours in the hospital at their bedside, forgetting my friend's dog. In my absence, Nellie shits the house, which I discover when I am finally able to look in on her. But right then, my friend returns. Finding me cleaning up, they look puzzled. I explain. Suppose they reply, "I shouldn't have trusted you." That would be off given the clear, extenuating conditions. My agency does not abandon them but attends to something else that has a greater claim upon it.

INSIDE OUT

By setting discretion at the heart of trust, thereby rendering it unscripted, even improvisational, I regard trust relations as fluid, meaning they often find their character in their execution. But they are not shapeless. Improvisation is always situated, and responsively so.

Imagine you lend me your car for a week. I do not have one and you want it driven every now and then and I am happy to have wheels. Presume, too, that you know me fairly well. We socialize often but we are not particularly close. We do not share personal feelings and we do not seek each other's advice. But we probably see each other or run into each other at least once a month. If asked, you would say you trust me. "He seems like a good guy."

Now, what can I do with your car? Drive errands? Sure. Take a longer drive in the country? Probably. Take two, exceedingly long trips, about five hundred miles each? Not so sure. Take it off road (it's an average sedan) and damage it, but agree to pay for the repair? That seems too much. Not that I damage it but that I use it in such an extraordinary way. Of course, we might disagree. And that seems interesting. It suggests that trust's intersubjectivity involves a presumed, but somewhat open, mutual understanding of what should be done in determinate if unscripted settings. As Carolyn McLeod argues, what the "trusted person stands for morally speaking is similar enough to what we stand for . . . that we can count on that person to do what we trust her to do," although that should not preclude us from recognizing extenuating circumstances—why did I head off road (McLeod 2002, 27)? Nor should it foreclose opportunities to learn new ways to care for persons, places, and things. Suppose I lend the car, in turn, to someone hiding from a stalker who knows her car and keeps a watch out for it. I have not planned to do this, but the occasion arises, and I respond. That might strike someone as too much, and to the degree that I become less trustworthy in their eyes. Or it might lead them to think, "right call," and transform how they more generally regard me and their possessions. (I might be similarly transformed and think, "I really should get a car and be the person who lends.") Or some mix of all three might transpire. The discretionary heart of trust exposes people to one another in a scene that is not only dependent and epistemically fraught, but potentially transformative.

COMING TO TERMS WITH TRUST

We are exploring trust as a kind of conduct that is carried out in scenes of expectations and competencies, as well as in unforeseen circumstances.

By insisting that trust is situated in this manner, my view runs counter to Paul Faulkner, who believes that trust is principally a two-term relation: I trust another (Faulkner and Simpson 2017, 123). When it proves to be a three-term relation, as when you trust me with your car, he believes that trust inclines toward the contractual. But trust's stretch into the unscripted suggests that it always exceeds the contractual, even in specified circumstances. You might not trust me again with your car if I take it off road, but that would be because I've proved careless or too free with your stuff, not because I have violated some agreement and so led you to doubt my word. And while the stretch of trust involves a presumed mutual understanding, what is presumed is a range of possibilities and a somewhat vague sense of what is allowed within them, which also runs counter to the explicitness of the contractual.

I think Faulkner's conception of trust, what he terms "attitudinal trust," is based on the example of intimates. Among intimates, my trust does have a relatively broad reach. But even then, I do not trust others in areas where they lack competence, which effectively binds trust to a range of situations and thus the terms of those situations. While Hilary trusts me to trim the hedge alongside the driveway, she would not trust me to prune our vast array of bushes and shrubs. In fact, I think she trusts me not to get above my raising. Does this mean that trust is always three-term in some specified sense? No, and so I appreciate the spirit of Faulkner's claim, which Domenicucci and Holton also defend, albeit in their own way (Faulkner and Simpson, 2017). Trust can be and often is a thorough regard for a person or a general orientation or disposition. But through its ties to competence, trust is worldly in a Heideggerian sense; situated, bound to the factical. The possibilities it imagines (and figures) essay the actual and so remain tied to it.

AND THE PURSUIT OF HAPPINESS

Trust grounds John Locke's conception of state power. It is worth wondering, therefore, how that conception relates to what has been argued. On Locke's view, rulers (in the sense of representatives of the law) are trustees of the public good and, to use Locke's language, must act pursuant to that good or contradict the basic form and telos of their office (Locke 1988, sec. 22, 134, 149, 155, 231). And should their conduct fall into such contradiction, they forfeit less their right to rule than their standing as rulers, thereby making room for revolt, or what is better described as a new assertion of popular sovereignty.

The kind of trust Locke has in mind occurs among those who have achieved maturity. If that should be absent, the agent in question lives under the will of a trustee. Lockean trust thus flows among sovereign subjects who "hath attained to a state of Freedom," and whose "Understanding be fit to take the Government of his Will" (sec. 59, p. 307). Moreover, the terms of a Lockean trust tend toward the explicit and are underwritten by the explicit and implicit consent of the governed (sec. 59, 171). Not that everything is spelled out. Rulers wield some prerogative in matters concerning the public good that are insufficiently covered by existing law (sec. 210). But natural law remains the measure of such decisions, with the judgment of the governed prevailing in disputes over whether the public good has been served (sec. 240). The political Trust that Locke envisions is thus fiduciary in character—that is, responsive to moral norms rather than a set of contractually specified terms. (And note, he often capitalizes Trust to underscore the objective character of the arrangement.)

Locke's feel for the fiduciary nature of trust is welcome and essential in my view. But trust relations are rarely as well-defined or as explicitly articulated as Locke's imagined social Trust, which seems drawn from his experiences as Chancery secretary, a post he assumed in 1672 (26, 114). In its root form, therefore, as well as its imagined extension, Locke's Trust is far from paradigmatic for ordinary trust relations, at least as I understand them.

First, people often trust others without informing them, and without the kind of sovereign self-possession that Locke imagines when he proposes trust as a form under which the rule(r) of law can be legitimately instituted or recalled from tyranny. The moral psychology of ordinary trust is thus opaquer than what operates in Lockean trust. Second, Locke can imagine cases of implicit consent that, if applied to ordinary trust, would erase the difference between trust and reliance. (In other words, actions entailing implicit consent are consistent with distrust.) Third, ordinary trust considers a wider range of goods. Locke's public good is centered on property, so even when prerogative is exercised, it is limited compared to our trust in neighbors, friends, acquaintances, family, and coworkers, in part because the latter can concern things that I am not owed or do not have a right to (or proprietary control over) but which a trusted person presumably will look after or even generate, such as social and/or business opportunities. Fourth, the trustor is not the final or principal arbiter of what is and is not in accord with the trust. Whether one lets another down remains potentially contestable. Did I fail to look after your dog when it ran out into the street after I rushed out the front door to aid a car crash victim? I do not know. But the final call does not rest with you. Fifth, Locke's trustees and trustors do not relate to one another as private citizens, whereas many do (and at times beyond a context of identical or even operative citizenship). More ordinary trustees may have needs or obligations, therefore, including to themselves, that condition what they can consider in exercising discretion. But Lockean trustees only may consider their own welfare when exercising discretion as a function of their share of the public good, whereas a trusted acquaintance, say, regarding a professional opportunity, may look after themselves first without letting me down, let alone betraying me. Sixth, ordinary trust usually does not authorize the trusted to act on my behalf—namely, as my representative—but only in my interest. Returning to a professional opportunity, an ordinary trustee may mention my name when an opportunity arises, whereas a representative trustee may commit me to it. The trust that Locke valorizes, therefore, imagines that we are functionally interchangeable under some social compact, whereas ordinary trust must travel rougher, uneven terrain, and face more contestable results.

MIRROR, MIRROR

A trust that is worthy of the name is dynamic. It risks the unscripted, which the trustworthy brave on our behalf. The incipient "we" that courses through trust is thus also unscripted; or rather, its script is often revised as we encounter ourselves in what we expect from others, in how they meet, frustrate, or exceed those expectations, and how we bear the trust placed in us. An image of who we might yet be, trust also discloses who we currently are.

But trust may also involve a kind of avoidance or keep us from some unpleasantness. If we knew everything about everyone, every flicker of doubt, twinge of regret, and grasping desire, would we play ball? If I saw every waver in my peeps, could I trust them? In effect, trust may not only empower us but protect us from what would stick like a pin.

Emily Dickinson has a poem that plumbs this idea (Dickinson 1979, 424). It begins by suggesting (in two ways) that we often act on what is taken on trust.

Trust in the Unexpected—
By this—was William Kidd
Persuaded of the Buried Gold—
As One had testified
(lines 1–4)

But it closes with a less common thought.

The Same—afflicted Thomas—
When Deity assured
'Twas better—the perceiving not—
Provided it believed—
(lines 13–16)

How are we to take the suggestion that "the perceiving not" is better provided we still believe? One reading holds that the divine rewards faith, which does not require or seek confirmation. But the poem also seems to suggest that perceiving the bedeviled details may make it more difficult to believe. If the latter also applies, it affirms finitude, if backhandedly. Having to act on trust spares us the fate of knowing each other and ourselves too well.

TRUE COLORS

The "we" imagined in (and figured by) trust and partially generated by trust is far from undifferentiated. We are never a simple aggregate of discrete parts, nor a seamless whole. Rather, "we" names you and I in the company of us. And you and I are not substitutable, as the phenomenon of trust clarifies.

Trust courses through a domain I have called the personal, which revolves around actions that no one can do for another, like persevere or understand. I cannot trust *for you*, nor you for me. Others can influence whether we trust or not (and the degree to which we trust), but our trust (or lack of it) is just that—ours.

Whom to trust? To what degree? Our replies individuate us. So, too, whether we prove trustworthy. The unscripted tests our commitment, discloses our allegiances. How we endure and resolve these trials discloses, in part, our character. Trust images more than an incipient "we." It also discloses an unfolding *me* (and you) in relation to you (and me).

THERE GOES THE NEIGHBORHOOD

You have recently moved. Time for a new dentist. One is recommended. Same last name as a neighbor you once had—Ghiron. Good family. You make an appointment. Sitting in the chair, Dr. Ghiron enters. African American. Does your trust flicker?

You are a firefighter. Big fires. Wilderness aflame. People die when mistakes are made. Your crew chief appears. Small. A woman. How will you receive her orders?

Reread these scenes. Who are the presumed agents? What do they look like? Sound like? What happens if we change their demographics? Do not oversimplify. "There is nothing more painful to me at this stage in my life than to walk down the street and hear footsteps," Jesse Jackson has said, ". . . then turn around and see somebody white and feel relieved" (Page 2016). A lot courses through trust. Some currents incline us toward mistrust, even fear, and despite who we take ourselves to be or even hope to be.

ENOUGH ABOUT ME

Implicated in deforming social currents, the conscientious can fall prey to an ironic narcissism. What begins as concern for the other culminates in self-interrogation, even unhappy consciousness. A counterforce can be found in Nancy Potter's *How Can I Be Trusted?* (Potter 2002). Imagining a community that includes victims of incest and sex abuse, or rather, simply addressing our communities, she wonders what it means to be trustworthy on the presumption that you are interacting with those victims even though they are unknown to you as individuals. And while she explores the issue in terms of pedagogical relations, it is obviously vaster than that. The National Center for the Victims of Crime reports that "over the course of their lifetime, 28% of U.S. youth ages 14 to 17 [have] been sexually victimized," most of them female (NCVC 2021). Interventions such as Potter's acknowledge the traps of bias but also propel us toward response-ability. Here are several thoughts sparked by Potter's analysis but taken outside the confines of a pedagogical relationship, although they apply there as well.

1. Trust is given but not a given. Trust relations are results, even accomplishments. The trustworthy know this. This is more me than Potter, who finds more trust in what I regard as broad, social reliance. The difference makes a difference in just this context.
2. Trust should not be presumed or expected as a default regard. Nor should its absence be taken as unwarranted suspicion or criticism. "Trust me" may very well solicit a silent incredulity and felt isolation.
3. The more power one wields in a relationship, the more of a threat one may appear. Profound harm intensifies feelings of vulnerability. That should provoke sadness, not frustration. And outrage at the crime. Again, distrust is lonely. Try not to make it worse.
4. Because trust is something to nurture, where possible, one must know how to relate in its absence, which requires generosity, fairness, and honesty. That is, one should behave in clear accord with other characteristics broadly held to be virtuous. Because these character-

istics, when evident, help nurture it, trust might emerge over time. But it might not, hence the need for patience as well.

5. No one is substitutable, which requires an epistemology of love, a thought lurking in *Walden*, in "Winter Visitors," in the pure love actuated by poetry according to Thoreau (Thoreau 2008). Love? In the sense of a philein whose desire should refuse to rest with generalizations. But that may ask too much, at least on the side of affection. But the epistemic point holds for the goodwill that orients the trustworthy. It particularizes its regard, and that is what I hear underwriting Potter's insistence that the trustworthy take their epistemic tasks seriously, knowing the broad fates of various peoples while striving to learn another's particularizing traits and circumstances, including their responses to generalizable fates (Potter 2002, 27–28).

6. The wronged and wounded need to decide when to entrust their suffering to another. Thinking of trustworthy people, Potter imagines them trusting survivors (Potter, 117). But that may say too much in most cases that involve modest familiarity. The issue may be one of more general respect and concern. Do not pry. Most wounds reopen when poked. Also, receive disclosures with one's full attention, and comport oneself in a manner that conveys a readiness to be supportive and caring. Find ways to acknowledge the magnitude of the issue without virtue signaling.

DON'T BE A TOOL

Whether and how we trust discloses our character. But in what way is our trust *ours?* Do we decide to trust? Presume a minimal understanding of decision such as Aristotle's. On his account, we need to determine whether the action derives from forces in us or outside us. If the answer is "inside us," trust belongs to the voluntary.

Apart from sci-fi forms of mental manipulation (wires to the brain, airborne drugs, psionic powers), I doubt trust can be generated coercively. Forcing another to say they trust me will probably ensure the opposite. They might say it, but obedience is not trust. As Benjamin McMyler says, "Trust is something that must be cultivated rather than incentivized" (Faulkner and Simpson 2017, 169).

But coercion may not be the only way in which our trust can be brought about "outside" us, as it were. We can be deceived by another and so trust them when we should not—and would not, if they had been honest. And trust of this order seems different—less voluntary—than what arises in scenes free of deception or manipulation, as the French roots of "manipulation" convey. *Manipuler* involves handling an apparatus, whereas the Latin *manipulus* indicates a handful or bundle as well as a cohort of soldiers, *maniple* in the plural. The metaphor is thus apposite. When manipulated, our agency diminishes and we become implements, extensions of the will of another. But this goes too far, no? Even when manipulated, it is not as if the other trusts for me. I remain the trusting party.

Being manipulated is oddly active and passive at the same time, or something *jenseits* the distinction. It is because we are not apparatuses but reflexive beings that others manipulate us. The possibility of distrust needs defeating. Allegiance must be secured. Even a manipulated trust bears witness to our agency, if only indirectly, which may be why we feel ashamed when we discover we have been deceived.

But do not obsess over the negative. What about charisma? Not all winning personalities are up to no good. And when we trust them, as we often do, what is our role in the result? Something appreciable, otherwise it would be odd to learn about ourselves from the result, which we do. Voluntary vulnerability and an act of abandon, trust twists inflexible grammars.

DREAM #33

"Can I help you?" becomes a way to say hello.

MORE THAN THEORY PROVES GRAY

The psychomechanics of trust further thicken the forest. "Trust can come with no beginnings," Baier writes, "with gradual as well as sudden beginnings, and with various degrees of self-consciousness, voluntariness, and expressness" (Baier 1995, 105). Sometimes I just trust someone, and nothing like a "decision" or "commitment" takes place. "I found myself implicitly trusting her" is a perfectly sensible statement. Sometimes I trust another despite sound misgivings, resisting the conclusions of reflection: "I don't know why I keep thinking this time will be different." Other times (and over time) another earns our trust: "It's taken time, but I've really come to rely on them, and happily." But even then, the time at which one feels another has earned their trust is rarely marked by something like an explicit decision. And this intrigues me. Not only does trust concern the unscripted actions of others; to a degree, it is itself unscripted. Its current moves beyond what we normally associate with voluntary—that is, explicit, self-conscious commitment.

THROUGH A GLASS DARKLY

A bank loans me money based on my credit rating. If I default, how likely are they to say, "But Mr. Lysaker, we trusted you"? Very unlikely. And if they do, "Come off it" will be my reply. Not that I do not have to cover the loan. But I do not think trust enters our relationship. They are not looking out for me, and I am not looking out for them. Instead, we have a contract, and a verbose one at that. And while contracts face their own epistemic gaps, those distances are typically filled with gambles; in loaning me money the bank gambled based on data that also dictated the terms of the loan.

It is precisely the expressness of the bank's agency that trust lacks—a clear, linear process of inference that terminates in an explicit decision to lend (or not). And this leaves trust somewhat mysterious. To be clear, I am not claiming that discoveries cannot influence whether and to what degree I trust others. If I know you have let others down, that will impact my trust. So, too, if you have let me down. One could even speak of someone's "trust history": "Be careful with old reliable." But even then, I do not have a method of calculating another's trustworthiness based on that history. Trust involves a deliberate leap.

LET'S KEEP THIS BETWEEN OURSELVES

Trust's relative opacity as a phenomenon is no doubt compounded by the fact that its current is intersubjective. When trusting, I relate to myself, considering what would be entrusted, its relative importance, and what I know of the other. I also relate to how that other relates to me, to their manner, such as their posture, eye contact, tone of voice, etc. (If someone tries too hard to win our trust, we grow suspicious.) And here again, expressness or explicitness is often modest to minimal. In fact, if I need to ask, "Can I trust you?" I have my doubts. But also, I rarely announce to others "I am trusting you." If someone tells me that, I hear anxiety. And "trust me" rarely if ever sets me at ease.

ONCE BURNED, TWICE SHY

I find myself at a dead end of sorts. The backwall is a weave of "cognition," "affect," and "desire." Not that trust is spontaneous and thereby pure, some native instinct to be freed rather than educated. Trust can be (and should be) enabled by inferences. I say this because trust involves learning processes that interpret the intersubjective, worldly situations in which we find ourselves.

But how should we characterize a learning process that results in an affective, cognitive, conative braid—or rather, something that suggests we are a bit clumsy about the psychomechanics of ethical life? Does one gather all kinds of information from various sites (modes of intelligence, say, including emotional)? And is that somehow sorted and weighed, leading to something like a belief that "X is trustworthy," which in turn forms the basis of our trusting them? Unlikely, I think. Leaving aside the third man problem, which lurks at every joint, I am often unsure if someone is trustworthy but trust them anyway. Or I do not. And there are times when I simply trust another without explicitly bothering to determine if they are trustworthy in some general way. At once, in the face of uncertainty, I trust them. But I cannot just bring myself to trust others, even if I lack a good reason to deem them untrustworthy.

In the alchemy of our souls (or selves, or minds, or organisms), trust flows (or not) along an ambiguous moral-psychological terrain, one poorly captured by models of inference that involve express steps toward explicit conclusions. Trust must cross more than one epistemic gap. We don't quite know whether another deserves our trust, and we are often unsure why we trust (or won't) when we do (or don't).

THE THICK OF IT

In *Giving an Account of Oneself*, Judith Butler observes some of the ways in which we prove opaque to ourselves (Butler 2005). Why, for example, did Foucault's studies incline toward the philosophy of the human sciences, and what led him to pick up Nietzsche when he did, and emphasize the genealogical strains of his thought? Or, more generally, what leads one to elect a profession or pursue one set of interests over another? Or, thinking now of Montaigne, why does one get on so much better with this one, singular person?

To find opacity in such phenomena is to acknowledge that we cannot fully account for why (or how) we come to do, feel, or believe a range of things, including things that characterize us. Not that we'll have nothing to say by way of explanation and justification, but the ways of trust are more like moods in which we find ourselves than stances we explicitly take. And that fluidity (if not quite fickleness) seems worthy of observance. Because trust relations are not explicit, contractual relations, and because the roots of our trust are relatively opaque, we can (or should) remain poised to catch our own prejudicial missteps. Trust and distrust can be couriers of bias, or worse. Better then, when the dust settles, to return to the variable character of those with whom our lives are bound, and our own as well.

Not only deforming habits circulate in the recesses of our character, however; surprise and renewal percolate as well. An acknowledgment of the implicit and unscripted character of trust, therefore, should also keep us alert to what hovers at the limits of self-conscious inquiry and reflection, just past the reach of our justificatory practices—say, gut feelings, nagging doubts, or the grip of an idea that is just hard to shake. In the context of trust, we might group them as "affinities," stressing the word's sense of attraction, kinship, borders, and limits, which openly bears its finitude.

"Why give voice to an incapacity? Why acknowledge this limit regarding currents like trust?" A second reason comes from Aristotle. Ethics shouldn't seek more specificity than the phenomenon allows. If we over-intellectualize what requires adjustments on the fly, we will miss the mark. This is what I find in accounts that characterize trust too expressly. McGeer and Pettit argue that when I trust you, I "manifestly rely on you to do X: I make clear to you my assumption that you will prove reliable in doing X" (Faulkner and Simpson 2017, 15; see also 29). This seems too specific, both in its "manifestly" and, to a lesser degree, in the specification "to do X." If I go away, I trust that Hilary, should she play records, will do so with care— keep the stylus clean, put the LPs back in their sleeves, shelve the albums. We have never discussed this, but she has a good enough sense of their importance to me that should she be careless around the stereo, I will feel put out. In an unscripted site where goodwill is expected, she would let me down. Similarly, should Hilary go away and be unexpectedly detained, she will expect me to water the plants, inside and out. Their care is entrusted to me simply by her being away. She need not tell me this, and she does not remove herself from a trust relation by not telling me this. Said otherwise, the "we" brought about by trust, one in which we have each other's backs, remains in play even when we do not expressly announce this to each other. And should I forget this, or lose the point in philosophical reflection, I will become less trustworthy and less able to trust.

The good of trust, at least in part, lies with the incipient "we" it initiates and images. Not that "we" is an unquestionably redemptive figure. When predicated on false universals, it can prove a smothering, totalitarian leveler. But trust eludes this dialectic, at least when we observe the limits that give rise to it. By observing trust's opacities, the finitude of its incipient *we* is embraced. Because it endures two epistemic gaps, trust acknowledges my dependence upon others as well as their alterity and freedom. All that? I think so: (a) Trust enables shared agency, thus unveiling the power of dependence. It embraces heteronomy and helps unleash its power. (b) Trust also relies on another's discretion in unscripted scenarios. It thus recognizes (or acknowledges) the trusted as distinct, and (c) as a distinct agent (someone capable of acting deliberately in my absence). Trust thus situates us within our finitude, amending without repudiating it. As well as any facet of our lives, it discloses the human.

TRUSTING TRUST

Alphonso Lingis suggests that trust, like laughter and sexual desire, breaks through "images and representations and labeling of things." In doing so, trust makes "contact with the singular reality" of another (Lingis 2004, xii). "But to *trust you*," he writes, "is to go beyond what I know and to hold on to the real individual that is you" (Lingis, ix). I see things differently. Lingis converts the vulnerabilities that trust embraces, its exposures, into a kind of immediacy. But that does not follow. Yes, trust exceeds contractual scripts and probabilistic assessments, but the leap and feel of prereflective life still carries its habitus (or habitudes, for there are more than one). Moreover, an acknowledgment of your difference and my inability to know what you will do does not amount to direct contact. Instead, the *you* I hold on to in trust is a figment of my imagination, one solid enough to orient my conduct but elusive enough to guarantee nothing, a problem intensified by the passage of time in which we change, ever slowly, sometimes suddenly.

AT YOUR DISPOSAL

Many regard trust as a feeling. "Affect" indicates the extradiscursive character of the phenomenon as well as its motivational force. But that threatens to both pull the currents of trust outside learning processes and underplay their positionality in ecosocial history. Moreover, feeling does not quite capture how trust also involves conduct. I prefer to think of trust as a *disposition*.

Trust and distrust dispose us in particular ways; they give us a tendency, and whether they are habitually operative or not. If I trust you, I tend to interpret your motives as inclined toward my benefit, and I tend to place some aspects of my welfare in your care. And note how "tendency" does not force me to locate trust in cognition, affect, or desire. Rather, tendency refers to the organism in general, and how it comports itself. Tendency also displaces activity/passivity dichotomies, which, as we've seen, obscure more than they clarify about trust.

The tendencies that trust (and distrust) establish are always positioned in the world; trust's character modulates established situations, from intimates to strangers, family members to coworkers, relations that are themselves situated in broader ecosocial networks that are both synchronically and diachronically complex. The presence or absence of trust is thus never just a fact about a discrete being. Like any human phenomenon, trust is a function of a dynamic field of interactions, and the language of disposition underscores that dimension.

Finally, trust, as we have seen, renders one vulnerable. But no less being trustworthy, which may make us targets for manipulation. The currents of trust thus leave us at the disposal of others, placing our welfare (or some slice of it) in their hands. And this is something "disposition" captures down to its roots, from *ponere*, to put or place, to the Old Latin, *posinere*, to leave (*sinere*) away (*po-*), a fate echoed in "expose."

ENOUGH ABOUT YOU

According to Emerson, self-trust is a cardinal virtue for scholars, one that underwrites their duties to cheer, raise, and guide others (Emerson 1971). To fulfill them, one must trust that they are duties, and one must trust that one is competent to realize them. Without self-trust, one hovers between reflection and commitment, and between commitment and enactment.

A broader application is also in order. Trust is a powerful, even vital way to fill epistemic gaps within subjective as well as intersubjective fields. As an educator, I work with students struggling with the weight of impostor's syndrome. They feel they cannot hack it, they do not belong, and they believe this will become apparent to all. All students have some of this; professors, too. Most people do. But the weight of it often multiplies among students from underrepresented groups, particularly those that have suffered multigenerational, systematic oppression. Their internal audience has an extra set of haters, a chorus wrought in part, as Mari Mikkola has argued, by discriminatory speech and stereotypical representations, though also, I think, by a kind of passive racism where educators are unwilling to push students from underrepresented groups, which indirectly intensifies the "you can't hack it" motif (Dormandy 2020). The result is a self-undermining risk aversiveness, what Alessandra Tanesini presents as timidity, although she casts it as a predictive self-regard, which is more a lack of confidence (Tanesini 2020, 226). We learn by extending ourselves, by working out ideas whose future (and value) is uncertain. The metaphor "learning curve" is on point. Growth requires steep terrain. And a lack of self-trust undermines our ability to ascend.

MORE THAN YOU KNOW

Self-trust is more than a self-relation. If I do not trust those around me, say, their feedback or their willingness to stand by me should I falter (or even trust the relative safety of my setting), my self-trust may contract. But the worldly character of self-trust does not minimize its import for human action. In fact, if I am wracked by self-doubt, I may prove unduly skeptical about the dependability of others. Their "I think you can" may not interrupt my "I doubt I can." In fact, the latter may even intensify if I really doubt their sincerity (or evaluative competence).

KNOWING THE INS AND OUTS

Trust intensifies agency in multiple ways. Trusted others can act on my behalf, extending my reach. Self-trust enables me to pursue things amid doubt, known indeterminacies, and vulnerability. And, to some extent, each enables the other, as if they were knotted in a way that keeps our mainsails braced and battened.

Carolyn McLeod wonders whether the language of self-trust is meaningful, and if so, how it compares to interpersonal trust, which she regards as prototypical (McLeod 2002). I appreciate the latter concern, but the former strikes me as odd. People communicate quite effectively when they appeal to self-trust. If a young person heads off to college and wonders if they will meet the right people, choose the right major, and so on, "trust yourself" is normal advice. If someone heads into a meeting about a divisive and complex issue, "trust yourself" offers common, unmysterious support. And when someone needs to make a difficult decision with gains and losses on either side, one can say, "trust yourself" and not befuddle most addressees. Not that one cannot clarify how that notion functions—say, by comparing it to other uses of the word. But philosophy needs to forgo the temptation to police language under the aegis of the "meaningful." Terms and phrases can be spun to good use, and such usages can, over time, lead the history of language to fork. Moreover, when one intervenes in a language and encourages distinctions, the gains to be made should be articulated, and in a manner that doesn't exile some language users from the "meaningful."

Niklas Luhmann looks at trust as a social attitude that facilitates cooperation and simplifies our lives. If I can trust A to do B, then I don't have to worry about B or deliberate about how to achieve it. This seems a misstep in the manner of being overly broad, but not at the level of meaningfulness. *Zutrauen* can mean "trust" or "confidence," and while that blurs trust and reliance, the two also blur in English. Regardless, when Luhmann says such things, we know what he means. But something is lost in that usage, and that is what prompts my wish to amend it. Thanks to trust, Luhmann writes, the "problem of complexity is divided up and diminished" (Luhmann 2017, 29). In part, but trust adds complexity as well. Moreover, Luhmann's conception renders trust a supplement to calculative, strategic action, which obscures how trust relations generate an incipient *we* oriented around good will. But I know what he means.

WORKING-CLASS HEROES

The trustworthy lead with their chins.

BACK TO ME

McLeod's analysis of self-trust led me to rethink and revise, even when I wanted to rephrase it. As she sees it, self-trust is optimistic about one's competence relative to a particular domain of action (McLeod 2002, 40–41). As with our trust in others, trust in ourselves targets situations where we consider ourselves equal to the occasion. Her example concerns Janet, a woman who believes she is pregnant but faces resistance from her doctor. McLeod—following Janet—reads this as a conflict between two ways of knowing, or epistemic competencies, Janet's working knowledge of her body and the doctor's professional knowledge, which braids medical education (past and ongoing), the experiments that inform that education, and the doctor's own experience with pregnant patients.

I, too, think self-trust concerns one's competencies. I don't trust myself in situations where I am incompetent. But McLeod's language drifts in an obscuring way. Optimism strikes me as a calculative stance within the scripted; it reflects a judgment based upon the likelihood of success. But with self-trust, we face unscripted conditions that call our competency into question in a way that optimism cannot banish but trust (hope, too) can help us bear.

As McLeod reports it, the doctor's contrary opinion leads Janet to doubt that she is pregnant and, more generally, to question her knowledge of her body. This raises a second but related issue. Prior to this encounter, does Janet trust her knowledge of her body, or does she just believe that she is pregnant? Self-trust becomes a variable when one has reason to doubt one's belief (or plan) and one's reasons for holding it. Not that a doctor cannot undermine Janet's trust in her knowledge or judgment. As Lily Levy has shown, institutionalized health care is an ongoing site of epistemic injustice for many women (Levy 2021). Dismissive remarks, particularly from professionals wielding various social powers from expertise to arbitrary social privilege, may intensify our doubts and lead us to abandon positions. They may even lead us to doubt our ability to generate sound positions about such things. But that is not my concern. Rather, I am arguing that simply believing in something that might be false does not require self-trust. That arises after we wonder, Can I do this? Am *I* right? Some source of felt doubt, internal or external, is needed to open the gulf that self-trust then shoots.

Because trust is keyed by uncertainty, and because it proves itself amid the unscripted, I do not want to lose the leap that is integral to trust. Like hope, trust is extrafactual, claiming more for itself than the evidence warrants. Govier claims that our "trust or distrust of ourselves is generally based on our knowledge and beliefs about what we are able to do and our sense of ourselves, resulting from experiences in life" (Govier 1998, 96). I generally agree, but I would stress that self-trust is more than an inferential self-assessment. We begin to trust ourselves when we are unsure if the future will be like the past, or whether our past has adequately prepared us for a given future. Not that self-trust, like trust in others, abandons inferential assessments. But Govier is more on point when she writes, "Issues of self-trust come closer to the surface when we are challenged in some way and have to respond" (Govier, 92).

If we are relatively optimistic about our competencies, I would rather speak of self-confidence, as when I am confident about my ability to prepare food for a large group (rather than hire a caterer), mediate disputes between coworkers (instead of bringing in an outside party), or assess the adequacy of political candidates in an environment of intense disagreement. Following Luhmann, McLeod believes that self-confident people are sufficiently secure in their competency to forgo consideration of alternative courses of action (McLeod 2002, 50). This says too much. One can survey various rival options and remain confident that one's approach is best. Confidence does not preclude deliberation. Trust is distinguished from confidence—to the degree such things are distinct (or need to be)—in its acknowledgment of the limits of our competence and in its sense that we can nevertheless muddle through. According to McLeod, with self-trust "you appreciate the risk but you are committed to trying to avoid it" (McLeod, 50). I would say self-trust acknowledges the risk but, whether avoidable or not, trusts that one can surmount it.

FRENEMIES, YES, BUT ENEMIENDS?

By exceeding the confidence that self-assessment can generate, by remaining undeterred despite the grip of doubt, self-trust establishes an oblique relation to skepticism, what we might regard as radical doubt about the validity of what we believe and plan to do, either in general, or with particulars in view.

Needing doubt to arise, trust cannot flow in a world where the threat of skepticism has been removed in every case. But it also cannot exist in a world where skepticism becomes a full-blown mode of comportment. I thus want to say, leaning on Cavell—I am thinking of "Knowing and Acknowledging"—that trust resists skepticism without having to refute it (Cavell 2002). This puts me at odds with Keith Lehrer, who claims that while we can doubt the validity of particular beliefs and plans, we open an abyss should we doubt the general trustworthiness of what we find acceptable. We should accept the following, therefore: "I am worthy of my trust concerning what I accept" (Lehrer 1997, 9). Not that Lehrer has rendered this proposition indubitable; on his own admission, he has not: "The point of the argument is the explanation of the reasonableness of accepting that I am worthy of my trust concerning what I accept, even if I cannot prove that the argument is correct" (Lehrer, 9). But where does this leave us? If I distrust whatever I accept simply because I accept it—as if I were an epistemic blight—we will go nowhere. (This would be an example of being unable to resist skepticism.) But I am unsure what Lehrer means by "reasonableness" even if I understand the general point. The fact that *we* believe something might give us a reason to accept the belief even in the absence of knockdown evidence. But only sometimes. Right? "I do not conclude that I am infallible," Lehrer continues, "or free from error in all that I accept, but I do conclude that my best efforts are worthy of my trust" (Lehrer, 9). I presume that our evaluation of beliefs, plans, and deeds are what is "best" here. The term thus reflects a meta-assessment of sorts. Trust those things that you have already identified as your best efforts. But this position is not covered by his claim, "I am worthy of my trust concerning what I accept." That applies to whatever we accept no matter the quality of our efforts. Moreover, our evaluations of our own beliefs, deeds, and plans seem like just the sort of things we want to keep open to doubt even when we act upon them. After all, we can do our best and fail. Given our partiality, such is the plight of the finite.

"Are you denying that it is reasonable to trust one's best efforts?" No. I am trying to make a point about what it means to be reasonable presuming one's best efforts. In turning to trust, one acknowledges the possibility of error, and thereby inhabits one's commitments alert to how the road will rise to meet them. In trust, one cozies up to skepticism rather than leaves it behind.

I THINK I CAN'T, I THINK I CAN'T

Despair awaits the complete erosion of self-trust. The future is occluded, and one circles a paralyzing doubt. Aimee Mann's "It's Not" travels the rim of this drain.

> So here I'm sitting in my car at the same old stop light
> I keep waiting for a change, but I don't know what
> So red turns into green turning into yellow
> But I'm just frozen here on the same old spot
> And all I have to do is to press the pedal
> But I'm not
> No, I'm not
> *(Mann 2002)*

This scene directs us toward difficulties that sometimes afflict those suffering from schizophrenia—commitment to a course of action seems impossible (Lysaker, Davis, and Lysaker 2006). But one doesn't know why. The inability hogs the stage.

> I keep going round and round on the same old circuit
> A wire travels underground to a vacant lot
> Where something I can't see interrupts the current
> And shrinks the picture down to a tiny dot
> *(Mann)*

But this scene also images what would befall us if the currents of self-trust were continuously interrupted. Our world would recede into unmanageability. And crushing vulnerability.

MY SIDES

Goodwill is a factor in trust because the trusted might be indifferent or ill-disposed toward us. Are such things possible in self-trust? A stoic indifference toward our welfare is possible, but that does not preclude self-trust. I can trust myself in a particular pursuit and remain sanguine about whatever happens. Also, stoic indifference is sought for the equanimity it supposedly brings. It reflects, therefore, a more general concern for one's well-being.

When I think of situations in which I do not trust myself, issues of temperance come to mind, or, more generally, *akrasia*—weakness of will. I tend not to trust my restraint around cured meats. Or, if someone gets under my skin, I do not trust myself, at least while cranky, to productively address the conflict. In these cases, my self-distrust focuses on my current state or disposition—one way to think of my "will." It seems insufficiently in line with the good. And so, I wait until congruence is possible, say, by waiting until I have calmed down. Or, doubting that congruence is possible, I keep my distance from situations that put me at odds with myself, say, by avoiding a buffet where salami lies in wait. Self-trust presumes we are properly oriented toward the good, that we are acting with what McLeod terms "moral integrity," although that may overstate the disposition (McLeod 2002, 40–41). I doubt self-trust assumes our moral integrity in general, only the sense that an operative disposition is not self-destructive, and I want to repeat that self-trust only arises when we're unsure of ourselves. If I become so habituated that cured meats are no longer siren calls, then self-trust will no longer be a variable around the buffet. Similarly, if a conflict never gets to the point of really pissing me off, I do not need to trust myself to address it.

MILGRAM'S 37

For Emerson, self-trust stands in opposition to conformity. We are inclined toward a stance or position that runs contrary to those held by others, and that difference initiates a problem—maintain the position, defer to a rival, or generate one that eludes or overcomes (or ignores) the conflict. On Emerson's view, self-trust helps us avoid undue deference and enables us to stay true to what strikes us as the best way to go, which may in fact call us to abandon our initial position. In Emerson's sense (which Tanesini seems to second), self-trust is as much an enemy of pride and arrogance—which often lead to a foolish consistency—as it is of conformity (Tanesini 2020).

What do we distrust when we feel compelled to conform? It might be our competence, but sometimes it appears that people believe, at some level, in some way, that they do not deserve to individuate by way of distinction. Fearing to prove too tall a poppy, they conform. Not that one could not conform due to prudence. Herodotus, in Book V, stages one way for a leader to treat those who distinguish themselves—cut them down. (Livy reports a similar story with poppies instead of wheat as the plant in question.) But I have something other than prudence in mind, something like doubt that one deserves individuation and the recognition that might accompany it, a doubt that one is worth trusting irrespective of one's competencies. It interests me because it evidences something other than goodwill toward oneself. It doesn't rise to the level of a death drive or self-loathing, but it is a self-undermining bearing that corrodes self-trust.

Nonconformity is probably enough to raise doubts about the propriety of one's plan. Not for all, but many, probably most. For self-trust to quiet those doubts, it might help to believe that one is capable and worthy of something like independence. In such a scenario, self-trust is strengthened by the sense that one is entitled to speak and act in accord with one's mind.

Interestingly, entitlement of this sort, which provides authorization, might derive from a wish to maintain one's integrity, echoing McLeod. Emerson certainly thought so, proclaiming, "Nothing is at last sacred but the integrity of your own mind" (Emerson 1979, 30). One need not go this far, however, to appreciate the point. When there are pressures to conform or withdraw, self-trust asserts self-worth. This becomes more apparent when I think of the things people say to those who resist conformity: "Who do they think they are?" "Do they think they are better than us?" The suggestion conveyed by these rhetorical questions is that nonconformists have an excessive estimation of their self-worth. But it is not the quantitative issue that catches my attention. Instead, it is the recognition that nonconformity involves thinking well of oneself, that one deserves in some loose sense to think for oneself and to act accordingly. And that offends?

UNDERFOOT AND THUMBS

Self-trust, like all trust, is fragile. In the thick of the unscripted, we and those we rely on can falter, even fail. When that happens, trust suffers. But there are also haters, direct and indirect, who plague our ability to trust. Even among the privileged, self-trust is rarely welcomed. Adult life as I've known it favors the conforming nod. The less said, the better. And as one pulls back those scenes of privilege—or rather, as one adds exposure to undermining, oppressive social forces—self-trust seems positively beset.

I have entered a complex, varied, sad scene. Govier reports that trauma, through tragic self-incrimination, can undermine self-trust (Govier 1998, 89). For those beset by derogatory stereotypes, fear of failure (which might seem to confirm the stereotype) may intensify self-doubt and leave one risk averse and/or dampen one's powers. Webster's presents "uppity" as a broadly used, derogatory term for people who think too well of themselves. In my lifetime, the term is usually raced. Regardless, patriarchy and white supremacy as well as Eurocentrism have ways of getting into the heads of those they wish to subordinate. "You're not one of us." "At its roots, your culture is uncivilized." Not that all charge arrested development, but oppressive social orders constantly tell those they oppress, "You can't hack it."

Not that this is the only accompaniment. And even when it predominates, many lives have proven it wrong. Is self-trust the reason? I am unsure. It might be more appropriate to speak of courage than self-trust, although the two may build upon one another, as Lingis observes: "It takes courage to trust someone you do not know" (Lingis 2004, x). Moreover, in its presumption that you have my back, my trust in you (or us) may make me more courageous. In fact, the sense of self-worth that helps fuel self-trust may be distributed: "Let's show those fuckers what we're made of."

STRANGE ALCHEMY

I often think of self-trust from the perspective of a teacher and mentor, where the goal is to help students cultivate and realize their potential. The scenes I have in mind concern a will-to-believe or its absence (or its waning to a flicker). Thinking (or trusting) that one can do something can render a positive result more likely, particularly in the absence of sufficient evidence or warrant. But I cannot trust for them, only in them. And particularly in a pool of social poisons, it is difficult to turn the lead weight of self-doubt.

In my experience, it is a mistake to regard student distrust as an impertinence, let alone an insult. In a world of widespread oppression, distrust from those subjected to oppression comes with the territory, particularly if one occupies a position of authority and one's apparent starting points reflect broad social entitlement. Moreover, evaluation and feedback are risky sites. Those continually told, "You do not belong" may hear sentences such as "This paper lacks clarity," "Vague," or "Your main point was underargued" differently than students who have been gifted self-trust. The point is not to avoid negative feedback, but to be conscientious about how one delivers it. Literacy requires one to acquire a feel for how things sound to others regardless of one's intentions.

ALL TWISTED UP

To embrace trust, even celebrate it as a figure of finitude, as if it were a snapshot of humans near their finite best, is not to absolve us of the task of trusting well. "Trust is not pure faith," Govier writes. "We need not trust blindly" (Govier 1998, 7). And should we, blame ensues. "Naivete" is a term of derision. Moreover, suspicion serves one well, even amid success.

I'm a poor man's version of a rich man
I've got a small van swerving through a big land
I've got a road map that's looking a lot like a math test
A blocked phone number and a bunk home address
(Francis 2005)

"Lie Detector Test," by Sage Francis, pushes these questions: Is this what it means to make it? Is adding numbers (counting money) all there is to navigating the world? Does success require that most others not be able to reach or find me? The album as a whole, *A Healthy Distrust* (2005), spreads the concern across hip-hop culture, confronting, for example, trends that merge hypermasculinity, homophobia, and gun culture. "I see the world through the scope but get no insight with it," we hear in "Gunz Yo," Also:

This dick is a detachable penis
An extension of my manhood, positioned like a fetus
(Francis)

So much for being a grown man.

Self-trust, like trust in others, is not a simple current that we rely on when doubt takes hold. Its terrain remains something we must negotiate, which poses a conundrum. But first let me complicate matters. Self-trust can underwrite distrust. Sage Francis trusts himself even when his thoughts run counter to previous ones. "The Buzz Kill," which opens the album, begins:

I used to think that rappers had it figured out
Brass Monkey, St. Ides, Olde English, and Guinness Stout
Once a man, twice a boy with a choice of vice, a voice of spite
Not enough poisons to pick to enjoy this life
Then I thought suicide was a suburban myth
I couldn't see my own hands being the one's I'm murdered with
That is until I traveled this world a bit
I understand now if I lose my nerve, I'll get the girl to do it!
(Francis)

Sage Francis's distrust refuses a foolish consistency and a certain kind of conformity. But self-trust, when left unmoored, contracts into isolation and skepticism, hence the threat of suicide, and the clear isolation which these later lines convey.

It's not lonely on top
I'm kept busy with shivers and cold shakes
Sitting on snowbanks
Waiting to be delivered some soulmates
(Francis)

The knot is plain, if thick. A kind of self-trust moves within whatever renders distrust healthy even as that trust is haunted by its own potential naivete. Second, even the self-trust that allows one to resist conformity reaches out for "soulmates" who can second one's resistance, suggesting, again, that self-trust and trust in others underwrite one another.

LEARNING TO LISTEN

In *Intellectual Trust in Oneself and Others*, Richard Foley eschews foundationalism and imagines what rationality looks like in (or at) its wake. He offers a basic, orienting thought: the "degree of self-trust it is appropriate to have in one's opinions and faculties is a function of how much epistemic confidence one has in them and how invulnerable to self-criticism this confidence is. The greater and deeper one's confidence in the accuracy of an opinion, the more one is entitled to rely on it" (Foley 2001, 47). Because I doubt we have the same phenomenon in mind, I don't want to pretend I object to Foley's position. (Exploring rationality, he turns to trust, whereas I begin with trust and find myself unsure of its best or most rational patterns.) But I am struck by his formulation because it suggests that as our confidence increases our trust should too, which misses, I think, how trust is generated by doubt and indeterminacy. Should the latter disappear, trust will as well.

How does one relate to trust, measure it, without twisting it into a measured gamble or prediction? That is my conundrum. And I'm averse to resolving it in the manner pursued by Trudy Govier, which proposes a deliberative protocol. But I don't think anyone will be surprised and thus reoriented by the "sources of information" she believes one should consult when wondering whether trust is warranted: direct personal knowledge, indirect personal knowledge, book knowledge (this might surprise, if for the wrong reason), knowledge acquired from the mass media, and knowledge based on social roles (Govier 1998, 122). Second, and more tellingly, in each consultation, trust will again prove an issue. More like Potter, I take trust to resemble and involve but not coincide with induction: "In trusting others, we always extrapolate from available evidence. In the final analysis, no decisive grounds for reasonable trust can be offered" (Potter 2002, 26). And if they could, I hasten to add, trust would not be called into play.

For some, infants and young children exemplify trust at its most intense. In *Trust*, Alphonso Lingis seems to align trust with a kind of infantile innocence (to be contrasted with the representations and images that organize songs of experience) (Lingis 2004, 42, 189, 198). Without valorizing it, Govier also locates a kind of trust in infancy, claiming that "early trust is absolutely fundamental in personal development. It is the first trust, essential for developing a positive attitude to other people and the world at large and fundamental for developing further trust" (Govier 1998, 69). I am not arguing that people should not regard infants as trusting, and I agree that safe environments enable the capacity to trust. But infant trust is far from paradigmatic, standing closer to blind faith, although even "faith" gives me pause. On my view, trust arises in contexts of doubt and indeterminacy, and the trusted must be intersubjectively available. Are either operative in infancy? To the degree they are not, and this is a matter of degree, infants are poor examples for those perplexed by how to trust well.

Foley's measure for self-trust involves immunity to self-criticism. My resistance lies with "immunity." But one could also hear this as an honesty requirement. If one is going to trust well, honesty is essential, more essential than rules or protocols, which might lead one astray. Not that a call to honesty, particularly in the context of self-trust, is terribly helpful. But it does remind me of Dizzy Gillespie's reply to Dick Cavett, who asked, "What's it take to make a great trumpet player?" "Well," Gillespie replied, "the first thing is to be a master shit detector" (Gillespie 1971).

When I think of Gillespie's advice in the context of trust, I also wonder when and where, and regarding what with whom. And so, while I resist Govier's turn to something like a protocol for trusting well, I find her ongoing engagement with differential sites very instructive—friendship, family, and intimate partners, to which one could add civic relations and doctor/patient scenarios (a concern shared by McLeod and Potter). This variety seems essential because what passes as trusting well (and being trustworthy) will have to prove itself somewhat differently in each case. A trustworthy friend is not the same as a trustworthy doctor, and the kind of trust my wife deservedly expects would be unwelcome from a colleague or a student.

YOU HAD TO BE THERE

The unscripted dimensions and individuated character of trust relations limit the usefulness of generalized advice about trusting well. But they do not preclude it. There is a broad social consensus that some ability to trust and prove trustworthy is desirable, even praiseworthy. Knowing how and why should open paths toward richer trust relations, which extend agency and acknowledge dependency in a manner that recognizes the alterity and agency of the trusted and so course with utopian energy. In trust we affirm a sociality in which we look out for others beyond the reach of formal rules and conventional mores. An ethically beautiful *we* is, in a sense, held in trust alongside whatever has been entrusted. But both can be compromised when trust's discretionary core is enacted. We fault naivete as well as undue suspiciousness. One is careless in the face of vulnerability and dependence, thus unduly risking the goods it affirms and the mutuality that a genuine *we* requires. But one can also be overly cautious, thereby unnecessarily limiting the ways in which those goods can be realized and preventing, from the outset, the inceptual *we* that trust enables. Regarding trustworthiness, we can show insufficient care for the welfare of the trusting, undone by our love for "number one," say, or through not really knowing what their welfare entails. Indifference may thus be the deficiency of trustworthiness, which poses threats to the particular and general good at work in trust relations. And while it sounds odd to say that another is too trustworthy, one can prove overbearing and so smother the agency of the trusting. Think of those who are "too helpful" and so, through a kind of arrogance (which I would mark as the excess in question), they think they know better than the trusting and so fail to suitably care for the good in question. But even when they do, note how they manifest a lack of respect for the judgment and abilities of those being told, "You can trust me," which compromises who we might become by preventing mutuality.

Should one want to cultivate a capacity to trust, one might conceive of it as a virtue, following Nancy Potter (Potter 2002). The question concerns, I think, what we gain and risk, ethically, by doing so. From the normative side of things, trust strikes me as a key to the happiness or flourishing of social animals. As I suggested at the outset, like friendship, it is difficult to imagine someone preferring a life without trust to one with it, barring profound changes to the finite character of our existence. It therefore seems rational to cultivate enduring dispositions to trust well and be trustworthy, as we do with other virtues. Moreover, we can imagine both dispositions operating within a continuum marked by deficiencies and excesses in the exercise of discretionary agency oriented toward goods pursued through and on behalf of others. It thus makes some prima facie sense to look at trust relations as based on virtues.

Of course, trust among thieves, like honor, seems a problem, but that is true of other virtues. Courage is a vice in an unjust war, for example, as

Karen Jones has observed (Jones 2012). Moreover, again following Jones, each virtue, at least for Aristotle, is only a dimension of happiness, and one needs their full breadth (over the full length of one's life) to fully flourish. In particular, one needs a feel for justice, which allows one to determine what each is due, and I find this emphasis throughout Potter's discussion of trustworthiness, almost to a fault. At points, say in her discussion of trustworthiness among intimates, the trustworthy intimate simply gives their partner what they are owed (Potter 2002, 121–46). But the slide is understandable. Without a sense of justice, most of the virtues will run aground. What appears temperate in my case may be unjust if I am in conditions of scarcity and there are others with needs that trump my own. Those seeking justice must also know how to trust if the ends sought are to be broadly realized, and if they are not to turn their fellows into manipulable means. And I can imagine people with a fine sense of justice who are unable to entrust its enactment to others, thereby eclipsing the result and the *we* that its pursuit requires. I am confident, therefore, that trust has a place of its own in a complete portrait of the good life.

While Jones is sympathetic with this line of thought, particularly at the points specified above, she is unwilling to regard trustworthiness as a virtue. As she sees it, trustworthiness can require us to let another down— that is, betray them (Jones 2012, 82–85). This becomes possible when we have come to be regarded as trustworthy by two groups seeking incompatible ends. She imagines a case where someone belongs to two community groups, one seeking historic preservation (HP), the other social inclusion and neighborhood diversity (SI). Belonging to both, one can be trustworthy in a general (she says "rich") sense so long as no project arises that brings the groups into conflict. But suppose a developer wants to build a high rise in the neighborhood that offers affordable housing, and suppose all designs fail to accord with the preservationist goals of HP. HP thus wants to prevent the erection of this building while SI vigorously supports it. In order be trustworthy to one group our exemplar must betray the other, and this shows that trustworthiness is unlike other virtues.

Jones's view seems wrong to me. With each group, I am trustworthy relative to the ends of those groups, which I regard as worth pursuing. But my being so is conditional; trustworthiness always is, even when it operates in a general sense. In fact, justice requires that I set each group into the larger web of social life that runs through their pursuits. Neither is oriented toward the good per se, just a dimension of it, and thus each group should know that under certain conditions, what they want may not be the best option. Said differently, just as trust should not amount to absolute faith, trustworthiness should not involve absolute loyalty.

Admittedly, one could simply favor one group and so betray the other. But one needn't. I can be trustworthy and disagree with those who trust me about what an unscripted scenario demands. I remain accountable in disagreeing, but disagreeing does not entail betrayal. And if they met my considered and considerate disagreement with a charge of betrayal, I would regard them as mistaken about the case at hand, what trustworthiness entails, and about what a comprehensive sense of virtue requires.

EXPECT THE UNEXPECTED?

On the moral-psychological side of things, trust, like virtues of character, has a dispositional character. Moreover, enacting trust requires *phronesis*, that capacity to specify the where, among whom, how, and regarding what that trusting entails. And regarding trusting, it does seem to seek a mean between naivete and undue suspicion, whereas the trustworthy empower the agency of the trusting without absorbing it. This is not to say that one must look at trust in this manner. But should one agree that it is better to be prudentially trusting and responsibly trustworthy, and that a capacity for both is something to be cultivated across one's life, casting it as a virtue allows one to imagine it as something to weave into the fabric of their character.

Cultivating character is no easy task, however. No one is mere clay in the hands of moral potters. And the positionality of trust relations further pluralizes the task of trusting well. In fact, I am unsure whether one should conceive of a generalized *phronesis* when thinking about trust (or proving trustworthy). Potter's book burrows into the nuances of crisis counseling, and many of those demands do not clearly translate to many of the other social positions we inhabit in relation to one another. On the trusting side, as a patient, I may (and may need to) trust my counselor (or doctor) with information that I would not share with anyone else, possibility even an intimate. And as a crisis counselor, one may find oneself compelled to lie to save another's life—Potter, in fact, did. But those scenes are heavily scripted, down to professionally articulated normative expectations, and they face scenarios unlikely to arise in social life more broadly. Not that they are not scenes of trust. They are. But it is difficult to imagine a path of cultivation flexible enough to cover those scenarios and the push and pull of everyday sociality. The discretionary demands of trust relations may limit what one can build into a disposition.

But the difficulties posed by trust's positionality also contain an insight. Potter wants us to think about trust as a virtue to bring trustworthiness into our sense of (and preparation for) enacting various social roles, particularly when social power is distributed asymmetrically. And once we see that it is not easy to generalize, we realize that being trustworthy requires one to consider the many ways in which one is socially positioned, which requires an ever-expanding social literacy that maintains a feel for how those fates have been individuated during a particular life. "A violation of trust is especially damaging to a woman," Nancy Potter writes, "who has already been a victim of abuse. Often there seems to be no one to whom that person can turn for help and protection" (Potter 2002, 53). And yet, as I suggested earlier, given the number of women who are subject to harassment, assault, and sex abuse while children, this thought should orient most professional and social relations, as Potter also argues. Similarly, people suffering such fates should be able to acknowledge them as legitimate variables in their search for a disposition between naivete and undue skepticism.

I'M SORRY

These are only a few paths toward the thought of trusting well. And I have managed to place only a few provisions along the way, some only in the form of flags to mark points that might waylay us. And there remain scenes of trust that I have left unexplored, such as epistemic trust, say, regarding testimony. But no essay can be exhaustive, and an effort to be so exhausts.

Because essays are always (r)essays, permit me to close with another of Potter's insights that I want to second and repurpose, thus aligning myself with the lines that run from Baier to her and beyond. As noted, Potter recalls having to lie to a patient over the phone to save her life. Even though the patient asked that she not, Potter, who was working as a crisis counselor, called an ambulance. Moreover, when the patient directly asked her whether she had called one, she said no. While the lie seems justified, Potter directs us to a different matter: even if it were justified, lying rendered her untrustworthy to the patient. Moreover, doing so undermined the trustworthiness of the agency for which she worked, possibly also the profession in general. And that, on Potter's view, calls for redress.

Justified actions can cause harm. A justified action can undermine a relationship. And this is a crucial insight for those who care about trust. Sometimes we are required to trust strangers and sometimes strangers trust us. Attending to such cases may help clarify some intuitions and commitments, but trust lives, more than less, in ongoing relationships. And in that context, remaining trustworthy can be difficult. Recall me dog sitting for Nellie, who died through no fault of my own. The loss will still prompt grief, and if I prove numb to that or fail to show any sorrow, my friend's trust in me may contract. Not because Nellie died but because, failing to show proper concern for my friend's loss, my goodwill comes into question.

Imagine a different scenario. Suppose you frequent a shop, even when it costs more to do so. You like the owner, the employees, and you want them to do well. One day you buy something and it proves defective, and in a manner they should have noticed. No big deal. You just want to return it. But the owner proves oddly defensive, complaining about the challenges of owning a small business, insisting that no one could have caught such a defect (even though you both know that to be false), etc. In such a setting, I would be hard-pressed to trust the business in the same manner, at least not without sorting through the problem. The problem? Not that they sold a defective item, but that they could not own up to it and relied instead on BS and clichés to cloud the issue. What Potter gets importantly right is that trustworthy people acknowledge the fragility of trust by following up on misunderstandings and missteps, even accidents, as if to say, I am still looking out for you. We are still *we*.

Interlude
Become Who You Are Not

*I am writing all this down in blue ink, so as to remember that all words,
not just some, are written in water.*

MAGGIE NELSON

OFFPRINTS

"My body is traversed by a cluster of invisible lines which link each point
of intersection to the center of the sun. I move about unharmed among
all these threads which pierce me, and every point in space breathes a new
soul into me" (Leiris 1987, xi). At times I can almost see into this scene that
one night claimed Michel Leiris. As if he and I might meet in the light—or
rather, realize in its shine how we had already met somewhere else. But
now that I'm here, I'd rather wait for the moon—less glare, and lit from
elsewhere, like us.

KNOCK, KNOCK

Self-knowledge finds an object (and so itself) on the move. "Who are you?"
becomes "Who are you becoming?" The known self is subject to influences, including those wrought through knowing and responding to (or
ignoring) what is found. "Who are you becoming?" becomes "Who would
you become?" This is one way to recount the call of conscience, which accompanies possibility.

Conscience does more than reflect. Tugged by aversions and attractions,
it imagines, deliberates, revises (or not), and commits. "What to do?" accompanies the pulse of self-consciousness, which lives in reply. Conscience
thus stands, sits, walks, and talks accountably. This is one way to explain
the emergence of ethical life without overdetermining things with meta-

ethical commitments. Like all animals, if loquaciously, we track how well we fare in order to steer the ship.

Stanley Cavell has termed this feel for ethics "perfectionist." Less than a "competing theory of the moral life," perfectionism names "something like a dimension or tradition of the moral life," one that "concerns what used to be called the state of one's soul, a dimension that places enormous burdens on personal relationships and on the possibility or necessity of the transforming of oneself and of one's society" (Cavell 1990, xxxi). "State of one's soul" names the length and breadth of one's life, from greetings to commerce to getting it on, from interpersonal bonds to how we further and/or resist reproductive, civil-social, and political orders. Perfectionism leaves us answerable for the physiognomy of those tracts and aims to (r)essay our part therein.

PLURAL IMPERFECT

The essays assembled here participate in the reformulation of perfectionism initiated by Stanley Cavell but also pursued by others such as Eddie Glaude and Vincent Colapietro. Its archive is an expanding set of texts and questions drawn into proximity, which does not preclude contestation or transformation.

Given this bearing, I should recount my course, its commitments and aversions, its negotiations and anticipations, also its sense of "should," even though, as recounted elsewhere, I am averse to securing a tradition of perfectionist thought (Lysaker 2008). I will not pretend, however, that American transcendentalism is not central to this project. It is, but in certain ways, and with certain resistances. At this juncture, that of feeling answerable, accountable, Thoreau goes too far: "Nothing was given me of which I have not rendered some account" (Thoreau 2008, 45). As Borges demonstrates in "Funes the Memorious," a full reckoning halts one's days. But even if Thoreau has a narrower range of events in mind (Funes tries to remember everything that happens to him, which takes just as long as the happening), what has been given me (you too, I presume) rends my accounts. And that should be acknowledged. "Our being is descending into us," Emerson writes, "from we know not whence" (Emerson 1979, 159).

COUNTING WHAT COUNTS

"Conscience" is a name for how we track our welfare. "Yours or mine?" For beings whose current is possibility, such questions may always arise. But that division need not constitute conscience, and it rarely does. The welfare of another, you included, may be and often is integral to my interest. In friendship, what interests me is your flourishing. If things go your way, I am rewarded. "Ah, so you get something out of it." Of course. I am happy for you. If I weren't, I would be the worse for it as a person, as would we, whether we are friends, acquaintances, partners, fellow citizens, author and reader, and so forth. Moreover, experiencing that pleasure is not the goal or end of my interest. You are. And this is what egoism trips over again and again. What interest explains its persistence?

KNUCKLE UP

Conscience need not have emerged. In both a historical and developmental sense, ethical life sprouts among the adventitious. But it does sprout, and so characterizes the species—which is to say, most of its members. But not always.

When I was in high school, squabbles would break out between people and groups. Insults or food might fly, or fists. Sometimes a grievance would be aired in the hopes that an aggressor would see reason, cease, and desist. And that often happened. But someone occasionally would say, "Kick my ass"—that is, make me stop. And in those cases, which were not uncommon, the aggrieved's hope or belief that the addressee felt answerable would meet with disappointment. Unconscionable in an almost literal manner, the menace did not give a fuck. And that attitude could spread. For one practice or an afternoon or several weeks, even a year, some set would be disposed toward one another with this kind of abandon.

At times, ethical life comes and goes. Its form crumbles and the gloves come off. To be clear, I am not imagining a position like "might makes right." That completely misses "Kick my ass," which says, "I am uninterested in the right that might be made. Make . . . me . . . stop." But we do not need to be so dire. "I felt like it, that's why." Not an answer. And not a declaration of not having to answer, say, because the asker lacked the illocutionary authority to demand a reply. So not a manifestation of being answerable. Just a refusal and, if I am right, an exit (presuming the ethical was already operative).

I am imagining (and recalling) characters whose entrance signals a breakdown in ethical life. I know of others. One often hears "It's only rational" to justify self-serving actions that seem prima facie unethical—lying on taxes, faking an injury, making a coworker look bad to advance one's career. But not really; that is, I do not consider the remark a sincere justification. Rather, it is a cynical explanation that corrodes ethical life from the inside. It drains "rational" of anything resembling an expectation that might check a desire in the immediacy of its occurrence. The remark could evidence an egoist ethic where the pursuit of one's own well-being is deemed praiseworthy, but that would invite a reply, whereas "It's only rational" is (usually) a conversation stopper.

WHEREVER YOU GO, THERE YOU ARE

Perfectionists neither take holidays nor accept cultural divisions of labor that render their demands and pursuits merely personal, private, or the final fancy of a retired life. In responding to others, in pursuing justice, our what, when, with whom, and how persist as questions, and the shape of our lives lies, in part, with how we reply—thoughtfully (or not), half-heartedly, cynically, fanatically, modestly, etc.

"Our whole life is startlingly moral," writes Thoreau. "There is never an instant's truce between virtue and vice" (Thoreau 2008, 148). He imagines life as a testimony to character, each act an *apologia* for the life it exemplifies, whether conscientious, modestly careless, or nearly oblivious. And I do mean each act. "Nothing was too trivial for the Hindoo lawgiver," he writes, "however offensive it may be to modern taste. He teaches how to eat, drink, cohabit, void excrement and urine, and the like, elevating what is mean, and does not falsely excuse himself by calling these things trifles" (Thoreau, 150). But also, life remains morally startling. Always becoming someone else in a world becoming somewhat else, life takes place in the changes. How, then, to play them?

EASIER DONE THAN SAID

"When you are on the point of putting your hand to any undertaking," Epictetus writes, "remind yourself of what nature that undertaking is" (Epictetus 1928, vol. 2, 487). His example is bathing—"those who splash you with water, those who jostle against you, those who vilify and rob you" (Epictetus, vol. 2, 487). His goal is action that accords with nature. But how do we determine what we've done or what is to be done, which requires a feel for where we've begun and where and when that will come to an end? Contexts upon contexts run through our actions, shaping, in part, their character, their consequences, our responsibilities. Water flows. From where? How, and who built and maintains the pipes? Bathing inherits and perpetuates that social labor, which has multiple tributaries, some fading into ecosocial history. Suppose, unwittingly, I play patient zero to a virus that travels through and beyond the pool. It's not the same as intentionally doing so, but it remains my action—I was patient zero. Our actions implicate us wherever *our* impact is felt, and the details are our angels and devils. Bathing, voting, driving, consuming, eating—delimiting conduct, whether beforehand or after the fact, is more than a full-time job.

NEITHER HERE NOR THERE

Heidegger and Nietzsche part over the primacy of valuation in scenes of compearance, Nancy's term for the relational multiplicity of existence. The possibilities of a day give way, never to return. And we feel that, their significance, which indicates some operating valuation, even when we conclude *comme ci, comme ça*. What befalls us matters. Not all in the same way, or with equal intensity, but, unlike brute facts—red car, empty glass, mutating virus—the possibilities of a day indicate our relative welfare here and now, refracting the past, forecasting the future. Not that significance or even sense (*Sinn*) rests with "what X means for me." What might seem like our doing also undoes us; what carries significance also manifests "what my life means in relation to X." Sense is a two-way street, as am "I,"—or rather, an intersection designed by uncivil engineers.

"But one can unfold scene after scene of relations that do not bear upon me or you." I agree. Take the bizarre orbit of Exoplanet HD 20782 b, which lies in the constellation Fornax, some 117 light years away from Earth. It takes light one year to travel 5,878.5 trillion miles, a distance—687,784.5 billion miles—that makes the word "distance" sound sly. About the size of Jupiter, HD 20782 b "comes within scorching distance of its parent star before catapulting back out to 2.5 astronomical units away. To put that in layman's terms, that means that if it were in our solar system, it would go much closer to the sun than Mercury, and then all the way out to the asteroid belt," which lies between Mars and Jupiter (Wenz 2016). We are not variables in that loopy (or not loopy) journey. But the scene has significance, as does the decision to unfold it, particularly to prove a point.

WHAT IS TO BE DONE?

Constitute, ignore, or smash the state, ethical life, demanding discretion, individuates us. Its concerns return with every revolution.

LIVING THE LIFE

"Ethical life" is a standard translation of *Sittlichkeit, Sitte*, naming the conventions that one can also hear in the word εθοσ, or *ethos*, which can mean custom, or, more generally, a "habitual gathering place" (Halloran 1982,

60). On this view, a kind of code is instilled in our upbringing, and it helps us know how to greet elders, act neighborly, even manage the difference between friend and acquaintance, and all beyond the reach of clear duties and obligations. But when I bring hope and trust to ethical life, the stress falls on life, the living, even.

Hope stretches toward the better. It circulates ecstatically, addressing a future lying latent in the present of an unfulfilled past. But its course is closer to longing than custom. Not that it is thoughtless. It orients, determinately. But hope arrives like a current; it jolts, sparks, initiates. Its better is impulsive. Trust as well. I don't exactly choose to trust another, but I find myself trusting and giving in to it. Or not. I might resist that tug. "Trust and distrust are feelings," Annette Baier writes, "but like many feelings they are what Hume called 'impressions of reflexion,' feeling responses to how we take our situation to be" (Baier 1995, 131).

Surprisingly, I can say something similar through Heidegger, turning to *Befindlichkeit*, which names the fact that we find (or encounter) ourselves, and in ways that are mooded or attuned through *Stimmungen*. Hope and trust are attunements that disclose, in part, our life, our situation—the new year, the trusted friend, that fella's shifty look, or the task and pleasure of being a son, a partner, a neighbor. Each dispose us toward extrafactual possibilities and what has (or might have) worth therein. Each names a way (or ways) in which, among other things, we enact and thus link, negotiate, even stretch and revise customs and social roles.

THE GRAVITY OF THE SITUATION

Ethical life does not institute relations. Relations are everywhere, in every "are," harmonious or violent, passable if banal, liberating or oppressive. Ethical life names a way of deliberately inhabiting those relations, of bearing them by moving among points that draw one another like magnets, rotating and drifting—you, me, I, us, we, and our expectations. The force of that evolving field stems in part from our capacity for accountability. Amid its sallies and returns, scenes of moral concern and valuation open that shape the course of conscience: (a) the what: behaviors, beliefs, flicks of desire, the character of persons, the character of relationships, the whole of a life; (b) the who: friends and family, those in the tribe and those without, perhaps the unborn or future generations, the welfare of nonhuman animals, the state of a planet. But so, too, (c) the very character of our expectations and what it feels like to be answerable—they also morph. "Thou shalt not . . ." is only one idiom.

EXPECTIONALISM

Expectations (standards, measures, norms, values, etc.) deliver us, dispose us toward one another and ourselves. They are part of what renders us deliberate in our bearing, or conscientious. "Meets expectations," or not, has become part of the fabric of the human. Not that we agree on what those expectations entail, or whether a certain bearing has met them, but we live under the awning of expectations—some shared and some contested, some explicit, others subtle as eye contact, some little more than a hunch or gut tug.

Expectations imply the possibility of failure. One expects nothing in the thick of the inevitable. As truth is bound to error, moral success is bound to failure, praise to blame. We aspire because we tire and fall short, or run off the rails, taking others for the ride. The unethical is a moment within ethical life, haunting it, an underworld with an undertow.

BETWEEN RULES AND THE USUAL PLACE

Because customs function prereflectively and, moreover, clash, one might explicitly designate duties and obligation and formalize prohibitions, which has led some to distinguish morality (or *Moralität*) from ethics in the sense of *Sittlichkeit* (or ethical life). Unhappy with the implicitness of the latter's know-how, morality presents itself in maxims and imperatives (principles more generally), and it favors contracts and laws. A distinction between morality and ethical life conducts life in valuable ways. To refuse their categorical distinction is not to refuse them in general. Rather, it is to cast them as differing orientations, both of which can operate—compatibly or not—in the same situation.

Suppose I borrow someone's computer without asking. In assessing that action, it matters whether we are strangers or friends (or roommates or siblings). And it matters how long I keep it, and where I take and use it. Sorting through the resulting tussle (presuming one arises), we might eventually rely on some mix of informal custom and formal principle. If we're roommates and you're away for a week, and upon your return I say, "I used your laptop while you were away," you very well might reply, "No biggie; that's what friends are for." But if I take it on a trip without asking, and only speak of doing so when you find it in my bag upon my return, you not only might say, "I thought we were friends" but call the police, telling me I didn't "borrow" it, I "stole" it! Both prongs of moral theory provide workable pitches.

But when it comes to the "good" that I hope we'll continually realize, and in better and better ways, I do not simply defer to extant principle or convention. I seek broader, richer realizations. And our feeling for our most precious moral terms conveys this. We are still discovering and pursuing what "equality" entails. Given the range of material dependencies that enable (and undermine) our conduct, no one can credibly argue that the absence of formal constraints to various goods and services, including political-legal orders, establishes equality of opportunity. Equality of opportunity is a social achievement whose character moves with the dynamism of the social forces that empower human agencies. And no imperative can incorporate all the needs, opportunities, and demands that will accrue therein. One of my hopes is not only that we will rededicate ourselves to equality as a principal social good, but that we will do so in a manner that acknowledges the self-overcoming and ongoing renewal which that requires.

Imagine now that some significant population shares my hope, and we get down to it. As we learn to trust each other and glimpse the incipient *we* that trust enacts, and as we rediscover what a good trust is, our conduct will be, to a degree, unscripted. We will learn about who we are and might yet become, maybe even regarding trust. I say this because it took intimacy to show me how to trust another with my happiness, releasing it to their sheer presence and regard and tethering it to their own well-being. The improvisations of ethical life are generative in ways than neither lynchpin of moral theory calls to mind nor settles.

CHECKING OUR PULSE

The prereflective operations of hope and trust recall what John Dewey says about "impulse" in *Human Nature and Conduct*, lectures delivered at Stanford in 1919 and expanded and published in 1922. Returning *Sittlichkeit* to conduct, Dewey argues that habit lies at the core of ethical life. We learn the ropes, and that know-how settles into prereflective modes of conduct, as with "please" and "thank you," catching someone as they fall, calling your mother on her birthday (if not more regularly). But habits are only adept in situations akin to those that give rise to *Sittlichkeit*, and even then, every situation has nuances that individuate it. In short, habits are not always equal to the occasion, and that gap is felt—sometimes after the fact, sometimes ahead of time, often in the thick of it.

"Impulse" is Dewey's name for what arises when our capacities negotiate a scene in an unsatisfactory manner. But rather than take the resulting burr as a failure, Dewey turns impulse into a potentiality, a "pivot of readjustment," or, more fully: "Impulses are the pivots upon which the re-organization of activities turn, they are agencies of deviation, for giving new directions to old habits and changing their quality" (Dewey 1983, 75, 67).

A friendship has hit the rocks. In a moment of frustration, I became intemperate and overstate my frustration, which hurts my friend, and deeply enough that whatever I do to redress the hurt only recalls it. I find myself at wit's end. I want the friendship to continue but don't know how. I keep trying in the hope that a far side to this impasse awaits. In this case, hope rises like an impulse, oriented toward a situation that exceeds my grasp, and in two ways. I don't know what exactly it will entail, what "friendship" will mean post-fuckup, nor do I know how to get there. As Dewey also says, taking himself to be recasting *will-to-power*, "Each impulse is a demand for an object that will enable it to function" (Dewey, 98).

The whole situation is not free of *Sittlichkeit*—friendship has its habits. And our actions may also have to answer to *Moralität* regarding lying, cheating, stealing, etc. But in trying to preserve the friendship I have torn, I find myself bereft. And no doubt my friend, twice shy, is now averse to the tugs of trust once felt in my company. How might we proceed? Where might we meet each other again on the rise? The dream of *Moralität* is to bring all these currents into accord with explicit rules, even if only through implicit contracts. My experience has been that when life remakes itself, it stutters and hovers near whatever remains ajar.

FAREWELL TO THE EPOCH OF THE EPIC

One might try to elude all dichotomies, particularly when they implode under their own weight. I still recall realizing that the distinction between Dionysos and Apollo was thoroughly Apollonian. I was seated at a picnic table, late summer in Tennessee, a graduate student just out of coursework. An undergraduate asked me to explain the distinction. I looked across the lawn, still green, crisply mowed, and it hit me. "That very distinction . . ." Later, I wondered where that left *Birth of Tragedy*, and where that left me relative to conceptual-grammatical orders and the lives they took as their subject. Did it signal how deeply significance belonged to concepts and the judgments in which they resided? Or (and/or) did it unveil the infinite deferral that every concept suffered when it tried to name its origin, and on that basis legitimate its grasp of its object? And that twist continues to coil, having since corked through Emerson, for whom such dichotomies "resolve" into questions concerning the conduct of life. Each term becomes a usage and so a disposition, and one to be assayed (and not just as a single term). The usages and habits of *Sittlichkeit* and *Moralität* are currents in ethical life, each an inception to assess over the course of its enactment. Perfectionism is one name for that task.

AFTER ALL THESE YEARS

Better is a worthy enemy of the good. Become who you aren't.

MISPRISON

"Ethical life" is apt for *Sittlichkeit*. But the reverse withers.

MY UNBEAUTIFUL LIFE

Perfectionism is impossible without some sense of shame, that creeping unease in our own skins. Inflected with normative expectation, shame is the "moral response we should and tend to have when we fail to uphold principles we affirm on our own account," and when we regard our failure as inexcusable and unjustifiable (Lebron 2012, 18). Sometimes we catch ourselves being less than we imagined, even hoped we might be— impatient, unjust, cruel, dishonest, and so forth. Shame can help turn those discoveries into departures. It might even, by returning us to the normative expectation that orients it, renew, at least perceptually, the good that has been wanting.

"But shame undermines agency and traps us in illicit prohibitions that risk self-loathing." No doubt it can, and in gendered ways. Shame can rip a life apart from the inside. But I cannot think of an ethically charged disposition that might not go wildly astray: generosity, courage, prudence, hope, trust, forgiveness, even a sense of justice—say, one misled by overly formal conceptions of equality. In our finitude, we can fuck up anything. But we are never just our shortcomings, as "illicit" indicates, exposing an evaluation that sets the shame in question at arm's length. One reason I invoke Lebron, besides his instructive account of shame's role in perfectionism, is his insistence that the expectations in question have been affirmed on our own account. When that is the case, shame can "be redemptive," he writes, "as it alerts us to the potential to be better than we are" (Lebron, xv).

"But those expectations might be oppressive strictures that have been internalized!" Indeed, although be alert to how this thought can be (a) an injunction to conscientiousness or (b) a skeptical denial of our ability to be conscientious. (The former I affirm. The latter has the sound of a disappointed metaphysician.) Regardless, moral maturation, at least for perfectionists, demands that we work through such crises in the company of others—quoting in an originary manner (Emerson), reauthorizing the language of our upbringing (Thoreau), authentically repeating that into which we have been thrown (Heidegger), freely returning to our commitments, explicit or implicit (Beauvoir), and, following Paul Taylor's reading, recommitting to one's orienting values by recurringly reinterpreting them, often in the wake of shame (MLK) (Taylor 2018, 46). And as we twist and turn our own guiding lights, we may find our goods proving less clear, even less wholesome than we had presumed. I thus agree with Taylor's suggestion, made while reading King, that the "appropriately sensitive ethical agent will have the experience of self-loathing, irrespective of whether he or she wishes it. The burden is to harness this experience so that it is productive rather than destructive," or both, since to grow is also to leave behind (Taylor, 56).

IN ABSENTIA

Addressing those who refuse to venture their own thoughts (as well as those who might yet), Emerson says, "This conformity makes them not false in a few particulars, authors of a few lies, but false in all particulars. Their every truth is not quite true. Their two is not the real two, their four not the real four: so that every word they say chagrins us, and we know not where to begin to set them right" (Emerson 1979, 32). How does "false" operate here, and what is proving "false"? If every word chagrins, even another's use of numbers, the problem is more general than a failure to calculate properly or apply concepts according to rules. This is why it is difficult to true such characters. Going about it the wrong way, they get it wrong even if they get it right.

But what does that mean? Cavell argues that for Emerson the problem is conformity (Cavell 2003). I may not know the logic of a base ten number system, or even be aware that one is in operation, but that misstep leaves me naive in a way that can be righted with a "Did you know . . ." intervention. But if my basic bearing is conformist, I'll never look away from the cool kids long enough (or the boss, mentor, or expert) to find my own way. And for those who take themselves to be answerable, that proves fatal. Perfectionism requires us to think for ourselves, to inhabit our "therefores," to render beliefs commitments, and to accompany commitments into conversations, ready for the reply of interlocutors, or the world's brush and bump should the working touch of anticipation falter. It thus requires a kind of honesty that exceeds sincerity; the perfectionist aspires to share the considered, interrogated, even tested. Euthyphro's problem, or one of them, is that he rhetorically hides when the issue of what is pious or holy (*to hosion*) arises. His replies are somewhat dishonest, therefore. Because of his self-proclaimed expertise in theological matters, and because of his concern for the gods and their ways, his replies to Socrates ring false. (One might even say he sounds impious, which is part of Plato's point—to contrast Euthyphro's faux piety with Socrates, who has been charged with atheism.) Imagine now a scene in which someone within philosophy "dares not say I think, I am, but quotes some saint or sage," another line cherished by Cavell (Emerson 1979, 38). To be clear, the problem is not quotation; if anything, the absence of quotation is dishonest in historically saturated practices, a point made by Emerson across his career (Lysaker 2008, 35–37). The misstep lies with quoting to avoid answerability. Not that we are refusing to present our real view behind the cloak of another. Rather, we are presenting that view as ours when it is not, at least not yet.

WHITEY'S IN THE ROOM

Some conformity is unwitting, some unwilling but mortared with cowardice. Other absorptions are willed, even longed for. For some, whiteness is a racial marker tied to an imagined slew of historical accomplishments and future promises as well as stark negations of a descriptive and normative nature. For such people, it is something to be protected and perpetuated. "Whiteness" defines them, provides them with a self-concept. It answers the question "Who are you?" And it answers it in a manner that desperately seeks to distance itself from those bearing other racial markers, particularly blackness. (Dialectics is hell on purity.)

"Whiteness" is deliberately not among my self-concepts. Its matter is Platonist in a cartoonish way, and ironically disorienting, given what those who constitute the class bear in all directions, and in ways that embrace rich veins of Black life. And its manner floats aimlessly in negativity. One might as well chant, "Haters gonna hate" during roll. But more than that, whiteness, desperately outsourcing dignity, is just sad. If it were not evil, I would pity it.

For some, whiteness manifests in dispositional tendencies built around the negation or disregard of Black life and other Others: the clutch of a purse, a tremble of fear, doubt in another's abilities, indifference to who gets killed by cops or is poorly schooled or is given equal pay and so on and so forth along too many soul seams. Patricia J. Williams underscored the phenomenon for my generation of graduate students in a piece that recalled her not being admitted to a Benetton in New York City in 1986. At the height of the Christmas shopping season a teenage salesclerk refused to buzz her into a store full of white shoppers. Through the window, he claimed they were closed. "He had no compassion," she writes, "no remorse, no reference to me; no desire to acknowledge me even at the estranged level of arm's length transactor" (Williams 1992, 45). But the event did not end with the clerk, as Williams demonstrates. Her efforts to recount it suffered further exclusions. Editors of a law review seeking to publish "Excluded Voices" elided Williams's use of the active voice as well as her outrage, and even removed references to Benetton and her race, although, in the end, she convinced them to allow references to her race. Both sides of this tale are instructive. Dispositional whiteness can disregard directly or through an obliviousness kept safe by the weasel-words of neutrality.

George Yancy has demonstrated how common and varied such denigrating exclusions are, which has helped make "whiteness" a subject of academic and ethical analysis (Yancy 2012). "Whiteness" in this sense operates habitually and moves primarily in intersubjective contexts. From where I live (home, work, city, head, heart, and heartbeat—when and where it quickens), this order of whiteness is hard to shake. For the alert, it remains a possible modulation of numerous inclinations, reactions, and estimations, and one to be resisted in a way that acknowledges the tendency.

And then there is whiteness as a kind of privilege, which involves greater and easier access to the social endowment relative to other groups, as well as freedom from exposure to overt and potential harm, again relative to other groups. While whiteness of this order marks an objectivity of social existence, it also slides into dispositional whiteness, which can manifest in presumed entitlements—say, to various careers, as well as common decency on the street, at work, or on the phone. It might also manifest in a basic self-regard—say, self-trust—or in the felt sense that one is worth a listen. Outside a self-concept, therefore, whiteness maintains a certain currency that is sometimes but not always dispositional. Indifference to that fact discloses in part one's relation to it.

I have been quickly schematizing "whiteness" as a way into what Glaude, citing Baldwin, terms *the lie*, a designation also invoked by Yancy (Yancy, 32). I am drawn to this formulation because it addresses "whiteness" in an epistemic register that sets itself beside (rather than wholly outside or wholly inside) the horizons of meaning and action that whiteness informs. This not only resists, theoretically, a kind of worldview relativism or skepticism, but it keeps whiteness in the world where its objectivity, multiform and shifting, operates. But this does not prevent Glaude from rightfully looking at whiteness as a set of thoughts, practices, and institutions that overdetermine human agency and underwrite, differentially, human fates—that is, as a form of social power.

The lie is more properly several sets of lies with a single purpose. If what I have called the "value gap" is the idea that in America white lives have always mattered more than the lives of others, then the lie is a broad and powerful architecture of false assumptions by which the value gap is maintained. These are the narrative assumptions that support the everyday order of American life, which means we breathe them like air. We count them as truths. We absorb them in our character. (Glaude 2020, 7)

And yet, my commitment to nonjuridical models of power—as more appropriate to broad, differential phenomena like race, class, and gender—leaves me wary of casting this multilevel network of phenomena in the figure of a speech-act denoting intentional deception. I think the language of character, grounded in habit (which Glaude deploys in *Democracy in Black*), cuts deeper than this, which is why the task at hand is so difficult. I also am unsure that many in the grip of this multiform habitus count its various commitments as truths. I know too many stuck in the dispositional currents of whiteness who know what those currents involve but who, nevertheless, fail to be their better, aspirational selves. But *the lie*, unlike "the nonsense" or "the bullshit," underscores that we are talking about currents of evil.

THE KILLER IN ME

Whiteness is the kind of phenomenon that perfectionism should address. "It is the eternal testimony of the soul in man to a fairer possibility of life and manner than he has attained," writes Emerson, "that agitates society every day with the offer of some new amendment" (Emerson 1972, 259). That was 1840. He was more intense in 1860: "A man should make life and Nature happier to us, or he had better never been born" (Emerson 2003, 141). But before we let these lines call to mind additions and advances, do not forget that for Emerson, the way of life is abandonment, and that is as much an event of departure as it is of arrival, as Branka Arsić has stressed (Arsić 2010).

"We thrive by casualties," Emerson wrote (Emerson 1983, 39). Eddie Glaude writes, "If we are going to change how we see Black people, white people—and only white people can do this—will have to kill the idea of white people" (Glaude 2016, 201). And later, with a softer touch, and more pain:

What do you do when you have lost faith in the place you call home? That wasn't quite the right way to put it: I never really had faith in the

United States in the strongest sense of the word. I hope that one day white people here would finally leave behind the belief that they mattered more. (Glaude 2020, xvii)

But I prefer the earlier conditional, in part for the doubleness in Glaude's insistence. White people, who must be more than the idea of white people if they are to do as asked, should disperse the idea of white people, break its hold at the level of self-concept, disposition, and social privilege. At each level this includes redressing dispositions toward those who are not white given how bound the phenomenon is to negation. Glaude's sentences thus say to me: you are more than the idea of whiteness, and I address you as such, hoping to awaken that more, to "awaken the sleeper" in Thoreau's words, which Glaude recalls, and which recalls in me: "Moral reform is the effort to throw off sleep" (Glaude 2020, 107; Thoreau 2008, 64). But, and here I imagine Glaude addressing Nietzscheans like me, prattling on about shadows of God: "It is the idea of whiteness that remains to be killed. You need to put *that* idea in the ground, John. Have you the sponge to wipe away that horizon?"

These (r)essays bring perfectionism to bear upon normative ethics. But they also try to interrupt the flow of whiteness. The task is to be that fairer—or rather, hotter—current that agitates with an amended way of conceiving of oneself (and others), of riding one's dispositions, and of undergoing advantages, but also of witnessing, resisting, and redressing exclusions, diminishments, and violence. But the most decisive blows will emerge in creative companionship en route to successor engagements.

TUMBLING RUNS

Perfectionism is a matter of leaping and landing, prepared to pivot.

VOICES CARRY

For many, metaethics is a distraction, a way of avoiding complex ethical snarls and replies. For others, it seems the heart of the matter—say, regarding the status of moral facts. I have tried to have my wake and survive it too, arguing that metaethics is a kind of reflexive conscientiousness, a recurring attempt to recount or (r)essay those histories of conscience that one has inherited (Lysaker 2017, 112–113). Set within perfectionism, the suggestion is that metaethics is more of an ongoing revision of usage, affect, and habit than a critique that clarifies, once and for all, phenomena like the genuine character of a good will, the *summum bonum*, the historical fate of humanism, what good actions have in common with good tables and chairs, and so forth. Not that perfectionism ignores (or should ignore) such fields of concern. But it pursues them through usages and practices, feeling them out for ideational and affective entailments and links to other engagements. Moreover, and in a denial of clearly demarcated orders, the perfectionist weaves metaethical concerns within normative (r)essays that consider what usages bear.

LESS THAN PICTURE-PERFECT

I cannot imagine a less promising name for my bearing than "perfectionism." Is "perfection" somehow the goal of the good life? The term connotes not only excellence (even "supreme excellence") but completion, reaching back to the Latin *perficere*, the present, active infinitive for "to finish," which combines *facio*, "to make," with the prefix *per*, "thoroughly." Presumably Aristotle's *megalopsuchos* is such a person, a "gentleman possessing the perfection of moral virtue," as Charles Griswold presents him, stressing his "self-sufficient" (*autarkos*) and masculine character (Griswold 2007, 8). But that seems like a flight from the human rather than its perfection, presuming that we err, fall short, even behave poorly, which we do. Moreover, the dynamism of ecosocial life presents novel conundrums that often befuddle us. Our lives are never wholly given to us. Karma extends us beyond our acts and deaths, from offspring to policies to those we inspire. As Nancy has it in a passage quoted previously, "We begin and we end without beginning and ending." Such is our finitude—infinite.

"Perfectionism" proves an even odder word given that its principal proponents have not identified themselves as such. Steven Wall lists Aristotle, Aquinas, Spinoza, Marx, and T. H. Green as perfectionists, later including Nietzsche (but peevishly omitting Cavell) (Wall 2017). But who among them subscribes to the name? It seems designed by critics to ease their negations, as with Rawls's reading of Nietzsche, and I resist aligning myself with terms gifted by opponents (Rawls 1971, 325–32). Not that the word fails altogether as a way of thinking about how various people think the good, namely as enactments of humanity's developmental potentials in either individualized or broadly human ways. But given how diverse such commitments can prove, "perfectionism" doesn't tell us very much about what is on offer, which is something like a second strike against it, or even a third, given that the idea of "perfecting" a human life seems, as I just argued, at odds with finitude. True, acknowledging finitude (and the inevitability of error) could be integral to perfectionism, but that makes the term even clumsier.

And yet, somewhat in response to Rawls's rejection, Cavell uses "perfectionism" to align himself with Emerson, Nietzsche, and Wittgenstein. The usage enables him to speak to aversions, loves, and longings, and to think human development, the "soul's journey," as a venture sought through acts of accounting, recounting, and revision where every word counts (Cavell 1990, 32). And it allows him to find in perfectionism precisely what Rawls thinks went missing: an effort to address a differential public in a manner that does not presume overlapping consensus about a comprehensive doctrine (Rawls 1971, 330; 1996, 195). In other words, in Cavell's work, perfectionism becomes a dependent, vulnerable, and answerable project even as it remains a radically individuated one. Refusing or ignoring the term thus seems a misstep given my project (r)essays Cavell's among others (including the Emerson he refuses). Eddie Glaude, Chris Lebron, Melvin Rogers, and Paul Taylor also employ the term, and I would maintain whatever allows me to remain proximate to their manifold efforts (Glaude 2016; Lebron 2012; Rogers 2014, 249–82; 2015; Taylor 2018). They help me think in the hyphen of "African-American," a movement caught, in part, in a multivalent Black-white dynamic that implicates me, even plots me. Better then—and more honest—to assume "perfectionism" as a usage and see what emerges as I enact it in the company of others, which is my way of agreeing with Paul Taylor, who writes, "Rather than refusing any external sources for their ethical judgments, perfectionists simply accept the burden of working through the meaning of these sources for themselves, in ways that are never immune to change or error" (Taylor 2018, 53).

THE WRITING LIFE

No matter how we recount, or how often, narrowness operates. But that is how we learn things. We focus, tarry, and submit to the push and pull of what we find in our way. The tasks I have aligned with "perfectionism" belong to a spray of authors and texts that exceed what the concept convenes. The phrases *epimeleia heautou* and *cura sui*, roughly translated as "concern for" and "care of" oneself, name activities that include but are irreducible to self-knowledge. I say this less to be ecumenical in my browsing and perusals (cynics, stoics, Epicureans, and Galen) than to open proximities, hence possible intensifications and redirections. One touchstone is writing. "But we must keep in mind," Foucault insists, "that very early in the government of the self the role of writing has been determinant," albeit not exclusively. Still: "The self as something which one had to take care of was a theme of a constant writing activity" (Foucault 2021, 23). How many of us meet here?

BECOME WHO YOU ARE

Pindar's second Pythian Ode, "For Hieron of Syracuse Chariot Race" (470 or 468 BCE), celebrates Hieron's victory. The poem offers the race as an allegory of the soul, which must, in its movement, struggle to hold the reins with help from gods like Artemis, Hermes, and Poseidon. The poem then takes a broader view, attending to all that fate throws one's way, recalling Ixion. Having been forgiven by Zeus for murdering his father-in-law, Ixion then seeks to bed Hera. For transgressing presumed orders of family and cosmos, the gods set him upon a wheel spinning ever after. Hieron thereby warned, the poem exhorts, "This song, like Phoenician merchandise, is sent to you over the gray sea: look kindly on the Castor-song, composed in Aeolian strains; come and greet the gracious offering of the seven-toned lyre. Learn and become who you are" (Pindar 1990, lines 69–70).

According to Pindar, each human is fated, and that fate provides the logic of one's becoming. The task is to become in accord with that logic and not resist it, which the poem indicates directly: "A man must always measure all things according to his place" (line 34). And: "But to be rich by the grace of fortune is the best part of skillful wisdom" (lines 56–57). And: "It is best to take the yoke on one's neck and bear it lightly; kicking against the goad makes the path treacherous" (lines 94–95).

Pindar offers something like a theologically moored, humanist perfectionism. The poem takes human becoming to have a settled, if divinely derived, logic. It instructs us to pursue our fates as humans rather than animals (refusing to defer to appetites and instincts), and with a keen feel for individual roles and projects. The latter must be discovered, but they are there for the finding and, once found, normatively preferable.

If perfectionism follows this path, its measure lies with who we truly are. But without a backdrop of gods and wheel-spinning Fates, too much ontological variability—and fungibility—haunts our condition to allow for a simple "learn and conform" perfectionism. Do the dimensions of your life have corresponding vocations? Can you see yourself as a Miller, Thatcher, or Cooper, and not just via your profession but across your sexuality, ethnicity, and gender, to name just three incredibly broad, differential folds of facticity? Moreover, without an aura of sacred authority, our simple facticity loses its normative force, at least the kind that could charge projects bent otherwise with something like contradiction or alienation. Finally, our fate includes a shared alterity and so is bound to a host of others—"you," "me," we're a jointed affair.

But my resistance is not simple credulity. Rather, I resist theo-humanist perfectionism within the arc of a learning process. I have discovered that our being lacks a deep, broad *eidos* that could categorically inform such projects. But that lack is not just an absence, and so that negation is something more than indeterminate. Yes, it begins in a general thought, such as: "In another dream an old woman told me that at my age, she wished she'd known that the soul never stops appearing" (Manguso 2015, 59). But what shakes out of such a working-through is an encounter with our dynamic partiality, which registers the thought that we need to, even should, become who we are always already becoming, and that leaves perfectionism with a task. Moreover, bringing perfectionism into a learning process leaves it accountable for the possibilities entertained and evaluated, rejected or accepted, pursued or postponed, possibly killed off or left to die. And it suggests that if one should refuse such accounts (or dodge them with a given myth), one's character will present itself as fleeing itself, hiding from it, denying it.

LEARN TO LIVE, LIVE TO LEARN

For the perfectionist, the goal is to become in accord with something like the *logos*, taking *logos* to name an account we offer ourselves—that is, you and me in the company of us. (Following Thoreau, this could also be called "living deliberately," or an aspect of it.) Such accounts spring from a kind of learning—a braid of know-how and know-that—that registers facticity in whatever becoming is eventually affirmed (and refused, or at least resisted).

"What does your conscience say?" (Was sagt dein gewissen?) Nietzsche asks in *The Gay Science*, section 270. He replies: "Du sollst der werden, der du bist" (You should become who you are) (Nietzsche 1988, 197). This is a perfectionist scene; conscience concerned with and accounting for how one should become in the sense of change, develop, grow, transform. And it establishes itself quite deliberately, invoking Pindar to displace the fate and natural law of the original with an act of reading and revision. But not just that, for Nietzsche's remark is also an act of writing that offers the revision not only to himself but to all who read him. (This *dein* and *du*, which bring intimacy to the scene, are terms for every *one* but no one in particular.) Faced with questions of becoming, one takes one's leave from others—perhaps what they say, perhaps their example—but in one's own way, which one recounts for everyone, though no one in particular, certainly never just "me." (Foucault is again pertinent: "What is remarkable in this practice of the soul is the multiplicity of social relations which can serve as its support" [Foucault 2021, 29]).

Not that one cannot read Nietzsche differently. Setting herself against Nehamas's *Nietzsche: Life as Literature*, Babette Babich announces:

We are poorly placed to raise the question of our own nature: even if we were, even if we could be, of a mind to do so. We cannot jump over our own shadow: we cannot get behind our own skin, behind ourselves, because of all the nearest and closest things that as Heidegger points out are distant from us due precisely to such proximity, what we are is most alien to us. For this and related reasons, Nietzsche's "become what you are" or Werde der du bist is not and cannot be about the cult - culture - cultivation - of the self, because, despite the cries of self-starved existentialists and academic enthusiasms or fashion, it is ultimately not about the self in the sense of self-transformation (or care) but being. (Babich 2003, 39)

I welcome the displacement of a settled humanism. But by valorizing being over selves, Babich institutes an ironically ascetic perfectionism, as if the effort to become oneself is what must be overcome, perhaps in a self-extinguishing amor fati. But as I argue elsewhere regarding Emerson's idealization of the rose, such pursuits are performatively contradictory, beginning with its address, continuing into the assessment of our poverty, and turning into the deployment of "should" (Lysaker 2008, 54). Each moment presumes that something remains for an addressee to do, even if it is just to *accept* the place set for us. But my point is not simply that taking Nietzsche in this way runs aground. Babich's turn toward being also loses sight of a discovery lurking in Nietzsche's revision of Pindar, which exposes the scene of address where selves inclining toward perfection arise and encounter one another. "The human being inventing signs," Nietzsche also says, "is at the same time the human being who becomes ever more keenly conscious of himself. It was only as a social animal that man acquired self-consciousness" (Nietzsche 1974, 299). By giving oneself over to the dynamism of an address, Nietzsche sets the project of becoming ourselves *jenseits* any simple opposition between autonomy or heteronomy. In fact, by displacing *nomos* with the reflexive offer of an intersubjective *logos*, perfectionism pursued through deliberate accounts allows us to encounter ourselves precisely because we are dependent upon one another. In making ourselves known we encounter ourselves in relation (together and apart), and in ways that might allow us to know and begin to conceive of those scenes otherwise.

These passages from *The Gay Science* clarify the scene in which perfectionists address their own becoming, together and alone. Not only is the project situated in a series of historical changes that overdetermine whatever possibilities present themselves, ones the perfectionist must enact and assess, but those possibilities course between speaker and addressee.

A kind of character and intersubjectivity underwrites how they are given in their objectivity, therefore. And that course preserves our lives for not only recounting but revision or abandonment.

ESSAY TO BE

The self-regard of the perfectionist, at base an activity, is experimental within an address that displaces the *nomos* of autonomy and heteronomy in favor of the possibilities that arise among beings-in-common. Quoting Pindar en route to a touchstone for conscience, Nietzsche offers a pragmatic hypothesis, much as he does in *Beyond Good and Evil* when he proposes the notion of a multiplicity of souls. "Between ourselves," he says, "it is not at all necessary to get rid of 'the soul' . . . and renounce the most ancient and venerable hypothesis. . . . But the way is open for new versions and refinements of the soul-hypothesis" (Nietzsche 1966, 20–21). "Hypothesis" keeps perfectionist determinations within the arc of a learning curve, while "pragmatic" tethers it to possibilities for action, perhaps even in a perfectionist manner if Vincent Colapietro is right to describe the pragmatic turn as a "turn toward signs in their myriad forms," and as a "turn toward the subject, though in the sense of moral reckoning, not an epistemic self-grounding" (Colapietro 2006a, 28).

RIGOR MORTIS

Not understanding is a confession, not an objection.

NO ONE IS EVERYONE

The scene of address is fraught, and differently so for different people, and varied kinds of people who are varied in their own ways. One can be hailed in a manner that contracts the site and disrupts the currents upon which perfectionism relies. Contesting Machery's reading, David Marriott affirms what he takes to be "Fanon's extremely subtle point"—namely, "that blackness does not have a language of its own; or: what it reproduces, what it utters, is a ventriloquy . . . blackness has no articulation, for even its difference is borrowed; the result is a language whose idiom is that of *n'est pas*"—*it is not* (Marriott 2020, 31). The claim is stark with overtones of refusal regarding the ease with which some speak of Black thought, Black experience, Black identity, etc. I take Marriott to be claiming that whoever is regarded as Black, whether by themselves or another, is haunted by something prior to misrecognition or even the refusal of recognition, which that "tall newcomer" in the "wee schoolhouse" delivered by reject-ing Du Bois's visiting card. What could be prior? A kind of ensnarement that precedes recognition as its condition of possibility, which undermines the very scene. How? That which ensnarement establishes casts those so identified as *not*: not white, not human or not fully so (maybe 3/4, more animal than rational), uncivilized, incapable, etc. The *ante* is anti, as it were, and so the game is rigged.

Perfectionism begins in quotations and usages, and it casts and recasts them in praxical efforts to locate and realize, in part, and only ever in part, potentialities, possible becomings. I find myself stopped short by Marriott's essay because perfectionism seems compromised at the outset for those enveloped in "blackness," at least to the degree that Fanon, as Marriott reads him, is right in his overall assessment: "Insofar as we are dealing with a prohibition that is itself absent, evanescent, decisions made in the name of freedom are then always in principle, however unknown in fact, imprisoned within the formal instituted framework of a racial law (what Fanon calls an 'imposition') within which anti-blackness is judged and pronounced" (Marriott, 35–36). Not that something more, something excessive, isn't operative in lives so ensnared. There must be for it to be received, enacted, felt with either identification or resistance; in existences like ours, a how accompanies every what. But this does not mean that the die is not cast. Marriott writes, "This means, says Fanon, that in a sense blackness has to invent, or more properly, reinvent the world as though for the first time in the discovery of it as lost. . . . This moment (however fraught) of reinvention then repeats, in however minimal a way, the found-ing violence of the exclusion itself, as already described" (Marriott, 37).

But things are even more complex than this, particularly for a per-fectionist seeking zones of proximity to Marriott's essay. Perfectionism (r)essay tropes—usages, images, sayings, practices, scenes wherein we are turned determinately toward ourselves in relation to others. But for Mar-riott, blackness is a "figure that is not tropological" but disclosed only in effects that throw "one off balance, out of kilter, off guard" (Marriott, 47). The negation that blackness announces in Marriott's reading is a "prohibi-tion that is itself absent," and thus not present as a trope (or nest of tropes) that can be contested, reworked, ironized, reimagined, etc.—say, like "dike" or the N-word. And so, "let us say that blackness cannot affirm," to return to Marriott, "or choose, itself, for it is already chosen—by which I mean that it cannot pass from indecision to a transformation of what subordinates it" (Marriott, 49).

I am engaging Marriott's essay because it marks a challenge that is obscured, if not erased, when one takes perfectionism to entail valences unchanged and uncharged by differential racialized fates. Nietzsche is hemmed in by Pindar's language, diminished, but he remains its addressee and an author who, in his own right, can resay that inheritance. But that is markedly different than trying to (r)essay a field of meaning threatening wholesale negation, and before anything like a creative, crescive self enters the scene. And that threat—misaligned with any speech-act—opens something, call it a question, even a grave doubt for those who would rework ethical life at the level of usages, affects, and some of our more elusive dispositions. But I also recognize the apparent distance of Marriott's intervention from authors like Glaude, whose temperament seems more in step with mine, and given how that distance complicates whatever sense I have of how to think racialized fates in the context of perfectionism, my own included. Any example is always a variant in varied scenes, and often, if not always, a contested one.

I have no way to resolve this contestation, and it is not for me to resolve, certainly not on my own, although insofar as a (r)essay of whiteness is ensnared in whatever "blackness" might mean (or not mean), I cannot say in good conscience that it is none of my business, let alone not my responsibility. One thought arises as a felt resistance to the claim that history reproduces itself through anything like the formal framework of a law. Following the first volume of Foucault's *History of Sexuality*, I take power to operate principally in a nonjuridical manner, without univocity in either its character or application, and via differential disseminations rather than simple exclusions (Foucault 1984b). Yes, any singular occurrence inhabits the atmosphere of ecosocial history and so does not create it, but that atmosphere is nevertheless the result of those occurrences circulating, in part through emphases, tone of voice, the how that often shapes the what. Moreover, these phenomena are cast into multiple trajectories that do not derive from or express any singular determination, even if a certain set of determinations impacts most or even all of those in which we find ourselves. Lines of kinship, friendship, eros, work, play, writing (which includes genres and a host of logical-rhetorical operations) are not subsets of any single category. They bring, therefore, their own currents into whatever fates they conduct. One thus assays a situation from multiple vantage points, whose result is a surfeit. But this may be Marriott's point, or rather, his resistance to and interruption of "blackness" thought as a historical current that is not a trope. The claim may be that, in its centripetal negativity, it fails to provide sufficient current for a reorienting (r) essay. Escape velocity from its orbit lies elsewhere.

But maybe that says too much. "I do not believe," Marriott says, ". . . that blackness can proceed without a certain undecidability as to its object," and he insists that one cannot resolve this situation via an appeal to lived experience as the arbiter of what a given fate might entail (Marriott 2020, 43–44). If I stress this line, the scene of address remains fraught but open to experimentation. Rather than undoing or excising (or atoning for), founding acts of anti-Black racism (because there wasn't any single one or sum to blame), the task is to work through the miasma from within. I am led here when Marriott writes, and this time I quote in full, "Condemned, unconsciously prohibited—and yet performed: let us say that blackness cannot affirm, or choose, itself, for it is already chosen—by which I mean that it cannot pass from indecision to a transformation of what subordinates it" (Marriott, 49). Perfectionism as I take it moves within this "and yet performed," believing that such performances hold within them, at least potentially, room for transformation. All that can be said can be said in many ways, which history discloses, and all that is said is positioned in vectors of interaction. Each scene thus contains reverberations that a perfectionist might track and modulate, speed up or slow down, comp or cut up and loop. Racialized fates are polysemic and inflected by other determinations that are themselves disseminations differentiating over time. And those currents and crosscurrents mark nested possibilities for performances that no life can avoid—greeting one another, ghosting, asking a question, ignoring a contribution, crossing the street, a hand on the shoulder, the cold shoulder, etc. The perfectionist question is: In the name of what do we take them up? One replies with performances that reinvent what we, you and I in the company of us, will live tomorrow.

COMMENCEMENT

Hegel purportedly chastised Schelling for having pursued his learning in public. I'll take that any day over *Collected Reprisals and Refusals*.

A DESK OF ONE'S OWN

Thanks in part to a conversation with Axelle Karera, I returned to *Spill: Scenes of Black Feminist Fugitivity*, by Alexis Pauline Gumbs, which receives and replays lines from Hortense J. Spillers's *Black, White, and in Color* (Gumbs 2016; Spillers 2003). Not in a literal manner. And not simply by recontextualizing them. Rather, prompted by a page, sited and turned, Gumbs initiates an original line of thought, thereby acknowledging the task that Spillers finds and elaborates in the hyphen joining African and American, that "contact zone of mutually incommensurable contents." Spillers explains, "Black writers, whatever their location and by whatever projects and allegiances they are compelled, must retool the language(s) that they inherit" (Spillers 2003, 11, 4).

But this is more than a writerly predicament, which I note because professors sometimes valorize the pen and lose its point. But also, I want to broaden the context to include streams in Black perfectionist thought. Glaude, for example, working with Baldwin, imagines a similar task, but with an eye on the "tasks of self-creation and reconstructing American society. . . . But obviously, I am speaking as an historical creation which has had bitterly to contest its history, to wrestle with it, and finally accept it in order to bring myself out of it" (Glaude 2007, 15; citing Baldwin's "White Man's Guilt"). And not just to escape, but also to emerge with bragging rights. This, again, is Baldwin: "One enters into battle with that historical creation, Oneself, and attempts to recreate oneself according to a principle more humane and more liberating" (Glaude 2020, 82; citing a 1968 interview).

I invoke Gumbs and her engagement with Spillers, and I have rendered it proximate to a recurring thought in Glaude's engagement with Baldwin because, to an extent seen, felt, and enacted (subjectively, intersubjectively, and institutionally), my fate (unthinkable without its proximities and pairs), is also part of that hyphen, that contact zone. Conducting it, inevitably, I am accountable for my part therein and to those I encounter there. But I am also struck by how a kind of perfectionism is forced by the task that these writers, in their variety, articulate, which renders my text proximate to theirs in a manner that I still am tracing with an eye toward a rim to burst, recalling Emerson's "Circles." I am thinking about what, if anything is . . . not entirely commensurate (which suggests a kind of sameness, hence substitutability) or even consonant (which connotes harmony) . . . but a turn that offers a kind of assonance, an inflection that might further a line in a surprising manner and invite a reply.

One of Gumbs's (r)essays takes its leave from Spillers's discussion of "how a cultural history of the African Diaspora and Continental Africa might proceed from the point of view of food and the foodways," arriving, perhaps, where the "interarticulatory logic of the *material* and the *symbolic* blends the universal and the particular at the same place—*inside* one and all" (Spillers 2003, 41, 64). One question, which Spillers puts on the table (or draws from it), concerns the creolization of various dishes, particularly those that blend a broad range of ingredients, whether in soups, stews, or so-called pouch foods, a mode of preparation and presentation that, Spillers reports, may be typical for 75 percent of the world's population. In Gumbs's hands (or through her fingers), "table" prompts another question, one also tied to the material and symbolic: "*How do you turn paper into food?*" (Gumbs 2016, 24). Gumbs thus converts the dining into the writing table; or rather, she approximates them through shared valences—a kind of nourishment. But the question intensifies for one that wants to retool usages, and precisely because she cannot trust the tropes at hand, as an earlier entry conveys.

> she thought she heard dogs barking. she knew she heard crows.
> she sensed a plague of locusts crowding her windows. she
> remembered how fast and choking ivy could grow. she expected
> poison sweets from the neighbors and toxic rain from above.
> anticipated everything but
> love.
> *(Gumbs 2016, 6)*

Plagues, toxin from the heavens, choking vines, poison delivered as sweets or lacing laundry, crows gathering in a murder, dogs cornering prey—the triadic scene of poems or prose seems overwhelmed, with loneliness blotting. And never a capital letter for a proper name.

How, then, to (r)essay? Certain picture frames must be broken, cuts borne until "she was prism reborn. she was sharp refracted everything" (Gumbs, 29). But that takes radical hope, that "crawling part of every day," which gathers "somewhere at the base of lungs," and provides "the sense to want something else" (Gumbs, 7).

ON THE RUN?

Gumbs convenes and manifests a scene of enormous pressure. One also hears something like this in Ralph Ellison, who made "blackness," according to Spillers, "a *process*, a *strategy*, of culture critique rather than a condition of physiognomy [*nomos* again]" (Spillers 2003, 5). An essay begins, "In those days it was either live with music or die with noise, and we chose rather desperately to live" (Ellison 2001, 3). While the essay revolves around the noise of an upstairs neighbor that makes it difficult for Ellison to write, a noise he fights off with an increasingly elaborate stereo, it becomes apparent, over time, that she, the neighbor, is also trying desperately to live. But her music lies in not-quite-gifted singing. Return to that opening line, therefore, and look for a more general noise assailing both, one capable of drowning out lives that would follow their own paths. Doing so will bring one to the noise of . . . choose your term . . . say, anti-Black racism and its insistent "You can't," "Never have, never will," "You don't belong," and "Not one of us," a kind of hateful internal audience playing chorus to more personal angels and devils.

Ellison's essay is not simply about flight, however; or rather, it shows how disciplined flight, even flights of fancy can be. And this opens, I think, a perfectionist scene proximate to Nietzsche's transvaluation of Pindar. Writing of jazz musicians, Ellison says, "I had learned too that the end of all this discipline and technical mastery was the desire to express an affirmative way of life through its musical tradition, and that this tradition insisted that each artist achieve his creativity within its frame. He must learn the best of the past, and add to it his personal vision" (Ellison, 6). And the proof will lie in the pudding, with what is enacted and what avenues it furthers, loses sight of, opens, and forecloses. And we, multiple we's, or just you and me, might disagree.

SCIENCE!

Experimentalism suggests empirical sciences and their celebrated "method." "Science" in this sense operationalizes key terms, controls variables, and proves itself through replication on the presumption that, as Horkheimer and Adorno have observed (following Nietzsche), its phenomena are substitutable or equivalent (Horkheimer and Adorno 2002, 12; Nietzsche 1974, 169). Perfectionist tests, however, conducted in the elaborations and revisions of a (r)essay, lack, even resist, that kind of precision. Not that this converts them into poetry or literature—those terms say so much that they obscure the tasks at hand. Rather, just as Nietzsche saw no need to abandon the word *Seele*/soul (only its usage in the context of atomism), we too might (r)essay the cardinal tropes of empiricism in the context of perfectionism—experiment, hypothesis, revision, perhaps even confirmation bias, given our partialities.

"Why not *science* too?" We could. But why? At some point, certain ships have sailed, at least for the moment.

INOPERATIVE DEFINITIONS

Contra Christine Korsgaard, who finds practical identity gathering around a law or principle that one posits as one's own, Vincent Colapietro asks us to forgo the language of law in favor of generalized ideals that one simultaneously affirms and contests through actions pursued in accord with them (Colapietro 2006b). Such ideals have their roots in the metabolism of culture, however, and in conspiring, (re)ssaying acts of inheritance, not the universalizing judgments of self-consciousness. And we rely on them, in part, because they have served us in some sense and scene(s). Not always, and not for everyone, and never fully. We thus need them to prove themselves to ourselves through their enactment, which requires that we consider them possibilities. In short, they are hypotheses, and their normative force is hypothetical, bound to what Dewey would term "ends in view" even as he and Colapietro hasten to remind us that ends not only become means to further ends but, in organizing action, they also are means for the kind of meaning a purposive present might bear (Colapietro 2009, 10).

In terming the normative force of perfectionist ideals "hypothetical," I do not want to ensconce them in the grammar of the imperative. If anything, the enactment itself is the hypothetical measure, a concrete exemplification of a living possibility pursued under generalized ideals and idealizations. This means that perfectionist pursuits are carried out under the guidance of exemplars rather than categorical commands or free-standing, regulative ideals.

Consider James Baldwin's approach to the blues, which complements Benjamin's revisions of historical materialism (Lysaker 2018). Both witness barbarism and name it as such, and the naming (its rhetorical grace and frank tone) offers a measure of counterresistance. "Now I am trying to suggest," Baldwin writes, "that the triumph here—which is a very un-American triumph—is that the person to whom these things happened watched them with eyes wide open, saw it happen" (Baldwin 2010, 72). And in saying what they saw (and/or singing or playing what they underwent), they provided images of eloquent survival amid difficult truths, which resonates with Albert Murray's suggestion that a blues musician is an "agent of affirmation and continuity in the face of adversity," and no less in virtue of (r)essays of down-home church music without the promise of salvation (Murray 2017, 38).

GETTING HERE FROM THERE

Thinking about, or rather with, Cecil Taylor, Fred Moten begins with a line from Charles Lloyd who told a reporter, when asked to speak about his music, "Words don't go there" (Moten 2003, 42). My first thought is, did anyone *seriously* think they did, in the sense of taking the words to be an adequate substitute? But the journalist did ask, and the question stages Moten's concern, which lies with those who think they can "read" Taylor, as if one could translate his improvisatory work. I suppose some think they can. But they are not taking either the music or listening seriously, and that is Moten's point, or a slice of it. My second thought is, what does "go there" mean? Or rather, that is my third thought, given that "words" is an abstraction from speech-acts and how they are phrased, which is another slice of Moten's point, one he believes initiates a task: How does one phrase when one is talking about how Taylor phrases? But my third point concerns pointing. Reference can be gestural; that is, words can indicate rather than represent, as Gillespie's phrase "You need to be a master shit detector" does, and with a mixture of bravado and restraint. Gillespie's remark points to the scene of playing trumpet rather than inscribing it with would-be equivalents. And it points with a thought that is richer than merely pointing. In particular, "detector" underscores where the real work lies—namely, not in Gillespie's reply to Dick Cavett, but in the playing (and hearing). But to be instructed in this way, one cannot simply traverse the line between sign and signified or hover where it breaks. One must recall one's place in the ensemble and receive the address, follow the indication, and loop between anticipation and execution, returning with what one hopes won't simply pile up.

UNCONTROLLED CONDITIONS

An experimental perfectionism does not simply reject *Moralität* in favor of *Sittlichkeit*, understood as a set of customary expectations regarding conduct (e.g., honor your parents), and/or virtues (e.g., the courage of soldiers, the honest work of artisans, or the justice of judges). Experimental perfectionism also subjects custom to exemplification to determine the kind of welfare it conducts. Like Hegel, it rejects abstract right, knowing that human action finds its bearings in historical precedents—what Emerson terms quotation—which overdetermine the deliberations of practical reason. But it equally denies that the "right of individuals to their particularity is likewise contained in ethical substance [*sittlichen Substantialitat*] for particularity is the mode of outward appearance in which the ethical exists" (Hegel 1991, 197). For the experimental perfectionist, action is not simply a mode of appearance but a (r)essay, a venture that assesses how life is conducted and offers it to others by way of example. To the degree we find and claim them, individuations (as opposed to the more platonic sense of participations) are ill-served by the language of outward or external (*außerlich*) appearance, whose implied dichotomy misses the discursive and praxical reflexivity integral to perfectionism.

"Experiment," particularly when cast along a learning curve, connotes falsification and revision. How do these moments enter perfectionism? Reworking his pragmatist inheritance, Colapietro turns away from empirical science toward improvisation in a manner that resonates with Albert Murray. Writing on blues in Afro-American music (in a passage quoted by Stanley Crouch), Murray presents that hyphen as an attitude.

What it all represents is an attitude toward the nature of human experience (and the alternatives of human adjustment) that is both elemental and comprehensive. It is a statement about confronting the complexities inherent in the human situation and about improvising or experimenting or riffing or otherwise playing with (or even gambling with) such possibilities as are also inherent in the obstacles, the disjunctures, and the jeopardy. It is also a statement about perseverance and about resilience and thus also about the maintenance of equilibrium despite precarious circumstances and about achieving elegance in the very process of copy with the rudiments of subsistence. (Murray 2017, 250–51; Crouch 2006, 94)

But "attitude" may obscure how the sensibility in question is bound to various know-hows and know-thats, what Murray elsewhere associates with idiomatic stylization (Murray 2017, 196). At stake is a capacity to work with instruments, musical traditions, and often other musicians, and in a transformative way. I thus prefer casting the matter in terms of praxis, as elsewhere I cast writing (Lysaker 2018). An imagination-fired skill set finds and refines its character over the course of its own enactment, which distinguishes it from a technique that draws rote patterns from various materials.

One can glimpse the distinction—praxis versus techne—in Stanley Crouch's praise for Thelonious Monk, as well as hear overtones of perfectionism. "What made him avant-garde," Crouch writes, "was his determination to sustain the *power* of the tradition rather than reduce it to clichés, trends, novelties, or uninformed parodies" (Crouch 2006, 87; emphasis in the original). Italicizing power underscores the doing involved, whereas locating the undercurrent in tradition insists that "jazz is more than improvisation alone," one that engages "4/4 swing, blues, the romantic to meditative ballad, and Afro-Hispanic rhythm as core aesthetic elements" (Crouch, 212). But those elements are reduced to academicism when they are preserved as mere techniques, whereas they are kept fresh in a praxis that (r)essays them, as Monk not only did with his inheritance (which was vast and multitraditional), but his own compositions as well, reworking them in live and recorded performances, something the saxophonist Steve Lacy did as well, and across several albums such as *Reflections* (1958), *Evidence* (1962), *Epistrophy* (1969), *Only Monk* (1987), and *More Monk* (1991).

Returning to an Emersonian idiom, I would say that perfectionism (r) essays what it finds in its way. As Elvin Jones says about the great Coltrane Quartet that he rode like a man possessed, "It was not so new as to do away with what was basic in jazz music, but to get involved in this thing offered a release to a great many minds. It was not that it was so much removed from the blues, but it was like another way of playing the blues—and a better way. It was a way that you could identify with in your own time" (Wilmer 2018, 38–39).

KNOWING HOW TO BORROW

Part of Emerson's genius lay in his grasp of quotation at the level of concept and *savoir*, of how it underwrites invention. But we should not render the fact overly diachronic, as Emerson seems to do. In most cases, experimentation, even when startling, like Monk's, isn't simply a relationship between soloist and material, but a response to others. "The background issue to keep in mind," Ingrid Monson suggests, "is that *at any given moment* in a performance, the improvising artist is always making musical choices in relationship to what everyone else is doing" (Monson 1996, 27; emphasis added). And, more specifically: "The shape, timbral color, and intensity of the journey is at every point shaped by the interacting musical personalities of band members, who take into consideration the roles [Monson mentions keeping time, comping, and soloing] expected of their musical instruments within the group" (Monson, 26). It is thus unsurprising that across *Saying Something*, Monson and the musicians she interviews speak of listening (or reading), responding, and, most generally, conversation, which suggests, she argues, "structural analogies between music and talk and emphasizes the sociability of jazz performance" (Monson, 97). And so, too, in reverse.

There and not—the peculiar way of being-in that characterizes existence according to Dewey and Heidegger, and which Thoreau, more narrowly, attributes to solitude (Thoreau 2008, 94). But that solitary emphasis, in virtue of which our "doubleness may easily make us poor neighbors and friends," misses the synchronous interplay that renders improvisational experimentation so vital (Thoreau, 94). Talking with Ralph Gleason in 1961 about conscious choice when a group is clicking, John Coltrane says it's the "sort of thing that you're here and you're not here" (Gleason 2016, 15). For Coltrane, being "not here" entails being immanent to the number, playing one's part, what Thoreau casts as being within nature. But whereas solitary reflection renders Thoreau aloof, leading him to claim that "we are not wholly involved in nature," Coltrane's way of "being here" remains tied to listening and responding, leading and being led. Not that one's ability to be there like Coltrane isn't fueled by the careful, disciplined work of solitude. These strands can complement one another. But to the degree perfectionism is bound to the art of conversation, it strives to be beside itself in the company of others, saying, with Stanley Crouch, "Given the necessary discipline, those who hear best sound best" (Crouch 2006, 111).

CHECK IT OUT

Deftly turning pragmatism and perfectionism toward one another, Colapietro locates the two in the phrase "checking one's experience," which Cavell acknowledges might be a "rubric [that] an American, or a spiritual American might give to the empiricism practiced by Emerson and Thoreau" (Cavell 1981, 12; cited by Colapietro 2013, 9). The thought is that one tests hypothetical futures in the course of their enactment, and in three ways: (1) one consults or checks in with one's experience; (2) one examines or checks it out; and (3) one learns to (and to a degree, how to) set aside learned expectations, checking them like a coat or hat to consult the experiences of others.

Not that experience is fail-safe. It rises with what exceeds anticipation, and that is one reason (or two) why one should recurringly check it, others being our own becoming and the asynchronous becoming of our world. But even that partial slice of nature is quite capable of resistance, even surprise, particularly if we absolve ourselves to it or take it into account. And isn't that in itself startling? "The paradox here," Colapietro observes, "is that in making our experience more truly our own we make ourselves other than we have been: in making my experience more fundamentally *mine* I make me into *someone else*, the most intimate of strangers, the most uncanny of intimates" (Colapietro 2013, 9–10). (Nietzsche revises Pindar while quoting him. Colapietro further turns the screw, disrupting any simple identification of who we are and are not.)

Colapietro also insists that "enactments" are never fully scripted. "If everything in one's past serves as a rehearsal for what one is now extemporaneously doing," he writes, "then that might seem to preclude extemporaneity. The opposite is, in truth, the case: no amount of rehearsal or preparation eradicates entirely the need for improvisation" (Colapietro, 10). The claim is empirical. Because our becoming is manifold and asynchronous, fully scoring the future is folly. We are rarely if ever univocal, together or alone. Our capabilities are never primed in the same manner. Our moods swing (or stick). And our transactions feature shifting and sometimes novel variables. "I cannot tell what I would know," Emerson reports, "but I have observed there are persons who, in their character and actions, answer questions I have not the skill to put" (Emerson 1987, 5).

Uncertainties and the improvisations they prompt are more than speed

bumps, however. In the resulting changes, discovery and creativity sometimes occur, and in tandem. Moving fully into an analogy with jazz performance, Colapietro writes, "The given forms give way to form-giving,
when just the right tone in an everyday exchange is struck or when jazz
truly becomes (in the words of Sonny Rollins), 'the music of surprise'"
(Colapietro 2013, 16). One might say perfectionist measures can grab us
with startling authority.

Or not. Take some of Coltrane's late experiments—various albums from
1965, including *Ascension* and *Om*—which Stanley Crouch has termed
"emotionally narrow" and located in an "artistic abyss" (Crouch 2006, 213–
15). I do not want to defend or resist these characterizations; what interests
me are the terms in which they are levied. Crouch notes the abandonment
of tradition, from a willingness to swing to an embrace of the blues (both
of which run through "Alabama" and a *Love Supreme*), but also, and this is
telling, a steep decline in intelligibility to fellow musicians. Crouch reports
that McCoy Tyner, the pianist in Coltrane's magisterial quartet, asked Coltrane what was happening by 1965, but the "pianist could get no answer in
musical terms, something that had not happened before" (Crouch, 213).

Tyner (or Crouch) are not alone at this juncture, and not just regarding
Coltrane. Val Wilmer terms *Ascension* a "meisterwerk" and a culmination of
Coltrane's work at the time, but never explains how or why (Wilmer 2018,
35, 45). And Michael Heller quotes Cooper-Moore recounting the approach
of his ensemble Apogee, founded in 1970: "At that time, it was just—BLOW.
Blow until you stop blowing. . . . Whoever is in the audience, they get it
or they don't get it" (Heller 2017, 90). But as Crouch observes, many did
not get it. He reports being one of three to attend a Coltrane show in Los
Angeles in 1965, which was the height of his fame. And my guess is that
among those staying away, many did get Monk, the two Davis quintets,
and Coltrane's *A Love Supreme* (1965) which sold five hundred thousand
copies by 1970.

The absence of felt intelligibility lies at the heart of Crouch's charge of
narrowness. The issue is not a failure to transcribe some "point" into words
but an inability to provoke or lead or touch with a communicative example
that might itself be (r)essayed. And note, one could iconoclastically provide
such an example, as the pianist Matthew Shipp suggests while reflecting on
what he terms Black Mystery School Pianists, artists who "developed profound ways of generating sound out of the instrument grounded in a technique they invented and one that cannot be taught in school." And yet—"It
is a code that somehow gets passed down" (Shipp 2020). But that cannot
happen if one reduces Coltrane, or any exemplar, to a *via negativa*—he refused convention, he refused traditional structure, he refused melody, etc.

"Refusal," leading nowhere in particular, is an inadequate perfectionist gesture. Not to say that one should take Coltrane's late work as failing to offer scenes of instruction, to employ Cavell's phrase. That's a longer argument involving inheritances within (say, David S. Ware) and beyond jazz (from the Byrds to Terry Riley) (Nisenson 1993). And one needs to take a broad historical perspective. Certain performances take time to come into their own. Guitarist John McLaughlin confessed that on first listen, he could not follow *A Love Supreme* musically or emotionally, but later recorded a section of the album (Kahn 2002, xviii). Experimentalism, at least as far as perfectionism is concerned, is bound to learning curves and thus scenes of instruction that prove themselves as such in (r)essaying inheritances.

GENERATIVE MUSIC

Working in the absence of a prior or emerging *nomos* is what forces the experimental improviser to become a master shit detector whose best argument is his or her or their example. So, too, perfectionists, who neither create conscience from the smithies of their souls nor derive it, even retrospectively, from oughts that shine like laws. But where does that leave us?

"The glorification of the artist as creator," Adorno writes, "does him an injustice because it attributes to conscious invention something that is anything but. Whoever creates authentic forms fulfills them" (Adorno 1997, 200–201). I get it, up to a point. Experimentation is a situated, overdetermined activity, and any appeal to spontaneity threatens not only to obscure that but to risk unwitting perpetuations. But I wonder if the distinction between universal and particular—a distinction fundamental to Platonism, and to an ontology of things more generally—is the right way to frame the dilemma. Perfectionism enacts a range of know-how and know-that relative to unsettled terrains, even when clear social roles are involved—brother, sister, citizen, friend, lover, employee, neighbor, etc.—or the broader identities that seem particularly aesthetic in presentation— say, gender and race.

To be fair, Adorno is writing about art, and thus has genre in mind, as well as forms such as the fugue. But *Aesthetic Theory* seems too Hegelian when Adorno insists, "The power of the subject resides in its methexis in the universal, not in the subject's simple self-announcement" (Adorno, 202). Praxis is irreducible to participation, aesthetic or otherwise. As Donald Davidson argues, everyday conversation, particularly among the witty, remains open to plays and ironies that are fresh and must be grasped as such—that is, without simple deference to rules or convention. Furthering undermining the scheme of the paradigm, he writes, "We must give up the idea of a clearly defined shared structure which language-users acquire and then apply to cases" (Davidson 2006, 265).

AGAINST KANT

Agency owes a thank you note.
A good will distrusts commands.
Responsibilities cannot be met ahead of time.
Dignity never stands alone.
Faith always has more than enough room.
Disinterestedness, like vanity, is ugly.

AND NOW FOR SOMETHING SOMEWHAT DIFFERENT

I come to perfectionism after the pitched struggle between British and German avant-garde music, which Michael Nyman has recounted polemically (Nyman 1999). It offers perfectionists yet another line of intervention.

Imagine a desire to have each moment of a work, no matter how fleeting, live as a function of that totality, and to the degree that it could be derived from a graspable rule or set of rules organizing the whole. One could explain why everything was where it was in the way it was. According to Nyman, composers like Boulez and Stockhausen belong to this group, working as heirs of Beethoven's *es muß sein*. "You must be really capable of really integrating the elements," Stockhausen insists, "and not just expose them and see what happens" (Nyman, 29). Imagine, now, an embrace of the adventitious, which allows elements to arise and resonate without any clear derivation from operative rules or even their surrounding elements. And they remain somewhat fungible in their arrival. This is what Cage helped enable, according to Nyman, and what led to the experimental music generated by composers like Cornelius Cardew, Gavin Bryars, and Brian Eno. Without relying on virtuoso improvisation, they composed in ways to generate unforeseen circumstances that rendered them artist and audience. But Cage reified that moment (and his own activity in the process), fetishizing chance occurrence. But we need not follow him to the letter. Brian Eno didn't, electing instead to creatively conspire with chance results, trust his judgment, and share its fruits in a manner that allows us to conspire in turn. One can listen to his *Music for Airports* in a variety of ways, or, like Bang on Can, transcribe the album for acoustic instruments and perform it. Or one can set up two turntables and layer the tracks against one another. The work invites one to join in without leaving one empty handed (Lysaker 2018).

INPARTIALITY

If the example of empirical science conjures more precision and control than perfectionist (r)essays employ, art, particularly jazz, indicates more freedom (from and to) *Moralität* and *Sittlichkeit* than we wield, although Foucault may have shrunk that gap by casting ethical life as technologies of the self, practices whereby you and I in the company of us become subjects and objects of moral concern. Regardless, whether one employs metaphors of science or art, they remain rough analogies to be wielded while observing the partiality endemic to such tropes. One checks experience during one's enactments, and hopefully in multiple contexts, at least as multiple as our selves. Learning to write sincerely is not the same as learning to be sincere in bed, and blowing sessions are not marriages or even friendships. Not that bridges are impossible. Some report, for example, that learning to be patient with oblique prose may cultivate therapeutic patience with people suffering from schizophrenia (Hamm et al., 2014). But the exquisiteness of science and art should not obscure how revaluation plods. Improvisation exemplifies creative power because it enlists technical know-how and a broad education in musical examples, and few if any are prepared to syncopate and swing across the full breadth and length of their lives and ethical source material. And even if you want to pursue your life as an artist, I'm averse to playing primer.

NO MASS?

Like all steps in ethics, perfectionism faces the question of measure— the good, the right, the just, virtue, flourishing, responsiveness, beauty, holiness—each term adding depth to the thought "well played." I do not have in mind a question like: How does one recognize perfection? One doesn't, at least not in any simple manner, least of all by way of a rule; one seeks and thereby (r)essays it in words and deeds, in one's character and across one's life. But in that seeking, in its deliberateness, one is called to account. For what?

- *The overt*—choices, actions, the manner of one's deeds, beliefs, and refusals
- *The implicit*—indirect endorsements, unhappy complicities, crimes of omission
- *The incipient*—what we enable (or could enable but fail to pursue)
- *The reflexive*—the terms with which we deliberate, agree, converse, commit, revise, praise, blame, apologize, or wash our hands

Not that you or I know how to navigate these straits without friction or error. One must ask, "What counts in and as an account, ethically speaking?" And please do not reply, "Asking that question is the perfectionist project." That just doubles the task by introducing second-order reflections on matters that will still require a first-order response. One might as well say, "We'll get back to you." I also would avoid appealing to the complexity of one's account and propose an "aesthetic perfectionism" in a modernist sense—every element counts, and the more thoroughly worked, the better. While it's an answer, it's a thin one; this "better" can't account for itself. Clever villains require and often provide clever narratives, hence murder's claim to fine art.

Another strand, bound to authenticity, can be found in Emerson's declaration: "Nothing is at last sacred but the integrity of your own mind. Absolve you to yourself, and you shall have the suffrage of the world" (Emerson 1979, 30). Thinking through Emerson's language after Cavell, the task is to absolve (in the sense of free) your facticity (and the ambiguity of the "you," singular, plural). This would entail translating, even transfiguring what Thoreau terms the mother tongue into a sense of self of your own making, *your*-self (who speaks with what Thoreau terms the father tongue). In this scenario, praise and blame are meted out according to the degree of *mineness* characteristic of your becoming. But: "What makes you (or me) so special?" I want to ask. Here, the villain still looms in the shadows (as does the wastrel). One can do it "my way" and fail to impress.

Return to Emerson's remark. What characterizes the integrity of a mind—or better still, a life? Does its wholeness lie within the reach of my self-regard and the terms it might generate? Our finitude, including the obscuring extent of our past and future but also the vastness of our dependencies, suggests otherwise. For example, the terms with which I regard myself may incline in directions that surprise us unhappily. For example, after Irigaray, I find the distinction between the mother and father tongue ensnared in a drama I would abandon because it opposes a masculine, free intelligibility to a feminine, material sensibility. Note, the issue is less dependency than ensnarement in currents energizing futures I wish to avoid. The integrity of my own mind may thus conspire against me in a way that "authenticity" as a measure cannot track. But dependency remains an issue, and in all directions. What is properly *mine*? Every role we play is played alongside others whose parts give the role its character. Professor requires students; brother requires siblings, parents, and others unrelated by blood. A citizen is only ever one among some, and our becomings impact more than ourselves. My self-regard, therefore, must register and account for that more or prove inauthentic, although in doing so, the very idea of what is authentic seems to disperse, as it does if we let Emerson's line indicate that one gains the suffrage of the world when one absolves one's self-regard—loosens it, releases it—to the world in which its integrity lies, and experiments in observance of that difference.

Forgiveness

PLAYING AMENDS

This is a story retold. Richard Davis, the bassist, heard it from a woman (nameless, to my knowledge) and relayed it to the musicologist Ingrid Monson (Monson 1996, 181).

Paul Gonsalves, a saxophone player in Duke Ellington's band, offended his bandleader. How seriously? I don't know. Enough for Ellington to be genuinely offended, and that's accounting for how bandmates grate. When Gonsalves arrived the next day, Ellington was at the piano, playing. Gonsalves, hungover, unpacked his horn and brought the mouthpiece to his lips. Reportedly, he blew as if asking for forgiveness. I imagine his tone conveyed contrition, possibly sorrow and regret, maybe even a kind of loneliness. I suspect his phrasing evidenced a searching quality, which showed a renewed willingness to listen and respond, to play along.

Two virtuosos making up in music. It suggests that apologies and forgiveness might come to pass in many ways—some discursive, some more like a makeup kiss. I wonder: Did they return to something lost or step forward into something new? Or the latter through the former? And would an attentive ear hear that when it came time to play?

The woman who recounted the scene relied upon a religious figure, as if Gonsalves were saying, "Father, forgive me, for I know not what I do." This reworks Luke 23:34, where Jesus begs forgiveness from God on behalf of those crucifying him. Here, Ellington is divinely cast (perhaps twice) and Gonsalves is the crucifier, thus muddling the role of savior. The scene from Luke allows the teller to make sense of what she saw and heard. What renders us intelligible to one another when a misstep dislocates the relation? Because wrongdoing can estrange, how do we refind each other in the mist? Luke establishes (or reestablishes) the most definite of hierarchies in which forgiveness enables a return to the most stable of orders. But is this stage paradigmatic, in terms of both what is reinstituted and what enables restitution—say, a thick, narrative third, where we forgive because a superior, infallible example already has done so? Or was it Gonsalves's tone, his phrasing, how he held his head as he played, how he looked at Ellington, how Ellington returned his gaze—were these enough to allow them to go on together? And whatever transpired, was that all it took, or was Gonsalves's offer and Ellington's reply just one step in a syncopated series?

CONNECTIONS

I'm in Seattle, awaiting a flight, my second of the day. It's delayed. Hilary and I are heading to England. In the area beside our gate, we hear a young man on the phone ranting about then President Obama—"liberal fascist," "He's not getting my ammunition," etc. Note, I'm not overhearing him. The guy, in his twenties, speaks loudly enough that no one must eavesdrop. Given the place (Seattle), the speaker's tone, volume, gender, prep shop whiteness, and talking points, his intentions feel unmistakable. He is trying to get under the skin of those around him, people he presumes sympathetic to Obama. He succeeds. Many cast him irritated looks.

After "Enough is enough" breaks through "It is what it is," I walk over and say, "I don't want to have to hear your voice." He pauses in surprise but replies, as if to prove his point, "What about freedom of speech?" "That's between you and the state," I reply. "This is between you and me." With some degree of menace, I am trying to meet him in ethical life.

WORRY BEADS

Poems of apology are nothing new. Remember Hass's poem about not going to New York? But that was more poem and this more apology, with its own course to plot. Hass's fret and fuss concerned an omission while I commissioned my broadside. I wanted to say stay true in the storm—I'm here for that—and to deflect the lightning. Instead, I fell like hail, cryptic words reaching terminal velocity. Just more storm.

Phones are crap for intimacy, but the thud and plunk of my words still echoes when we speak. There are rumbles in the pauses, a voice out of control, baying and berating when it should have consoled, or just hovered.

When we met, we were mostly future, still opening, a puzzle for some hipster Zeno—emptier hence fuller. But now my life is more past than future, with regrets to worry. Not the whole run of things, but some handful of beads pitted with shame and remorse, expanding through handling.

We know that email is a virtual medium, its shine a play of the light. But what was more real than that e-pistle, incautiously composed and sent? It lingers, smooth like the crescent above my eye or the zipper along my leg. Each recalls life lost in a moment I would have back. But my leg still walks and my eye still blinks, while we remain caught in descent.

Songs of praise are nothing new. Did I ever share the one I wrote about two Jacobs? Both grappled with God for the right to see and say what is good. I cribbed the title from that poem I wrote about our night's skate into surfaces pried from things. I think of it now, "Wrestling Angels," the backside of that bead playing at my tips, a weight to counter those words that struck you from behind. I finger each syllable, stress the one and the three, to remind me of that which I've lost and what remains to be.

OBLIQUELY ASCENDING

I have been reading Tim O'Brien's *The Things They Carried* in the context of Plato's *Republic*, thinking about the ancient quarrel (or difference) between philosophy and poetry that vexes Plato's text at several sites such as visual mimesis, affect-heaving speeches, or myths chastened by linear narrative. The difference is quarrelsome because the *Republic* concerns what should educate Greece: epic poetry, tragedy, or philosophy? Plato's answer is complex, possibly multiple, maybe even withheld, but poetry is clearly disciplined by philosophy, such as when Socrates suggests that Glaucon should prepare for those poets who return to contest their fate, although the presumption is that the contest will be Socratic. The fix is in.

O'Brien's stories recount experiences steeped in the Vietnam War. They also swerve into metafiction, explicitly wondering how to tell a true war story. The suggestion, which the book defends on and between the pages, is that no set of facts discloses the truth or truths of war—A was shot because B was careless; X killed Y; D's girlfriend left him ten months into his tour; over three million people died in the fighting, the overwhelming majority Vietnamese. Nor will that excess be caught through predication, as in "War is hell." "True war stories do not generalize," O'Brien claims. "They do not indulge in abstraction or analysis" (O'Brien 1990, 74). What escapes is less what happened than what it was like to be there as it happened, how it seemed, and what it was like to undergo that seeming, a seam itself wherein an event's significance emerges; "A true war story, if truly told, makes the stomach believe" (O'Brien, 74).

"That just sounds like subjectivity—how something makes you feel." But the object is "war," a scene of interactions involving mud and blood, the dead in heaps, flying lead, screams, last breaths, and genuine if sometimes misspent valor. War transpires where subjects and objects and other subjects meet, to the degree you would retain that dyad, even triad. Regardless, war is not simply a first-, second-, or third-person phenomenon, but like the world in the fullest sense, a scene of their ambiguity, their irreducible distinctness and inseparability: "There is no clarity. Everything swirls. . . . the only certainty is overwhelming ambiguity" (O'Brien, 78).

How could we enter that scene, dear Glaucon, with truth-telling speech? Doesn't a certain remove from what happened draw us closer? In cases like these, might the strictly false prove truer than a march of generalizations?

WEIGHT-BEARING GLEAMS

When the first term plays front foot, "moral psychology" is theoretical on behalf of the practical. It should bear fruit that nourishes us ethically. Butler's sermons "Upon Resentment" and "Upon Forgiveness of Injuries" are exemplary in this regard. They "take human nature as it is, and the circumstances in which they are placed as they are," to explore "what course of action and behavior, respecting those circumstances, any particular affection or passion leads us to" (Butler 1850, II.87). Butler approaches ethical life through the situated character of human existence—such as our capacity for reflection, commitment, various feelings—and he explores how various affections conduct life. But the goal is not merely explanatory power. The inquiry does not conclude when we delimit instances of resentment and forgiveness, explain the conditions that give rise to them, and predict what is likely to follow when either is enacted. Resting there flips the exercise into a psychology of morals. Moral psychology culminates in advocacy. Butler not only tries to clarify the nature of resentment and forgiveness. He assesses revenge based on those analyses, denying its legitimacy, arguing that we should forgive our enemies. Moreover, he proceeds to "some reflections, which may have a more direct and immediate tendency to beget in us a right temper of mind toward those who have offended us" (Butler, II.101). Moral psychology aims to further ethical life by venturing insights worth enacting and presenting them in such a way that addressees can imagine doing so.

THE ABYSS LOOKS BACK

Another story retold, this one by Simon Wiesenthal. It concerns a time when he was beset by crimes for which, until his death, he held perpetrators accountable.

For a time, Simon resided in a concentration camp, Janowska, in Lviv, Ukraine. *The Sunflower* recounts its ins and terrible outs—forced gatherings, transport, starvation, beatings, humiliations, conversations, distractions, survival techniques, multiple modes of murder. "See you on the soap shelf" circulated darkly among Lviv's Jews (Segev 2010, 49). But the text is not a death camp memoir. It stages a provocation around a bizarre, heartless request for forgiveness.

Simon was sent to work in a nearby hospital. Before he was given his task for the day, a nurse pulled him into a room where Karl, a Nazi soldier, was dying. An SS volunteer (a choice his father opposed), Karl desired an audience with "a Jew." Before he died, he wanted to recount a particular horror and receive forgiveness from "a Jew."

The horror was indeed a horror. In Dnipropetrovsk, a city in Ukraine (now called Dnipro), men, women, and children, all Jewish, were rounded up and crammed into a two-story building. More were brought by truck and forced inside. The building was set on fire.

As the story unfolded, Simon very much wanted to flee but Karl implored him to remain to recall the fate of a young family in whose demise he remained frozen. A father, already on fire, covered the eyes of his child and leaped. "Seconds later the mother followed" (Wiesenthal 1997, 42). Like all who tried to escape, they were shot.

Karl sought forgiveness. He had lost himself in his guilt and the enormity of his crimes. They had eaten him. "Karl" had given way to "Nazi," possibly to "SS," and then to one who insured that those being burned alive, should they try to escape, were shot.

The Sunflower closes with: "You who have just read this sad and tragic episode in my life, can mentally change places with me and ask yourself the crucial question, 'What would I have done'?" (Wiesenthal, 98). The book also includes short replies to its closing question, and over the years, replies have accumulated. In a 1981 edition, Cardinal König, then Archbishop of Vienna, finds three questions in the book's closing lines: May, should, and can one forgive (Wiesenthal, 173)? Is one permitted to forgive in such a case? (And note, while this question includes the possibility of the unforgiveable, it also concerns whether one may forgive someone for something they did to another.) Second, is one obligated to forgive in such a

184 | FORGIVENESS

case? (Christians, for example, might feel compelled to forgive, presuming they may.) Finally, is one capable of forgiving? The issue is personal in the sense that, unlike the previous questions, no one can resolve this dilemma for anyone else. I may be permitted to forgive, even obligated to, but still, in my heart, I cannot. And your being able to will not change that, although it may help me along the way (or thicken my difficulties).

But more is on the table. Suppose I cannot or should not forgive another. What then? Is that the end of the story? Simon did not forgive Karl. But he was patient with him and showed him a certain tenderness. Giving or withholding forgiveness does not exhaust the task initiated once a question of forgiveness arises.

I cannot refuse the request to transpose myself into the scene, which involves two questions. Was Wiesenthal right to withhold forgiveness, and would I have forgiven Karl if I were in a sufficiently analogous position? I will only pursue the latter, although I need time to reply, and not just because the question is as heavy as they come. I need a better feel for what forgiveness entails—or rather, what it could be, in this case and more generally.

TWINKLE, TWINKLE

Forgiveness belongs to a constellation of contrasts, each term opening a line of degrees. One is wronged and ignores it, forgets it, resents it, grows disgusted, or feels hurt. One is wronged and withdraws, sucks it up, retaliates, or waits between reception and response, stuck. Wronged, one views one's antagonist with fury, compassion, possibly pity. (I am trying to think if I have ever laughed when someone did me wrong. I think so. "How feeble," I've thought. Also, wearily, "Déjà vu all over again.") Wrongs can also weaken relations—they are never the same again. Or wrongs, worked through and resolved, can renew relations—they are never the same again. And wrongs can crack us, leaving fissures through which our goodwill drains.

Across the pulses and lines of this dark cloud constellation, forgiveness emerges as a possibility. Hurt, I resent but forgive. Or I don't, maybe can't—a knot of anger persists and tightens when their name comes up. Wronged, I view my antagonist with compassion and find it easier to forgive: "We've all made mistakes." Or maybe that just makes our parting easier. Or after some estrangement, we see each other more clearly. "This is what we're capable of," we think. I am imagining lines of possibility that run between forgiveness and some contrast term(s). But if I step back, take in the whole, each line bends around a center of sorts, namely wrongdoing, which threatens to become a black hole sun.

TALKING THE WALK

We judge all the time—distinguishing, evaluating, deliberating, refraining, committing, changing our minds. Where would I be without judgment? Who would I be? Imagine a group of bipeds like us but incapable of judgment. Imagine them isolated on an island. Presume they survive for generations. One day you wash upon their shores. What would you find? I have heard from time to time the suggestion that judgment per se is presumptuous, as if—

"The issue is normative. Look to Matthew 7:1–3. *Judge not, that you not be judged. For with the judgment, you pronounce you will be judged, and the measure you give will be the measure you get. Why do you not see the speck that is in your brother's eye, but do not notice the log that is in your own eye?*" (May and Metzger 1962, 1178).

There are many ways to read this remix of *Sirach 28:1–4* (where vengeance rather than judgment looms). It warns against self-deception and double standards. It also suggests that those who do not show mercy will not (or should not) receive it. But this just calls for fairness rather than a suspension of judgment. (Or it mistakes mercy as the suspension of judgment, whereas mercy refines it.) Perhaps the verse should begin "Do not judge robotically lest you be judged robotically."

But I have heard the lines from Matthew invoked to suggest that only the creator has the authority to judge what is right, what is wrong. We should mind our own, mortal business. Bad idea. And incoherent. Life is a constant expenditure whose ends, actual and sought, require reckoning. And such evaluations—of the good, the better and best, the wrong, the silly, the base and detestable—inform our sense of what, if anything, deserves allegiance, from friends to professions to texts. If the burning bush had said, "I have seen my people in Egypt and found it good," Moses might have pretended not to hear.

I HATE PEOPLE WHEN THEY'RE NOT POLITE

I am touchy; it is easier than it should be to rub me the wrong way: pedantic tones, presumed but unwarranted authority, inconsiderateness. Whether in lines, on the road, or at concerts, roughly getting in and out of your seat on an airplane, riding your bike on the sidewalk, holding a conversation on a public stairway . . . like I said: touchy. But social life is full of missteps radiating varying degrees of intention. Whoever finds it "all good" is asleep.

Margaret Walker also finds the grate of social life broad and noteworthy, distinguishing slights from improprieties from offenses—imagine unwarranted condescension, cutting in line, or continually withdrawing a dinner invitation the day of. But she interprets these as perceived threats to norms and social conventions that resentment, broadly construed, protects (Walker 2006, 123–25). I doubt that is why they grate. Cast as threats, they become causes of future, ill effects. But they get under my skin before I calculate. Moreover, the issue is the life thereby conducted and made, not tears in the webs of *Sittlichkeit*. I would say the effect that concerns me is life contracting, diminishing. Therein lies the wrong, which I feel morally and aesthetically. Petty people doing petty shit.

How should one respond? To everyone? Are affronts marked and then, in some way, forgiven? That also would be petty. One learns to let things slide, which blurs the line between forgiving and forgetting. Said otherwise, "forget about it" can be a way to forgive affronts. One aspect of finitude is a degree of constitutional, moral fallibility. It may be cynical to regard stateless life as nasty, brutish, and short, but reach past the rule of law, as ethics must, and one will find the vain, petty, and abrupt. Expecting more, we notice. Expecting more of ourselves, we move on.

NECESSARILY INSUFFICIENT CONDITIONS

Essaying forgiveness, one encounters the uneven ground of the "forgiveness territory," a phrase Adam Morton deploys to chart a "bundle of mutually sustaining practices, ideas, and theories that center on people doing something roughly like forgiving one another for wrongs" (Griswold and Konstan 2012, 4–5). Because it underscores varied locations, I prefer "territory" to "bundle," but I see the point in both—heteroglossia, which Alice MacLachlan also underscores (MacLachlan 2009). To think about forgiveness is to encounter multiple languages and multiple usages within those languages, often in different institutional and social settings, and then across different cultures, subcultures, and time periods. And there will be proximities, as with forgiveness and mercy.

Thinking of forgiveness as a "territory" makes it easier for me to imagine that this range of differences isn't always mutually sustaining. When one state apologizes to another and the apology is accepted, no one expects all or most of the citizens to feel genuine remorse for what had been done. (Moreover, those apologizing and/or forgiving may not even have been in office or alive when the wrong was done.) But in intersubjective settings, that absence of contrition is usually a deal breaker. Moreover, it would be odd, possibly improper, to apologize for something you did not do or forgive something you did not undergo. (Multiple published replies to *The Sunflower* insist that one cannot forgive Karl for what he did to others.) And while one usually distinguishes forgiving and forgetting, they sometimes blur. Consider, too, that when one forgives oneself, the process often lacks the mediating explicitness that usually constitutes forgiveness in two-person scenarios. Perhaps more so than Morton, then, I find anomalous features as well as complementarity across the forgiveness territory.

I also approach forgiveness as a territory because, unlike "bundle," which calls to mind strands requiring analysis, "territory" adds the need for orientation, which is what the analysis should provide. One wants to find one's way, and not simply as an observer. And to that end, I would like to recast "territory" and its locales as a stage upon which *scenes of forgiveness* play out. The shift is modest, but "territory" connotes land possessed by a political entity like a country or town, and I would rather not domesticate forgiveness in that manner. Not that different cultures or subcultures might not enact forgiveness differently, but forgiveness is not owned by any one group of enactors. Not only can it arise between them but, as with trust, finding our way through forgiveness is trickier than learning the ropes of convention. Because a stage (unlike a theater, say) is a figurative scene of enactment, it dislocates the forgiveness territory in helpful ways. Moreover, it reminds us that forgiveness arises in interactions that are dramatic in character—protagonist, antagonist, *mis en scéne*, deeds, resolution (or not).

YOU COULDN'T MAKE THIS STUFF UP

Jeffrie Murphy has argued that some wrongdoing must transpire for forgiveness to become an option (Murphy and Hampton 1988, 21). There need not be agreement that a wrong transpired, but unless the aggrieved believes they were wronged in a manner that would be broadly recognized, it would be infelicitous for them to forgive another. Suppose you give me a box of blood oranges as a New Year's gift. Oddly, and unbeknownst to you, I refuse to have oranges in my house. I explain my commitment and add, without irony, "I'll forgive you, this time." Annoying. And unwarranted. If you keep coming by with oranges, I might come to resent it. Barring a memory disorder, you are clearly trying to piss me off. But for forgiveness to be a legitimate response, a shared (or presumably shared) normative scene must be operative. (There are different ways to be "unforgiveable," therefore.) The parties not only meet in the deed but in the evaluation, which may be contested. Regarding forgiveness, intersubjectivity and normativity are equiprimordial.

SHOW ME WHERE IT HURTS

Resentment is a murky affair, even when we limit the term to reactive attitudes, which evaluate agents, in contrast to objectivating attitudes, which describe and predict the behavior of objects (Strawson 2008). What, precisely, grates when someone wrongs us or another? Not what does resentment feel like; rather, what prompts the grievance when we resent?

"The wrong." Indeed. But not very disclosive given different people conceptualize wrongs differently. Is the suffering caused by the wrong the issue, such that if it proves modest so does resentment? Or does everything lie with the intention? Suppose the deed in question was purely accidental, or due to negligence, or due to malice? Would each turn modulate our resentment? And does it matter who you are to me and who I am to you? Might I resent a stranger in one way, a colleague in another, and a friend in a third? Or is resentment a distinctly moral feeling that rises to contest the violation of norms such that the greater the violation the greater the resentment? Or do all bear upon resentment and thus figure in deliberations about whether to forgive?

One path through this muddle lies with wondering what might be relevant to one debating whether to forgive. If you were wronged, what would influence your deliberation about whether to forgive? The kind of wrong? The effect on you and others? Who it was that did you that way? Why they did it? Even how? I would consider all when entertaining forgiveness. You brazenly stole my bubble gum even though we were friends, and you know how I look forward to blowing bubbles after work. But you just wanted to piss me off, and you did. Gum thief! All would have a say in my say-so.

WELL PLAYED?

Scenes of forgiveness are normative in ways that exceed the wrongdoing that opens them. There are times when we regard people as hard-hearted due to their inability to forgive, or petty in the number and character of grievances that they observe and record. Moreover, one can not only ask, "Should I forgive?" but also consider how—say, quietly or demonstrably, publicly or privately—in a manner that slides into forgetting or that remembers. Histrionics make a farce of most things, including forgiveness.

And even in cases where one may not, should not, or simply cannot forgive, "What now?" remains. Scenes of forgiveness put us into question. We are accountable for our replies.

SHIT HAPPENS

Sometimes it is enough to forget, and not because we lack self-respect. Out of a certain fullness, the question doesn't arise.

NO HURT, NO FOUL

Following a wrong, forgiveness may not always be warranted. Someone might apologize for tripping and banging into me, but that is just being polite. If I were to reply, "I forgive you," "Get over yourself" would be a fair reply. But suppose someone hurriedly backs their car into mine. They were at fault, and they might apologize: "My bad." But suppose I reply, "I forgive you." That seems too much, whereas "Be more careful" does not. More precisely, it seems presumptuous in the sense of taking liberties, here with the act of forgiveness. (No doubt these are matters of degree, but such are the demands of ethical life.) I want to say something like, "The wrong-doing also has to hurt," by which I mean it must impact my self-relation in a manner that undermines my continuing relation with the culpable party. In other words, one only faces a decision to forgive if one suffers in a manner that negatively impacts the quality of one's relationship to a wrongdoer. That could include a careless driver, but it need not.

When a restaurant's valet ran a friend and me down, he was in the wrong. And we were injured. But if he had sought forgiveness, I would have found that strange. He did not mean to hurt me. Instead, he fucked up, broke a law, scuffed my head, and bruised my friend. It could have been worse, of course, and that might have made a difference. I genuinely do not know. Luckily, none of us needed to go there. It certainly would have made a difference, however, if he were targeting me (or people *like me*). That kind of attack would have hurt (and bewildered me), and it would have turned us from strangers into enemies, when in fact the accident had no qualitative impact upon our relationship. One day we ran into each other and then went our separate, grudgeless ways.

The role of "hurt" in forgiveness exposes a subjective loop in its inter-subjectivity, which helps me see why there are times when we may forgive but cannot. Forgiveness overcomes something subjective even as it rights a relationship out of joint. As Jean Hampton observes, forgiveness involves a change of heart (Murphy and Hampton 1988). Or forgiveness involves a second change of heart. The first is wrought by the wrongdoing, at least when it hurts.

SMOKE WITHOUT FIRE

Sometimes we hurt one another without doing wrong. A close friend starts dating, or simply meets another friend, and one feels slighted: "It's just not the same. And I miss how we were." To seize an economic opportunity, a couple agree to live and work at a distance for a year. It is stressful. One feels it more intensely and resents it: "It was too easy for you. Don't you miss me, miss us?"

When we hurt people we care about, we often apologize. But are we seeking forgiveness? In the cases sketched above, we could imagine a degree of inconsiderateness that proves blameworthy. But we could also imagine both scenarios without it. And those are the cases that interest me here. Someone feels hurt in a relationship, but no wrong has been done.

Interestingly, in these cases, apology and forgiveness part ways. When I hurt someone dear, I apologize. I am sorry for hurting them. If I could have avoided doing so, I would have, and so I look back with some regret. But should they forgive me, I'll pause and think, "That missed the mark—I didn't do anything wrong." I have readily apologized and sought to repair the relationship. But forgiveness should not enter the equation as I understand it.

WHERE IT HURTS

Not every relation is put out of joint by the same omissions and commissions. Imagine that someone is driving distractedly and jumps the curve, crushing a flower bed that I have been developing for a few years. I have had to amend the soil and find plants suitable for the resulting mixture, the climate, and the amount of sun the spot enjoys. Realizing what they have done, they might apologize profusely. That would make sense. And I might say, "It's OK, I can replant it," which passes for forgiveness in a limited encounter between strangers. Or I might not mean it in that way. I might just be diffusing the situation. The accident is irritating. Processing it only adds irritation. And that could make sense as well. Whether it hurts depends on how deeply I am invested in that patch of earth.

Are there limits, as far as forgiveness goes, on what should hurt? Return to my accident.

Because the valet broke the law, my friend and I were expected to attend his trial. The DA approached and asked whether we had sued the restaurant. "No," we replied. "We weren't really that injured. We'll settle those costs with the insurance company." A bit naive given the nature of adjustors, but so we stood, which changed the case in the DA's eyes. "I have a rather primitive theory of justice," he said. "If someone hurts you, they deserve to get hurt." I was irritated. The case seemed entirely impersonal, and the DA was trying to make it personal. He wanted to know what we expected as an outcome. "That's not our job," I replied. "You should determine how to punish reckless endangerment," which were the terms of the citation.

When I think about forgiveness, this scene captures some of my intuitions. Because the wrongdoing was not personal, the hurt modest, and the perpetrator a stranger, the resulting wrangle lay between the driver and the state; I was involved as a citizen of the latter. To me, a wrong becomes a candidate for forgiveness when it tears a relationship of interpersonal significance, and I incline toward forgiveness when I want to pop it back into joint.

But what makes something personal? Maybe this is just a symptom of my alienated relation to the state. Recalling Hegel, or a gloss of his *Philosophy of Right*, if someone harms a state that I regard as representative of me, then one harms me. And this makes sense. On January 6, 2021, supporters of then president Donald Trump stormed the Capitol to prevent Congress from certifying the results from the Electoral College, which would certify that Joe Biden would be the next president of the United States. The events of that day were infuriating in many ways. The orderly transition of power after legitimate elections is a cornerstone of the rule of law. The question, then, is how to respond to such violations. There are multiple options: blame, censure, warnings, punishment, etc. But what about forgiveness?

Imagine you are still at school (perhaps you are), and someone is teasing a friend. The antagonist is known to you but is neither a friend nor an acquaintance. All involved believe that the teaser is in the wrong. In fact, the teasing is cruel, and cruelty runs counter to your deepest commitments. Suppose another person intervenes and the teaser stops, is contrite, and apologizes to your friend. Should the teaser apologize to you as well? And would you be right to approach them and say, "I forgive you for being a jerk to George"? That seems misplaced, even if we render the scene epistemically secure. We rarely if ever forgive people for hurting others, even if the wrong violates our normative expectations. And wouldn't it be odder still if you forgave the bully for harming himself, presuming he, too, acknowledged prohibitions against cruelty? In the scene I have scripted, forgiveness seems reserved for George to bestow. You might be outraged on his behalf and intercede (and you should), but forgiveness is an act that moves between the wronged and the culpable.

DIFFERENT WRONGS, DIFFERENT RIGHTS

"You're begging the question!" I am if you insist that all advocates of an ethical order are among the wronged whenever that order is violated. I get it, and I don't regard that as crazy talk, particularly regarding *Recht*, "right" in the sense of positive law, whose extension is universal relative to some set of agents. That squares with certain usages of "wronged" that I am willing to endorse. But regarding forgiveness and when and where it comes into play, I do not want to lose the difference between (a) violations of my normative commitments and (b) wronging and hurting me as me, as someone who is not substitutable with another, even if our normative commitments are identical.

"I still think you're begging the question." To a degree, but I do so to resist framing the question in a manner that effaces the intimate, singular dimensions of ethical life, those in which no one can be substituted for another. Forgiveness, like trust and hope, course through that dimension. We lose sight of its character if we begin forgiving any kind of wrongdoing. My resistance to doing so is also normative in a first-order way. Forgiving X simply for violating our normative expectations seems to border on vice. It smacks of righteousness or moral peacocking and supplants genuine concern with histrionics, even with a sliver of sadism. And that transforms an act of repair into self-aggrandizement.

But the matter is genuinely slippery. If the bully in question is someone I have introduced to a group of friends, then he, representing me to a degree, wrongs me in hurting George. He misuses my name, as it were. But note, in this case, the hurt done to me is distinct from the hurt done to George, and if I forgive the bully for abusing my generosity, that is something other than forgiving him for violating my normative commitments.

"But might it be the case that violating the normative order is a distinct wrong, and one that might be distinctly forgiven?" It might. George might forgive the bully for the hurt and we might forgive the bully for violating our shared normative order. I do not think this is common, but if it became so, I would not be at a complete loss for words. There are times when someone is welcomed back into circulation from a deserved exile. Or, as Alice MacLachlan observes, people are sometimes censured for what they do to others—"I can't forgive her for how she treated Sally" (MacLachlan 2012, 118). But that change in view (or maintenance of censure) is not the change in heart that forgiveness paradigmatically entails. Reassessing someone's worthiness to be "one of us" is not the same as forgiving them for hurting us. I am happy to blame and punish the bully; I might even excoriate him. I also might become friends with him after I get to know him and the bullying ends. But I would limit "forgiveness" to cases when persons, in their singularity, in their irreplaceability, hurt one another and labor to resolve the fallout.

SCORCH MARKS

"Beneath contempt" is a contemptuous phrase, like mentioning that something is not worth mentioning. But it also bares an abrasion.

THOU SHALT NOT COMMAND

Requests for forgiveness strike me as modestly coercive. Having hurt another, one then asks for something? Such requests needn't be starkly selfish, although they sometimes are. Intent on resolving guilt, the culpable insists that the wronged absolve them. I discovered this in a roundabout manner. A friend had done me wrong. They abandoned me in a social situation where I was their guest, did not know anybody, and could not leave without them. I was on an island. After six hours, they found me and we departed. Fun times.

By the next day I had let it go. To be clear, it had hurt. But I knew that our friendship had plateaued, and romance was off the table, which I acknowledged by moving on and allowing us to drift into an amicable acquaintance, which we did. There also were mitigating circumstances, as there often are. Who has not been led astray by a flash of desire?

Unknownst to me, my equanimity intensified my friend's remorse, or so I was later told. But to the person's credit, they lived with it rather than provoke me into a reply that might alleviate their guilt. But others show less forbearance. Demanding forgiveness, they seek exoneration or a way to shift the blame if forgiveness is withheld.

In *The Sunflower*, the little life that Karl has left is consumed by guilt. He so wants Simon to take it away that his desperation renders him thoughtless, or oblivious to his thoughtlessness, and therefore all the less deserving of forgiveness even if Simon could forgive on behalf of others. But asking for forgiveness need not be so cynical. It can complement contrition by acknowledging the wrong done and the hurt caused, and by indicating a wish to refashion the relationship. (This is one way to understand begging for forgiveness.) And yet, those asking should keep in mind that, as with mercy, one may not compel another to forgive them. Forgiveness is never owed to another. Instead, it is a generous, life-expanding current that regenerates a *we* that has fissured, possibly foundered. Forgiveness doesn't reinstate relationality. We are stuck with that, at least in a certain sense. A relation persists in the hurt caused and felt, and it persists in the struggle to forgive or the refusal to do so. "I used to hang around with him" is still a way of relating, as is "Fuck him!" Moreover, being-in-common underwrites all our comings and goings. What forgiveness redresses is the character of a particular relationship: "It's OK, we're still friends. Shit happens." Or: "You hurt me, but I still love you." Or: "I'm over it. But if you do that again . . ." Like the incipiently ethical currents of trust, forgiveness imagines the parties on a course of mutual concern and perseveres. "You and me," it announces, "we're worth saving."

WAKING DREAM

I don't long for forgiveness, or even dream of it. What creeps up on me, makes me shudder, are the apologies I have yet to deliver. And looking back, this doubles what I now need to say. Until I die, I suspect I will rehearse for scenes that will never be shot.

BIBLICAL PROPORTIONS

It is difficult to think about forgiveness and not enter the orbit of Christian and Hebrew scripture, at least in the United States, which remains intensely Christian. Martha Nussbaum fronts *Anger and Forgiveness* with a reconstruction of what she terms a "Judeo-Christian worldview," which she contrasts, unfavorably, with lines of Greco-Roman thought (Nussbaum 2016). My focus on usages and their disseminating character and my distrust of the concept "worldview" leads me to (r)essay the topic without such a backdrop. Worldview reconstructions are broad to the point of distraction, even when addressing those who purportedly enact them.

In Nussbaum's text, at least at points, she presents forgiveness as sublimated anger: keeping score in a moral status game, forgiveness exacts retribution through a shaming demand for contrition. (This would be another way in which a kind of sadism slips into a forgiveness scene.) Forgiveness can certainly function this way. Murphy suggests that forgiveness restores what he terms "moral equality," which requires a blame ledger (Murphy and Hampton 1988, 22). And one can say, "I forgive you" in a way that suggests, "You owe me."

Such an account is narrow. Not that a historical reconstruction of forgiveness necessarily leads here, but such histories, particularly when brief, center patterns of thought at the expense of variations and anomalies. Forgiveness remains an issue for many who do not respond to wrongdoing with anger and a wish for retaliation. A hurtful withdrawal is also possible, and that opens another jumble that forgiveness might resolve, and in a manner that does not demand self-abasement. (Of course, if you feel that any acknowledgment of wrongdoing renders you abject, well, Jesus, get over yourself.) Moral condemnation is another possible response to wrongdoing, and that need not be fired by righteous indignation or lead to retaliation. One might simply be done with the culpable. Or, inversely, one may struggle to find forgiveness in one's heart precisely because one desires a way forward despite the wrong done, in which case forgiveness has richer goals in mind than keeping score and restoring some abstract state of moral equality. It culminates in finding a future together beyond the wrong and the hurt. Nussbaum has similar goals but sets them outside forgiveness, which strikes me as forced—in part by design, in part by her historical portraits.

A way to avoid the drift of these generalizations, even when they are generally accurate, and even when they square with certain paradigmatic examples, is to continually return to usages, and with a feel for their divergences. Reflecting on reading Celan, Derrida has said, "I try therefore to make myself listen for something that I cannot hear or understand, attentive to marking the limits of my reading in my reading" (Derrida 2005, 166). A similar sensibility orients me toward scenes of forgiveness (as well as hope and trust). But I do not stress the plural merely to unseat the centrality of ordinary senses or historical tendencies. A (r)essay experiments with what usage conducts, and that requires a feel for roads that do not lead to Rome.

ORIGINLESS STORIES

"Does cavorting with usages render the essayist ahistorical?" It could. But it also could mark the essay as a distinct way of being historical.

"Good, because 'love your enemies' seems to obligate us to forgive wrongdoers, which you deny is possible." Not quite—or rather, not yet. My claim was that the wrongdoer cannot legitimately demand forgiveness from the wronged, which a divine command does not contradict. But I see the point and recognize the usage, which underwrites a common scene of forgiveness defended by Martin Luther King Jr.

Several moments in Christian scripture imply something like a duty to forgive. Matthew 5:44 instructs us to love our enemies, and that might entail forgiving them when they wrong us. King reads the passage in this manner, inferring from the command to love a duty to forgive (King 1963, 44). Luke 6:27 also proclaims, "Love your enemies, do good to those who hate you, bless those who curse you, pray for those who abuse you." (May and Metzger 1962, 1251). And even though forgiveness is not mentioned, it again may fall under loving and doing good (although that leaves untouched cases where the wrongdoer is someone that is not an enemy and does not hate us). John 15:12 commands people to "love one another as I have loved you," which seems to suggest that if God can forgive mortals, mortals should forgive mortals, which is precisely what Paul infers at Colossians 3:13. After listing various virtues such as patience and meekness, he advocates "forbearing one another, and if one has a complaint against another, forgiving each other; as the Lord has forgiven you, so you must forgive" (May and Metzger, 1430). And the first letter of John underscores that Jesus "is the expiation for our sins" (2:2), adding, "Your sins are forgiven for his sake" (2:12), which echoes the premise in Paul's inference (May and Metzger, 1485).

This is a complex scene of usages, and in translation no less—or rather, translations, as Kevin Corrigan has helped me appreciate. Colossians involves the Greek *charizomai*, connoting general graciousness or favor toward another, whereas John's epistle uses *aphiemi*, which indicates that a punishment has been waived, or a debt erased. Also, the central imperative occurs as an inference: if the incarnation and eventual crucifixion of Jesus is an act of forgiveness, mortals should forgive those who trespass against us. But the details complicate matters. Jesus supposedly suffered on our behalf, thereby redeeming us, which seems more like paying a debt, and we usually do not forgive those who wrong us by suffering further on their behalf. It is not clear, therefore, that the love of God, through Jesus, exemplifies forgiveness in any paradigmatic sense. The authority of these lines also derives from a presumably sacred origin. As the latter fades, so does the former. I thus do not take these sayings to evidence any obligation to forgive those who wrong me. Without the illocutionary authority to secure their grammar—namely, the command—such lines are, at best, prudential maxims to be deployed with care, much as the faithful have done with *Thou shall not kill*.

Theism isn't all that bothers me here. Forgiveness comes into play when some *you* has or have wronged and hurt some *me* and so some *we* is out of joint. Forgiveness is directed to the wrongdoer, but not in some general sense—say, qua fellow citizen or a friend or sibling. Forgiveness concerns you and me. Upon its stage, we meet in our nonsubstitutability. To the degree forgiveness entails a change of heart, no one can undergo that change for another. Neither is anyone authorized to forgive another for someone if the wronged party is unwilling to forgive. (I can ask another to inform someone that I have forgiven them, but no one can forgive another for me.) In two senses, then, forgiveness is up to the wronged, and the moment of its consideration is a singular one.

To be clear, the possibilities circulating in scenes of forgiveness are not ones of pure immediacy. As I have argued elsewhere, self-experience and the responses it requires are synchronically and diachronically positioned, and that influences how wrongs and hurts transpire (Lysaker 2017). A lie from a stranger feels different than deception from a friend, and the betrayal of a lover has a particular sting. If a longtime friend becomes cranky and suspicious, we feel it one way whereas we typically grant new colleagues far less leeway. But in each case, those positions cannot decide for us whether forgiveness is warranted. Whatever scripts they entail fall short of determining such matters.

Return to "Forgive your enemies," taking it as a categorical imperative. Divine commands render us substitutable as children or creations of God, much like the rule of law renders us substitutable qua citizen. And on those stages, the culpable's singular relation with the wronged fades behind their standing relative to the divine and divine *Recht*. Immanent to such orders, we look away from one another and toward some class to which we presumably belong. And this is true of duties in general, which govern classes of persons regarding classes of actions. "Honor your father and mother" applies to children in relation to their parents, if under a narrow rendering. It announces that one is obligated to respectfully acknowledge, particularly in one's manner, who gave one life, which requires that one not treat them shabbily, say by belittling, denigrating, or humiliating them. But when wondering whether to forgive, one confronts, in one's singularity, a singular relation with another in their singularity, which the categorical logic of duties eclipses. That is the crux of the matter. Whether you forgive is up to you.

CAN, MAY, SHOULD

I have been circling the questions "Can I forgive?" "May I forgive?" and "Should I forgive?" The first individuates us psychologically—or better said, existentially; it concerns the kind of person we are. I cannot think for you, persevere for you, hope for you, or forgive for you. Forgiveness entails, in part, a change of heart, and no one can do that for us, although they might help or hinder us along the way. The trials of forgiveness thus disclose our bearing.

Regarding whether one may forgive another, certain conditions have emerged. One must have been wronged, the wrong must have hurt, and one may not forgive someone for what they have done to others. That kind of arrogation slides into arrogance born of confusion. Karl's request exposes a kind of moral immaturity that is negatively instructive for those who have done wrong, and it compromises his repentance by rendering his victims substitutable, even in death, and under the category of "a Jew" no less (thus deploying the same category used to round them up in the first place, and in the same equivocal, reifying manner).

What orients us, however, regarding the question "Should one forgive?" I have argued that we do not stand under any general obligation to forgive those who wrong us. Such an obligation renders us substitutable, and the scene of a hurtfully wronged and hurtful wrongdoer is a singular one. "Does this mean the question 'Should I forgive?' is wholly misplaced?" No. But the line of thought I am pursuing does free the "should" from any ethical or moral discourse that purports to bind the question to categorical obligations that render us substitutable. The wronged always have some discretion in deciding whether to forgive. That said, I might forgive another to preserve a friendship, in which case one might entertain a hypothetical imperative while wondering whether to forgive. Or, looking at one's life more broadly, one might think that forgiving is praiseworthy, and so aspire to forgive others when possible. The question "Should I forgive?" makes sense.

But let me pause even before the notion of a hypothetical imperative. I might want to preserve my friendship but still consider a betrayal unforgivable and so not forgive. But I am not withholding forgiveness because I no longer want to be friends or consider it a good, or because the person in question has proven to be false relative to friendship as I understand it. Rather, it is as if the wrong broke the friendship and I am at a loss about how to repair it. But that makes the issue sound too psychological, whereas my unhappiness is grammatical—the imperative is not hypothetical enough to capture what we go through when we consider forgiving another who has wronged and thereby hurt us. A hypothetical imperative resolves deliberation by providing us with a stable end we wish to realize—here, friendship. And no doubt there are times when one can resolve scenarios with just that kind of reasoning. But I also think that wrongdoing and the hurt it affects can raise questions that force us to rethink the ends we thought we knew. We find ourselves wondering, "Could I be friends with a person like that?" And over the course of a reply, our sense of friendship, what it entails and demands, might change, even if we decide that we cannot. The command structure of the hypothetical imperative presumes more stability than forgiveness scenes allot. By individuating a relationship, the question of who we might yet be reopens, sometimes radically.

WWJD

My position is proximate to Myisha Cherry's position in "Forgiveness, Exemplars, and the Oppressed." She claims that "we should be careful how and why we employ exemplars in our forgiveness arguments" (Norlock 2017). Cherry's concern is coercion through appeals to purportedly exemplary forgivers such as MLK, Mandela, and Jesus of Nazareth, the latter divorced from any presumed divinity (although that skews the usage). She thinks such appeals implicitly advocate for an "uncritical and irrational respect for authority." More tellingly, they risk metaethical confusion, mistaking the application of a moral reason for the moral reason itself. "Our respect for moral exemplars," she writes, "is not an uncritical admiration; rather, it is a respect for the moral law that the exemplars represent" (Norlock, 60). She thus insists that "we do not emulate the person per se, but rather the ideal of reason that the person represents and makes visible to us" (Norlock, 62).

What a difference two sentences make. I am inclined to agree with the latter suggestion that an exemplar represents an ideal that may orient us as we deliberate whether to forgive. Examples are bound to ideality—that is what allows them to apply to cases beyond their own occurrence. Unlike mere instances, they also mark the gap that their application must travel. To orient oneself through exemplarity opens the question, How alike are these situations? As with legal precedent, that question must be (and is, if only implicitly) answered anew every time, as Derrida has shown (Cornell et al. 1992, 3–67). And yet, I do not think forgiveness is answerable to moral laws, so something else must be in play when we take someone as a forgiveness exemplar. Profound examples often reorient our moral imaginations regarding who we might be, who we should be. They not only inspire but generate new ethical possibilities. (Take this to be the ethical version of existence preceding essence.) But that does not institute the kind of moral authoritarianism that Cherry rightly resists. If anything, the ordinary origins of exemplarity (as opposed to the a priori grounding that Cherry's essay occasionally invokes) clarifies that we need to determine whether someone's example applies in our case, and to what degree. And that may be something we surmise after the fact.

KEEPING IT FRESH

Charles Griswold opens *Forgiveness: A Philosophical Exploration* by demonstrating how classical perfectionism fails to register the importance of forgiveness in a well-lived life. Weaving a portrait from Plato, Aristotle, and various Stoics, he argues that a perfected human would neither err (and so stand in need of forgiveness) nor resent. As self-sufficient, even invulnerable to harm, the consummate perfectionist would be free from that which forgiveness overcomes (Griswold 2007, 8–13).

It does seem odd that forgiveness is not among the classical, non-Christian virtues. Virtues mark sites where life can go terribly wrong (when driven by fear, greed, intemperate desire, or lust for power). Resentment (even more so, revenge) seems such a site—something every sage would know if they recalled the crooked path that led to their apotheosis. Moreover, we change, and the world changes as well, and so a present-day saint is a latter-day bore, or worse. Third, we need others for support, love, and recognition, and that leaves us vulnerable to disappointment, anger, and hurt.

As Griswold sees it, perfectionists fail to register that everyone has moral standing and so deserves the kind of respect we show when we apologize, seek forgiveness, or see others in a fuller light and forgive them (Griswold, 9). But given that the sage does not err, that cannot be the sticking point. Rather, as Griswold also observes, the glorification of self-sufficiency favors conduct that frees itself from worldly dependencies through proper allegiance to the true, good, and beautiful (Griswold, 11). But that is flight from life, and those seeking it are not exemplars of what human beings aspire to, ethically speaking.

Perfectionism, however, is not limited to a set of authors working in and around the Mediterranean in the centuries before and just after the emergence of the Common Era. By the nineteenth century, and in resistance to the Enlightenment's presumptions of transparency, various Romantics (Emerson and Nietzsche, for example), often in dialogue with classical Asian texts, renewed the thought that one's life is a project built around an accountability that must acknowledge finitude: we err, never know enough (are even opaque to ourselves), have limited power, fall short of our hopes, and wish poorly, together and alone. Moreover, perfectionism has morphed into an experimental, even improvisational, approach to its own unfolding (say, in Cavell and Glaude), which enables it to not only transform through time but also contest distorting inheritances that unnecessarily limit our possibilities. In place of the wizened sage, Emerson valorizes youthfulness for its energy, rebellion, and creativity, all of which are compatible, even valuable, in scenes of forgiveness.

GET OVER YOURSELF

Apology, when honest, can be a line of self-overcoming. Forgiveness, when bold overcomes what transpired, refuses to be undone by it. It stares less into the abyss than into another, poised for adventure.

DREAM #9

Sorry's not the hardest word.

IT IS IMPOSSIBLE TO STEP INTO THE SAME RIVER ONCE

Forgiveness individuates us within normatively inflected, intersubjective currents. Rich in subjective eddies, the possibility of forgiveness discloses a relationship whose character hangs in the balance. And forgiveness emerges, if it does, by finding its own way. Not unlike hope and trust, it is, in part, unscripted. Not free of scripts. But not wholly overwritten either. Forgiveness is thus "voluntarist" in the sense that its whether-to and how exceeds prescription and convention. In a sense, it is up to you whether to forgive the one who has wronged and hurt you, and it is on you to figure how in either case. But in another sense, forgiveness is not voluntary—"I just couldn't find it in me to forgive him." Seeking to forgive, desiring to forgive, reflection can be pushed to an outside looking in, and in vain.

Forgiveness can be difficult because it is a manifold affair. At least three dimensions are operative: (a) a self-relation mediated by the wrong and the hurt it caused—"How could you!"; (b) a relation to the culpable as someone capable of wronging and hurting one—"I thought I knew you . . ."; and (c) an evolving feel for one's relation with the culpable and their possible futures—"I'm so over it." And note that the wrong can aggrieve in more than one way, which turns each dimension into a small house: what was done with what effects, how it was done, by whom and why. Moreover, forgiveness has a dynamic character. It often unfolds in degrees, as "too soon" indicates. And such movement is far from linear: "I thought we were past this?" "Well, I'm not!" A forgiveness scene marks a transition in which an out-of-joint relation is resolved, possibly renewed, or it stalls, maybe falls apart.

Importantly, these dimensions are irreducible, and each may resolve, if it does, asynchronously. Being hurt discloses our dependence, and that may prompt feelings of anger or shame, or just hurt. "How could I be so stupid?" as if someone fell for something that exposes them—say, their need or willingness to trust. And those feelings may linger, even reanimate with the thought of forgiveness: "Part of me wants to forgive her, but every time I think of her it's like it just happened." But the character of the culpable is also disclosed by a wrongdoing. Even as the hurt softens, we may see them in a new light: "It just became clear how little he thought of me." Or: "I realized he acted out of fear, and, oddly, I now know him better." And no doubt this process varies with the character of the relationship—lover, friend, parent, sibling, colleague, neighbor, fellow citizen, public official, etc.—as well as other social variables such as race, gender, and sexuality: "When I realized that he only ignores women, I decided we couldn't be friends." Not that forgiveness is merely retrospective or locked in a tussle with strong affects. It enacts a turn toward a future no longer eclipsed by hurtful wrong. And that suggests that forgiveness involves imagining a future with the culpable and gauging its worth. Certain friendships may seem so valuable that we are willing to endure the hurt and work it through: "If anyone else has said that to me . . ." Or, inversely: "What does he do to people who aren't his friends?"

BRINGING ALL OF HELL WITH ME

While forgiveness addresses a relation out of joint, it is an intrapersonal as well as an interpersonal affair. In fact, a good deal of the literature focuses on difficulties working through anger, resentment, and hurt and whatever retributive energies they initiate. While this focus obscures larger stakes, one cannot have an intersubjective disruption without it reverberating through the subjectivities involved.

What, precisely, is forsworn when we forswear revenge? It cannot be retribution per se. Most think forgiveness is compatible with punishment. Moreover, bypassing a prescribed and deserved punishment is more a matter of mercy than forgiveness, although theological traditions such as Christianity and Islam blur the issue (Abu-Nimer and Nasser 2013). Revenge must be something outside retribution, therefore, and the normative orders that prescribe it.

Suppose you kill my child. I then dedicate myself to your ruin. No measure guides me as I aim to lay waste to all you love. Nussbaum argues that the Furies depicted in the Athens of the fifth century BCE convey this well, conjuring an image of "unbridled anger" that is "obsessive, destructive, existing only to inflict pain and ill" (Nussbaum 2016, 2). I think that is right as far as it goes, but what, then, is the point of revenge? How does it function in one's self-relation? As Nussbaum reads the Furies, this is difficult to assess; "in its zeal for blood it is inhuman, doglike" (Nussbaum, 2). But setting it outside the human makes revenge appear as an immediate reaction to some trigger, and that obscures its intrapersonal logic.

One way to read revenge is to work back toward it from forgiveness and retribution, treating it as something like measureless retribution, payback beyond recounting, which seems all too human. Retribution organizes one's response with a measure, even if it is an eye for an eye. The wrongdoer becomes a perpetrator, the action a crime, and one's response retributive. Or, if a forgiveness scene opens, the wrongdoer becomes some-one more than their deed, someone with whom a future still beckons. Will it be defined by the wrong or evolve into something else? Can I see you and relate to you as someone more than the one who did me wrong? Revenge bypasses these deliberations. The loss might feel measureless, leaving one with only fury. Or maybe the wrong seems a simple exercise of power and so one returns the favor, but without the kind of measured distinctions that designate crimes and punishments, or that localize and contextualize wrongdoings and the scope of their effects.

In the company of measured retribution, revenge seems immature, even simple. And that, in turn, frames forgiveness as something quite differ-ent, something like a different kind of ethical subjectivity altogether, one more deliberate and imaginative. To use language employed by Victoria McGeer, even when it is withheld, forgiveness operates within a "negotiable space" that revenge does not enter (McGeer 2009). When the possibility of forgiveness arises, when we enter a scene of forgiveness, we ask questions that revenge refuses. Who can we be, who should we be, given what has happened? Arendt is right, therefore, to claim that forgiveness "does not merely re-act but acts anew" and so accomplishes a "freedom from ven-geance, which incloses both doer and sufferer in the relentless automatism of the action process, which by itself need never come to an end" (Arendt 1958, 241). But she is wrong, I think, to claim that forgiveness is thereby "unconditioned by the act which provoked it" (Arendt, 241). Forgiveness is often so difficult because wrongs cut deep. Also, the particulars of the wrong should not be ignored. A scene of forgiveness frees itself from re-venge, but only to appraise the wrong more appropriately.

A PAPER CUT SMILE

Revenge assumes many forms. Not all are apocalyptic. Sometimes vindic-tiveness results, say, through the exercise of bureaucratic power, whose harms are slow leaks. I imagine you have been told, "You do not want to piss him off." But while the paybacks are modest in comparison, the structure is the same. The presumed wrong initiates a payback scheme that precludes a more deliberate review and resolution of the relationship and why it went sideways.

WHAT SETS US OFF

Many believe that forgiveness forswears "resentment," taking that term to name all the ways in which we register wrongs done to us. That's a bit broad. Feeling hurt seems different than being angered or resenting. As Roberts suggests, anger or outrage is more intense (Roberts 1995). But I can accept it as a term of art, and I prefer it to anger.

Managing anger is its own task. Nussbaum's negative assessment of forgiveness focuses on anger. But anger can arise in cases where forgiveness makes little sense. According to Nussbaum, anger is almost always a response to a perceived wrong, but she casts that as "injury to something seen as important," including but not limited to status injuries (Nussbaum 2016, 20–21). But when I accidentally raise my head and catch the corner of a cupboard, I feel intense rage without having been wronged. And suppose a supply chain snarl delays the publication of an article that is, in the meantime, scooped. That would piss me off, but I would never claim to be wronged and so would never entertain thoughts of forgiveness. Also, many overly concerned with status are angered by the success of others without having been wronged. It strikes me that anger has too many modalities to designate what forgiveness tries to resolve.

Everyone notes that one can lose one's resentment, anger, or hurt and still not forgive another. I might let it go, ignore it until it fades, or fall into dementia. Resentment vanishes, but forgiveness never occurs. This suggests that forgiveness does not simply remove something (or attenuate its force); it is also generative. "Forgiveness is a catalyst creating a new atmosphere necessary for a fresh start and new beginning," King proposes (King 1963, 45). I agree given the performativity of forgiveness, which has illocutionary as well as perlocutionary force. Forgive another and your relationship changes. Or don't. It still changes. I agree with Kathryn Norlock's claim that "forgiveness is a negotiation of the relationship itself" (Norlock 2009, 103).

The transformational character of forgiveness makes it even more important to distinguish forgiveness from anger management, contra Boleyn-Fitzgerald (Boleyn-Fitzgerald 2002). Forgiveness repairs an interpersonal relationship, whereas anger management is only intrasubjective, a matter of self-control. Not that these dimensions are unrelated, but I can manage my anger and leave you out of the picture.

WAVE OR PARTICLE?

As Margaret Urban Walker notes, one can forgive even while working through the resentment and the hurt involved (Walker 2006). You have forgiven my insensitivity, but the thought of it lingers; you may even come to see me as somewhat self-absorbed, which I can be. From the standpoint of the receiver, forgiveness often seems like an act: "I forgive you." But within our self-relation, forgiveness, like grief, is usually nonlinear, tacking in the wind.

THE PROSECUTION RESTS

Walker casts forswearing resentment as a *"commitment to reject* backsliding into recrimination, anger, or mistrust, even if one cannot completely control these emotions," a position echoed in Griswold (Walker 2006, 157; Griswold 2007, 42). I like this because it acknowledges that working through resentment takes time and forgiveness regards another through a change in oneself. But something more than a commitment is required—one must come through. The issue isn't just unruly emotions, as the language of recrimination makes plain. Forgiveness culminates in conduct, in how I relate to those who have wronged me. I thus reject the idea that someone can forgive another but still terminate their friendship. That locks forgiveness within the heart, whereas it moves between us, preserves us.

A LITTLE BIT SOFTER NOW, A LITTLE BIT SOFTER NOW

Forgiveness attenuates the intensity of the wrong and the hurt it causes such that they do not center our regard for another. "Forgiveness" says: that is no longer definitive of who we are because it is no longer at the heart of my regard for you. I know you are more than that, better than that, or that mitigating circumstances apply. And when and where it still burns, I will act as if it didn't.

Importantly, forgiveness does not require forgetting. The issue concerns how a memory functions in one's regard for another, not whether one remembers. King is again on point. "Certainly one can never forget," he writes, "if that means erasing it totally from his mind. But when we forgive, we forget in the sense that the evil deed is no longer a mental block impeding a new relationship" (King 1963, 45). In fact, for a relationship to mature through forgiveness, both parties should remember the wrong that threw them out of joint and how they worked through it. (If the wrong fades into oblivion, so will the growth required to navigate it.) This is particularly important in a perfectionist context, which sets the course of a life along a learning curve. Again, forgiveness does not simply forswear revenge or even resentment; it absorbs those dispositions into a different bearing toward ourselves and the ones who wrong us. "I learned to be less sensitive." "We all fuck up every now and then." "Seeing the demons that plague her made me love her more."

FINDING YOUR FOOTING

Nussbaum presents anger as a disposition to seek the "pain of the offender *because of and as a way of assuaging or compensating for* one's own pain" (Nussbaum 2016, 24). What forgiveness attenuates is not just a desire to return the pain (if that even flares) but an unwillingness to go on with someone because of who they have proved to be. When forgiveness comes to fruition, the wronged resolve into something like a state of balance or equilibrium, a term that Walker uses: "Equilibrium means freedom *from* a sense of threat to one's standards, to one's well-being, and *to* that control of the future that comes from being able to move through a world with reasonable confidence in others meeting my normative expectations and my being capable of meeting theirs" (Walker 2006, 165; emphasis added). I find this persuasive in that forgiveness results in a refound balance, even ease—Walker's freedom from and freedom to. But she overstates things, I think, when she grounds this balance in the sense that one's standards are back in force, although everything hinges on what constitutes a "reasonable expectation." I would rather stress that forgiveness entails a willingness to have another go at being a *we*, which includes risk and maybe even a period of unsettled standards. If trust initiates a *we*, forgiveness renews it.

But my position is close to Walker's, who also sees forgiveness as an address to the wider community about one's normative expectations. It signals censure and, I would add, exemplifies one's character. But, and this is more a matter of emphasis than a disagreement, it also announces a commitment to being with another in our finitude. Forgiveness is prospective and retrospective, the former having the character of an invitation. "I forgive you" also says, "Come with me." And we are never sure what that will bring. Yes, we do not forgive (or should not) when we believe that someone remains an unambiguous threat. But we do forgive even when we are unsure how well our normative expectations converge. Forgiveness renews a work in progress.

ECCE HOMO

We are fragile, dependent beings, each perch a limit. Hope affirms our lot in its weakness and ignorance. Trust affirms shared vulnerability. Forgiveness finds new life in failure. Here we flower as no rose ever could.

STUCK IN MY CRAW

There are times when we want to forgive but cannot. The hurt remains raw, anger seethes, or we simply cannot see a future with the wrongdoer, at least not like the one we had. We would like to get over it, but we can't. The positionality of the agents is vital in such matters, and a reason not to set one's analysis of forgiveness among strangers. Who you were to me, the solidarity I presumed among us bears upon the knot that must be unraveled. "I expect more from other women," a student told me. I would certainly feel the snub of a friend more than the ghosting glance of an acquaintance. Children and parents have their own snarls to disentangle.

A kind of moral luck also runs through scenes of forgiveness. Sometimes carelessness comes to nothing or is barely visible whereas the same oversight or hastiness can prove catastrophic. Suppose you pick me up for dinner with a trunk full of drugs and nothing happens. But if we end up pulled over and I face drug charges, a trial, and prison time, a scene of forgiveness will open and challenge us. Even if I get off, I might never get past "You almost ruined my life."

THROUGH NOT 'ROUND

Resolving resentment, most everyone notes, recognizes that the wrongdoer is more than their deed, more than a "wrongdoer." One needs that "more" to go on together. But that can be precluded by intrapsychic forces, particularly if the wrong also brings about a sense of shame. In fact, a wrong may institute a kind of melancholia, a wound that reopens whenever we see or recall the wrongdoer. This means, I think, that forgiveness may require mourning. Wrongs are disclosive. We may need to let go of whoever we thought the wrongdoer was. I imagine many need to do this when forgiving their parents for hypocrisy or narcissism. But we also might need to mourn the loss of a self-conception. A deep hurt may call into question our sense of independence, and that may, in turn, require us to grow into our neediness. Or the issue may be the relation itself: "I thought we had this fairy tale marriage, but I was wrong. And I needed to see not only how that was OK, but how to embrace it, to live without that fantasy."

LUBRICANTS

What upset us? What do we really want? Are we ashamed as well as hurt? Forgiveness requires honest questions and honest answers. Hampton suggests that resentment often reflects the sense that we might deserve to be treated in this manner (Murphy and Hampton 1988). That seems a less prevalent phenomenon in my experience, although that may speak to how it is gendered. But Hampton's claim resonates regardless, particularly when the deed is public. And that is just the kind of intrapsychic baggage one often needs to work through when wondering whether to forgive or what to convey to another when imagining renewing one's relation with them, whether friend, intimate, colleague, neighbor, etc.

Humility also seems essential to finding forgiveness in our hearts. "I also am other than what I imagine myself to be," Simone Weil writes in *Gravity and Grace*. "To know this is forgiveness" (cited in Murphy and Hampton, 91). But that says too much given my failings may be quite different from those of my adversary. Also, one need not presume one's own perfection to withhold forgiveness. Someone in oppressed straights isn't required to forgive those who remain steadfastly clueless and careless about their privilege.

EXPECT THE UNEXPECTED

I have been singularizing forgiveness to underscore its challenges and possibilities. But one can be forgiving in a dispositional manner. Not that one never resents or hurts. Just as courage needs to know and undergo fear, forgiveness feels the wrong. But the forgiving among us keep their eye on the prize, which is the relation thereby put out of joint. Strong feelings of hurt or anger are contrasted with and contested by other feelings of affection and admiration, even pleasure in the company of that other. The imagination assembles futures undone and others reworked. They are patient as well, with themselves and whoever misspoke or misstepped. And they are generous in their interpretations of who the wrongdoer is, why the deed was done, and who the wrongdoer might still be.

And yet, so many variables seem relevant—who, what, with what effect, how, and why. Moreover, wrongdoings that wound come as something of a surprise. In this, they are quite unlike many dangers that call for courage. A wrong also establishes a kind of intimacy that rises like fresh terrain, and that, oddly, is also a site of possibility. Wrongdoings and the hurt they cause break through presumptions and worn-down habits, and with some patience, generosity, and luck, they allow the parties to ask: Is this who we want to be, and if not, who do we want to be? The prospective dimensions of forgiveness call for a spontaneity missing in the inertia of habitual currents. Said otherwise, a certain kind of forgiveness may be unduly conservative. This is not to say a virtuous character is not dispositionally forgiving. But that often sounds a good deal easier to manage than I have found it, particularly among those willing to be vulnerable and hold others accountable.

BARE BONES

A basic structure asserts itself in knowledge claims: appearance and reality. Would-be knowers live in a movement between the two, testing instances of the former in the hopes of establishing working touch with the latter. Forgiveness has its own scaffold—what, in a Christian idiom, we might term sin and sinner, riffing on Augustine and echoing Gandhi, as both Murphy and Griswold have observed (Murphy and Hampton 1988, 24; Griswold 2007, 54). I can forgive you only if you are or have the potential to be (or I have enough hope you'll be) more than that wrong. "When we look beneath the surface," writes King, "beneath the impulsive evil deed, we see within our enemy-neighbor a measure of goodness and know that the viciousness and evilness of his acts are not quite representative of all that he is. We see him in a new light" (King 1963, 45). In forgiveness, I distinguish you from your wrong, reaching out toward the former, negating the latter (which is not the same as erasing it).

How does one find that difference, and when is one warranted to act upon it? Unlike King, I cannot forgive another because God loves them (King, 46). I do not believe in God, and even if I did, God and I are not substitutable. (Also, it is easier to forgive when, as the Alpha and Omega, you know the whole story.) I also resist the idea that forgiveness is made easier when we recognize the "humanity" of the wrongdoer, a position supported by Griswold (Griswold 2007, 79). Presumably that was true before the deed was done. One might see something inhuman in wrongdoing, particularly in terrible deeds, but it is their humanity and the responsibility that comes with it that grounds resentment. Third, "humanity" also applies to many who have not wronged me, so it does not show me something particular about the wrongdoer that I can ride into the future. The question remains: What might orient our future together, you and me, whatever its character?

TWO-WAY STREET

Even as we struggle to manage feelings of hurt and anger, we consider reasons in scenes of forgiveness. They range across the kinds of questions wrongdoing poses concerning, to rely on Alice MacLachlan's list: "the extent of the harm, the wrongdoer's intentions, the victim's ongoing suffering, the suffering of other parties involved, the preexisting relationship between victim and wrongdoer, the wrongdoer's subsequent behavior, and the victim's broader moral commitments" (MacLachlan 2012, 117). Deliberating about whether to forgive, I need a working feel for the deed that initiated my resentment. Malice aforethought is difficult to overcome, as is prolonged negligence. And when the harm is severe, that tightens the knot that must be untied.

Another hand involves how the perpetrator behaves in the wake of having wronged me. Forgiveness is an interpersonal and intrapsychic process, which is why it behooves us to be patient when our ire is up. It is essential for the perpetrator to acknowledge their wrongdoing, which entails, I think, regret and a commitment not to do it again. (If I acknowledge a wrong but then say, "And I'd do it again," I take back the evaluation, as I would if I said, "Yes, that was wrong," but showed zero remorse.) Because I think that proving contrite is a single act or gesture, I resist marking it as four distinct conditions, as Griswold does, although I see the analytical benefit of doing so (Griswold 2007, 49–51). Still, someone seeking distinct acknowledgment of all four points would strike me as punishing the wrongdoer in a moralizing manner, thus falling into the kind of payback scenario that Nussbaum believes underlies many scenes of forgiveness. But there needn't be anything demeaning in expecting another to acknowledge their wrongdoing; in fact, it conveys that one already believes the perpetrator is more than the kind of person who does such things. Moreover, charges of wrongdoing are contestable. Working toward a mutual, moral understanding of what transpired allows for disagreements to be aired and settled, at least potentially. Finally, if one simply moves toward reconciliation without seeking acknowledgment, it will be impossible for anyone to determine, including the wronged party, whether one forgave or condoned the act, a distinction integral to forgiveness.

Manners are essential in such matters, and on both sides of the exchange. The set of one's jaw, the look in one's eyes, the tone of one's voice all inform others about our bearing toward them. So, too, does the number of times one addresses (or avoids) the issue. I have certainly been overpressed to account for failings, which has generated its own resentments. "I don't know how many times or how many ways I can apologize," we sometimes say, which amounts to: you have what you need from me to decide how you want to go forward.

KNOWING THOMAS

The interpersonal nature of forgiveness requires that parties meet on interpersonal terms. The issue at hand is not simply acknowledging a wrong but grasping the hurt thereby caused. This is particularly salient in friendships, where the wrongdoing may be modest but symbolically large, calling into question the depth of the friendship. Demonstrating that one grasps the hurt as well as the wrong reminds the wronged that one still has a good feel for their welfare. And if one cannot fathom that side of things, the only possible future seems an attenuated one.

For slightly different reasons, Griswold also insists that one convey to the aggrieved that one understands the wrong from their side of things, and he adds that perpetrators should also account for their actions (Griswold 2007, 51). "Why did you do that?" The request is reasonable. I would want to know whether my antagonist intended to hurt me. But there are limits here. It isn't only teenagers who find themselves at a loss to answer the question "What were you thinking?" The most common (or honest) reply, I think, is, "I wasn't." Thoughtlessness, carelessness, and, so, negligence lies at the root of many wrongs.

But even when there are other causes, explanations will often die out. Say you pursue an opportunity you know I also would want but do not tell me about it. You get it, and I think, "What a jerk. You could have at least given me a shot," particularly if more than one person could have taken advantage of it. "I was just being selfish," you reply. But that doesn't really explain much. It may only say: in this case, you favored yourself over me. But it can still give me enough with which to work: "That could have gone better, but I'm just going to be happy for you. It's a sweet job. Let's celebrate. You buy." Or I may conclude, "I'm done with your 'looking out for number one' approach." But to conclude this, I will need to set the deed in context. Was it an anomaly? How unique and limited was the opportunity? Distinguishing the sin from the sinner allows us to get a beat on what the future will be like.

MAÑANA

As it resolves, forgiveness conceives.

ABOVE AND BEYOND

I find myself in an odd corner. On the one hand, I think it is more than less up to the wronged party to forgive; they have discretion in the matter. But I also believe that it makes sense to hold people accountable for whether and how they forgive. Undergoing and responding to wrongs is part of our lot. And who we are is measured in part by those responses.

Griswold believes that if we want to regard people as blameworthy for withholding forgiveness in certain cases, then in some sense, we insist that they forgive in those cases. Imagine some set of threshold conditions that must be met for you to think, "X should forgive Y in this case." Once Y meets those conditions, "forgiveness is what is due the offender," according to Griswold, and should they not be forgiven, they will have been disrespected (Griswold 2007, 69).

Griswold's position is reasonable, but it does not sit well with me. I have a difficult time thinking that I could owe anyone who wronged me anything relative to that wrong. Amends do not negate the wrong; wounding is not a species of borrowing. Moreover—and I have been slowly assembling my argument for this—forgiveness is prospective, not just retrospective. And that makes a significant difference. If one makes amends in the full sense indicated, I would rather say that they become worthy of forgiveness. My position is not as odd as it sounds. In many cases, we praise forgiveness in scenarios where we would not blame someone for withholding: "You're a bigger person than I am. I don't think I could have remained friends after that." Or: "Yes, I heard they had 'a break.' I don't blame her. He is selfish and that makes for a tiresome colleague." In these cases, we praise an act for its occurrence but withhold blame when it does not take place.

"But surely there are times when we blame someone for being hard-hearted or cold." Indeed. And "hard-hearted," in accord with common usage, is Griswold's name for proving deficient in scenes of forgiveness (Griswold, 18). But is hard-heartedness a vice because the contrite wrongdoer is owed something by the wronged, and to the degree that the former is disrespected in not being forgiven? The sticking point, for me, is the notion of "owing," which drags the issue into a debt economy. (Incidentally, Griswold distinguishes contrition from the payment of debts, so I imagine he shares my discomfort.)

Consider an act of generosity. (Griswold uses courage as the comparator virtue, but one could argue that one has debts to the polis and so disrespects it by not facing dangers on its behalf.) I find a worthy person or cause and offer them my support in time, money, influence, what have you. I do not think that anyone would regard the worthiness of the person or cause to institute an obligation on my part to behave generously toward them. Nor do I think that anyone would blame me for not doing such things. If I were particularly well-off, I might be accused of selfishness or greed, but even then, I would neither owe the worthy party my attention nor disrespect them by withholding it. I would be less admirable in a general sense than if I had proven generous, and if I were overall obsessed with money, I might be pitiable. But I would not have failed to give another their due.

I find forgiveness analogous to generosity in this manner. It should be exercised toward the worthy, but it is never owed. "But what about acts of contrition? Those are missing in your analogy, and they seem decisive in the thought that one owes the contrite forgiveness." I do not want to disparage contrition. Particularly when done well, it evidences a slice of what might come to be: sincere, attuned, caring interactions. But thought prospectively, an apology is a request. It asks, "Will you have me back?" And the forgiven often say, with relief, "I thought I had lost you."

On my view, we praise forgiveness for its generous exercise of discretion. In the wake of a wrong, we need not renew our relationship with the wrong-doer, but it might be praiseworthy to do so, even beautiful. Like trust's willful dependencies, it pulses with utopian currents that move without reference to debit sheets. Forgiveness and trust are sources of hope, therefore. Without being commanded, we bind our lives to singular others.

"But surely we owe the contrite something." We do. An account. They have accounted for themselves, and so, should we withhold forgiveness, we should account for why we are no longer continuing as before. Admittedly, this may be as halting as the wrongdoer's account of their wrong. In numerous ways we remain opaque. But we owe them that: an account for an account.

ALL YOU NEED IS LOVE

In place of forgiveness as petulant scorekeeping, Nussbaum favors uncon-ditional forgiveness, or, even better on her view, an unconditional love and generosity that does without "both forgiveness and the anger that is its occasion, a love that embarks upon an uncertain future with a generous spirit, rather than remaining rooted in the past" (Nussbaum 2016, 81). Nussbaum prefers the latter because it is future oriented, whereas "[un]conditional forgiveness is still about the past, and it gives us nothing con-crete with which to go forward. It just wipes out something but entails no constructive future directed attitude" (Nussbaum, 77).

I appreciate the prospective dimension of Nussbaum's account. But I think she is too cynical about forgiveness and oddly naive about uncondi-tional love and generosity. Her principal example is the parable of the prod-igal son who squanders his inheritance and so returns to his family as a prospective worker. But his father will have nothing of it and welcomes him back with open, unresentful arms. If anything, joy orients his reception.

It matters, I think, that the example is a parent-child relationship. Most scenes of forgiveness are not underwritten by that kind of attachment or cultural obligation. One thus wonders how the father would respond to a distant relation or a neighbor. Moreover, parents are often too permissive and implicitly condone their children when they should not. True, parents can also be brutal with their children, but that is another side of the same die: the relationship is too charged to provide a baseline. I would bristle if someone who wronged me expected me to regard them as my child or even my friend. But even with a son, should I welcome his return, I would expect some recounting and evidence of growth. And that needn't devolve into a shaming ritual, particularly in the context of perfectionism, where accountability is an ongoing, individuating activity and a way of being true to oneself in the company of others. And because recounting is a two-way street, growth might occur across the relationship. Regardless, for the child's sake and for the sake of those who must live with them, a parent is responsible for raising a child. A process of forgiveness offers one way toward instilling that accountability, and it is reckless to abandon that post, even in the name of love. We should note as well that by seeking to be hired on as a worker, the prodigal son is contrite and arrives by humbling himself in a manner that worries Nussbaum about forgiveness, but that is not my main concern with the example and how it is being read. Paternal examples are too thick in presumption to characterize broadly desired modes of conduct, and even if we valorize the relation, in this case the father's behavior falls short of praiseworthy.

Nussbaum's other example of love beyond forgiveness draws from Mahler's Resurrection Symphony, which culminates in a disposition to "keep on being oneself and doing one's work" despite having been wronged, "not wasting time on angry thoughts and feelings, but just giving what one has to give" (Nussbaum, 84). I find this even less persuasive than the biblical excerpt. Whereas the father of the prodigal son refuses to hold his son accountable, here the relationship, whatever it might be, is ignored altogether, at least insofar as the wrong may have been disclosive of its character. "You cannot touch me," it says to the wrongdoer. And to my mind, that is a mode of flight, a quasi-Stoic contraction away from relationality to minimize vulnerability and intensify self-control. Nussbaum, however, presents it as a hero's transition into a light "that no eye has ever seen," about which Nussbaum says, "If one can venture a bold interpretation, this 'unseen' light appears to be music itself" (Nussbaum, 84). But this is precisely not a future with another who has wronged one but an abandonment of that relationship in its singularity. In fact, it carries a whiff of self-love at the expense of another with whom one cannot be bothered. When people hurt me, I want to know why, even if that exposes me to more hurt or, as is sometimes the case, provides us both with an enlarged feel for the character of our relationship, which may need trueing. Holding others accountable is a way of caring for them, and it is a way that goes missing if we altogether forgo resentment and the process it initiates.

JUST FUCK OFF

Even outside the thought of something "unforgivable," to which I will return, there are times when we withhold forgiveness. Someone wrongs us, and the wrong is either grievous enough or a backbreaking strand in a bale. But what does that really mean?

Although the phrase suggests an absence, withholding forgiveness maintains some degree of resentment. The result may settle into a judgment—"He's a bad person, what can I say?"—or it installs a button that gets pushed every time we see them. And in either case, the relationship diminishes—a friendship ends or cools, a familial relation drifts into formal obligation, collegiality is strained, possibly forced, or a stranger becomes a bad operator. ("Watch out for that one.")

Importantly, withholding forgiveness is not tantamount to exile from moral consideration. If I do not forgive you, you nevertheless retain your moral standing, meaning when my actions appreciably bear upon your welfare, I must take it into account. Should a sibling not forgive me for some mean-spirited deed, they still need to be relatively civil when the family gathers. They might remind me that I'm still on their shit list and act coldly, but they have no right to harm me or prevent me from attending. That would drift into revenge and be subject to justice assessments that would not be quieted by their saying, "But I did not forgive them." Not forgiving someone accounts for a diminishment of the degree or kind of relationship that had been operating prior to the wrongdoing. It does not license whatever you are now inclined to do.

Admittedly, I am relying on a slippery but common distinction between punishing someone and forgiving them, or not. When I withhold forgiveness, I effectively say: you no longer are entitled to expect from me a certain regard and comportment, including, in certain egregious cases, civility: "That man stole my discovery. I will not be in the same room with him." But more generally, the issue is a degree of consideration, warmth, etc., maybe even reticence or tact. Even when asked, I temper my remarks about those I find annoying, and I appreciate when others do the same with me.

"What about when we're just done with someone?" Then one avoids them, does them no favors, etc. But one is not thereby licensed to harm them. I can think of a few people I regard as unfit company, but that does not permit me to lie about them or undermine them. I consider it mistaken to think forgiveness or its absence as a return to or exile from "the moral community." Scenes of forgiveness, initiated by wrongdoing, hurt, and resentment, only open in the presence of a moral community, and withholding forgiveness, even holding another in contempt, locks them in their wrong, as it were. It is a move within a moral community.

Recall *The Sunflower* and Karl's request that Simon forgive him as "a Jew." The request still astounds. Refusing Karl does not somehow displace him from all moral consideration. And we see this in the conduct of Simon, who, though bewildered, listens patiently, and, at one point, shoos away a bluebottle buzzing around Karl's now-blind head.

> "Thanks," he nevertheless whispered. And for the first time I realize that I, a defenseless subhuman, had contrived to lighten the lot of an equally defenseless superman, without thinking, simply as a matter of course. (Wiesenthal 1997, 37)

Not that Simon owes Karl that. But the gesture raises a question that arises for all who withhold forgiveness: Now what? Sometimes forgiveness is the easier path; the inertia of the past can continue to flow. Withholding forgiveness requires us to adjust our bearings across all the places where the unforgiven nests in our life. To be clear, I am not echoing Camus's point, cited affirmatively by Murphy, that one forgiving too easily suffers from some "sentimental confusion," presumably that humans are good by nature (Murphy and Hampton 1988, 102). I am underscoring that withholding forgiveness raises more questions than the one it answers.

LOVE WITHOUT TEARDROPS ISN'T THE SAME

As I observe in my discussion of hope, Terrance Hayes confronts the poetics of Wallace Stevens in "Snow for Wallace Stevens," both in general and in his troubling "Like Decorations in a Nigger Cemetery." Despite dropping the N-word, Stevens's poem neither addresses the fates of those thereby named or the fates conducted by that word, which is itself a gravestone. Because the poem figures poetry as a commemorative decoration, this suggests that Stevens's massive imagination is nevertheless oblivious to the fate of Black life; his poetics has no room to poetize it. Hayes's poem digests this along with Stevens's ability to "bring a sentence to its knees," a wonderful image connoting a posture of praise, but also a writing in and on the grounds of language. But my observations threaten to obscure how Hayes's poem is keyed by a question never stated, at least not directly. Given *this* imagination, how then to regard the poet and his poetry? Hayes's poem stages a scene of possible forgiveness. And it checks itself with a typical but essential question: "Who is not more than his limitations?" (Hayes 2010, "Snow for Wallace Stevens," line 14). The reply is anything but typical, however.

> Thus, I have a capacity for love without
> forgiveness. This song is for my foe,
> the clean-shaven, gray suited, gray patron
> of Hartford, the emperor of whiteness
> blue as a body made of snow.
> *(Hayes 2010, "Snow for Wallace Stevens," lines 18–22)*

I did not see this coming, this redirection of the biblical presumption that love for enemies entails forgiving them. Of course, one could think the poem introduces a love that transcends forgiveness altogether but that would miss the overall thrust and tone of the encounter, which censures without categorical condemnation. Moreover, the capacity introduced does not follow from revelation but from two thoughts. One I have already noted: everyone has and is more than their limitations. The other is obliquely provocative: "I too, having lost faith / in language, have placed my faith in language." I term this "oblique" because it only announces a proximity rather than an identification. The proximity lies in using language to contest its limits and say what it cannot name—say, a world without us, or one with some of us under erasure. That disjunct marks the difference that keeps the two poets and their projects proximate without identification. Hayes's loss of faith acknowledges fates that Stevens refuses to consider even as, with careless hate, it perpetuates them. Hayes thus withholds forgiveness, marking the careless hate with the resentment it deserves, while nevertheless loving Steven's exclusive syntax, music, and vast if limited imagination.

IN THE BEGINNING WAS THE RELATION

My view aims to clarify the generative power, underscored by Cherry, that King also finds in forgiveness (Norlock 2017, 58). But some object to the thought in principle. Roberts, for example, states, "Forgiveness is an attitude of one person to another, not a pattern of interaction between them" (Roberts 1995, 305). Before addressing the objection, I again want to insist, like Walker, that we need to take forgiveness as a syndrome, and not expect every act that warrants the name to fall under a single set of necessary and sufficient conditions. If you break off a friendship and claim that you nevertheless forgave your new acquaintance, I will think that you are deceiving yourself. (I suppose your former friend would feel the same.) But it does make sense to forgive strangers who then return to being strangers. And yet, isn't that still a resolution, albeit a modest one? If we retain our resentment, we will no longer be strangers. Regardless, my disagreement with Roberts runs deeper than this.

Any intersubjective relation includes the self-relations of those involved. Each party's attitude toward the other pertains. But in forgiveness, the issue is another's wrongdoing, not just a set of feelings about that wrongdoing. We forgive the one who has wronged us for wronging us, and thus the principal object is an interaction between parties. And one of the chief questions is whether that wrongdoing has been and will continue to be a pattern. Second, one can refuse another's forgiveness. We may deny that a wrong has been done, or we may find forgiveness excessive in its manner. This indicates that acts of forgiveness concern our standing toward one another. And if you deny this, "I forgive you" loses its performative force and reduces to expression.

WHERE DO WE GO FROM HERE?

I have stressed that wrongdoing discloses the character of both parties and their relationship. Forgiveness works through those disclosures toward resolution. I chose "resolution" because at least four of its senses obtain: (1) to deal with a situation successfully; (2) to reach a firm decision; (3) to separate into component parts; and (4) to progress from dissonance to consonance.

Success is the renewal of the relationship, returning it to at least the terms that were in play prior to its being thrown out of joint. And I prefer this concreteness to the language favored by Griswold and Murphy, which renders forgiveness a move in abstract moral space. Murphy suggests that forgiveness returns the wrongdoer to a state of moral equality with the wronged (Murphy and Hampton 1988, 22). This seems off for a few reasons. First, why presume that moral equality was operative in the first place? Perhaps I just don't know what he means. If the issue is that wrongdoers become subject to punishment and so no longer deserve due equal treatment, then the issue is punishment and mercy, not forgiveness. But when I think of moral equality, I think of how praiseworthy or blameworthy someone is. Some agents are better people than others. And maybe it's the wrongdoer who has a long way to fall before reaching the level of the one they, in a rare stumble, mistreated. But more than that, tying forgiveness to a moral score sheet dissolves its prospective dimension into a retrospective one, and it makes it difficult to see that sometimes, the terms for going on together were not previously in play.

Griswold holds that forgiveness aims at the restoration of mutual respect and recognition in a "moral commonwealth," the "minimal state of civility that existed before the injury was done" (Griswold 2007, 49). This seems far too modest. It may make sense among strangers, the scene that Griswold presumes, but that undersells what we seek in most cases—to still be friends, loving siblings, neighbors, colleagues, etc. And each of those entails more than a minimal state of civility. Also, even when forgiveness is withheld, mutual recognition is usually obtained—the wrongdoer and the wronged know each other as such. What, though, of mutual respect? It does seem that one's respect for another contracts when one is wronged, and if one loses all respect for another because of what they have done, a future together seems eclipsed. But the language of mutuality sounds as overstated as the language of equality in Murphy. Isn't our respect for others a varied affair, both between people (we respect some more than others) and even regarding the same person across their many capacities, dispositions, etc.? Still, I see the point. Forgiveness signals that enough respect for the other remains or was generated in the meantime—say, through the sincerity of their contrition—to reembark together. This is its consonance. But even then, if I am honest, the process of regaining respect is as dependent on what follows forgiveness as it is on what leads up to it.

WHO ARE YOU, WHO, WHO, WHO, WHO?

"Catalyst" comes from the Greek *katalysis*, meaning "dissolution," from *katalyein*, "to dissolve," involving *lyein*, "to dissolve or release." I recall the word because King invokes it, and because I am resisting what we might call a restorative conception of forgiveness in favor of a transfigurative or catalystic conception. Both agree that forgiveness affects change. But the catalystic conception believes that the maximal potential of forgiveness includes qualitative transformation rather than the restoration of a baseline moral relation between parties. Not that the former is always operative, but it can be, and usually to the better.

Wrongdoings are also catalysts. They dislocate a relationship and estrange the parties involved. But that change is entropic, leaving a fissure filling with hurt and resentment (among the wronged), with guilt, shame, indifference, or perverse glee (among perpetrators). It, too, is dissolved, however, or loosened when one resolves to enter a scene of forgiveness. On the side of the potential forgiver, the wrongdoer separates from their wrongdoing. And resentment, which had oriented them toward their antagonist, becomes one possibility among others. On the side of the wrongdoer, their deed has been judged and so they now stand outside it, able to compare their own estimation of their conduct with how the aggrieved views it, which enables the question: Is contrition in order?

At this juncture, both parties and their relationship are put into question: Who am I to act and respond in this manner? Is this who we are? Who else might we be? Do we even have terms for such a future? A restorative conception of forgiveness mutes such questions, which is not to say they thereby become unimaginable. Griswold, for example, also observes that forgiveness may lead to growth, but that potential is a peripheral concern in his account (Griswold 2007, 108). But that is how it is in ethics; the most salient differences are often those of emphasis, of intensifying certain moments for the sake of goods sought and for discouraging certain emphases for the limits toward which they incline.

A scene of forgiveness has the potential to open into an intimacy, which includes the possibility that a robust resolution might release an unanticipated future. The hurt you caused made me realize how much you mean to me, and it makes you realize, in your regret, how much you care for me. Or, and/or, my standing up for myself by way of resentment may increase your respect for me even as my seeing you stumble may replace my fantasy of you with one closer to who you are. Admittedly, these concerns are inflected by the perfectionism I have been advocating throughout. Taking the course of a life to follow a learning curve or curves, I see forgiveness not only as a site of reflection and accountability for both parties, but as an opportunity to become more thoroughly who it is we are becoming. Some wrongs can be worked through easily. But when the deed is enough to generate hurt and resentment, it seems thoughtless to simply return to business as usual.

THE NOT-SO-AWFUL TRUTH

Another way to say the difference I have in mind is to contrast restoration with remarriage, calling to mind Cavell's readings of select Hollywood talkies that appeared between 1934 and 1949. On his view, remarriage involves the "reconciliation of a genuine forgiveness; a reconciliation so profound as to require the metamorphosis of death and revival, the achievement of a new perspective on existence" (Cavell 1981, 19). Here, as in most cases, the positionality of the participants is telling—vows of marriage, betrayal, and the possible renewal of intimacy on that level, hence Cavell's charged language. But whatever the relation, forgiveness entails rearticulating who I am to you and who you are to me, clarifying how it is that we matter to one another, and in what ways. These are some of the things we need to know to welcome a wrongdoer back into our lives and to demonstrate that we understand the wrong we have done. And while that may not require an entirely new perspective on existence, it will force us to think through the terms that bind us to one another—neighbor, friend, colleague, sibling, teacher, student, parent, partner or spouse, child, stranger, fellow citizen, etc.—and how they are inflected by variables of class, race, gender, and sexuality. We usually are good to each other and bad to each other under these conditions, and these modes of interaction underwrite what we expect from one another. Scenes of forgiveness provide parties with opportunities to revitalize those terms, and not simply by reminding each other of their conventional meaning. Rather, in the breach opened by a wrong, we often remake the terms of our relationship, tailor them to our circumstances, and so come to learn what they mean as if for the first time, although, in fact, it is only the next in an open series.

What Cavell foregrounds in these films, or one of the things he foregrounds, is how they depict conversation, as if change happens therein, and because of how they are handled or mishandled therein. This holds for forgiveness, as well, at least in its fullest and most valuable sense. Scenes of forgiveness are principally conversational (or aspire to be), something we elide if we overly focus on either partner's affect, namely resentment and regret (or its absence). Yes, a change of heart is essential to forgiveness, but that change is played, in effect, in words, looks, and tone, among other things. This claim, admittedly odd within the current literature, is tied to my other insistence—namely, that scenes of forgiveness open with more on the table than who did what and why to whom, and what is needed to make up for that. Those questions arise, but within a larger question: How do we now stand toward one another, and how should we go on? Parting is one way of going on, as is a shift from unknown stranger to asshole. Regardless, such matters are best worked through in deed and words (which are also deeds).

LESS IS LESS

Modest forgiveness leaves money off the table.

EQUAL TO THE MOMENT?

If forgiveness is potentially catalystic, it not only requires honesty, patience, humility, and generosity, but courage as well, and again, from both parties. Can I openly acknowledge a shortcoming? Can I confront someone about what they have done? And given that conveying a hurt also conveys vulnerability and intensifies it (Who knows how the wrongdoer will reply?) one might prefer to withdraw and nurse one's wounds. And change is not always easy. Forgiveness and contrition are inceptual acts that one makes good after the fact. Importantly, I am not talking about scenes where we think it right to withhold forgiveness; those contain their own lessons. Forgiveness is generative for ethical life, even intensifying.

DON'T MAKE WAVES

My emphasis on generativity obscures a common occurrence—namely, letting go of resentment to get along. Some argue that doing so does not entail genuine forgiveness, although Kathryn Norlock believes we need to tread more carefully around what she terms "peacekeeping forgiveness" (Holmgren 2002; Norlock 2009). Earlier I waved at a similar phenomenon. Forgiving and forgetting can slide into one another regarding inconsequential slights. But sometimes people make peace with others when the consequences are not slight. And sometimes this is because they are either expected to do so (and many women are, as Norlock observes) and/or they are seriously dependent on the wrongdoer.

Such cases are not only common but also forms of moral repair, all things considered, which seems Norlock's point, or a dimension of it. One might put up with things in order not to rock the boat, and precisely for the benefit of others with whom one shares it: children, family members, other friends. Rather than indicating a lack of self-respect, peacekeeping forgiveness manifests concern and care for others. But is this forgiveness? If no change of heart takes place, I would be hard-pressed to call it that, although I might praise the bravery and generosity of the agent in question. But as we've seen, "change of heart" can take time and occur in fits and starts. Moreover, we need a recounting of the scene—what, who, how, why, with what effects—and the deliberation that underwrote the decision. Only with that range of knowledge can we offer an evaluation that does not fall "short of taking seriously what women convey when they express forgiveness to wrongdoers we'd rather they resented" (Norlock, 21). But maybe they do resent those wrongdoers, and in a lingering way. (If they never feel resentment, a forgiveness scene doesn't even open on my view.) "I decided to be the bigger person, again," they might say. Not that resentment centers the relationship. But, as with a wound, it aches from time to time. And it's best not to talk about it. Remarriage abandons "happily ever after," and a genuine life is likely to carry a few scars.

YOU'RE NOT SO BAD YOURSELF

Karl wanted forgiveness because he could not forgive himself and suffered from an inability to think of himself as anything but a vicious Nazi murderer. He said he was not born an SS thug, but whoever that boy was, was gone. Karl's self-regard was unable to distinguish the sinner from his sins, and so he was haunted and riven. Did he resent himself? In a way—he felt shame, even moral horror. He thus was out of joint with himself, acutely so, and he hoped that forgiveness would allow him to die in peace.

Self-forgiveness is a celebrated activity in pop psychology. A quick Amazon search locates many titles, including *Forgiveness: How to Make Peace with Your Past and Get on with Your Life*, which nicely conforms to the logic we have been following (Simon and Simon, 1990). Or it can, if one is the wrongdoer and the wronged. Otherwise, the usage is strained to the point of incoherent. Scenes of forgiveness singularize the parties, render them nonsubstitutable. I cannot forgive myself on behalf of another.

If the issue is self-acceptance or self-love, a scene of forgiveness doesn't commence. Being odd or unusual is not a wrongdoing. In this, managing internal negativity is much like controlling anger. And if discriminatory cultural narratives are a root cause of one's inner turmoil, it is vital not to invoke the language of forgiveness. That would suggest that one has done something wrong when, in fact, one is the aggrieved party. "Don't be sorry, be angry" seems more to the point. And if anyone is a candidate for forgiveness under such conditions, it would be whoever instilled those self-undermining conceptions and narratives or allowed them to accrue uninterrupted.

Waxing Platonic, I might forgive myself if I thought my wrongdoing harmed me as well as another. But here I would counsel caution. Certain misdeeds might do well to settle into our self-conception. They keep us humble and attentive for possible repeats. And it does a body well to dispel the notion that a blameless life is the true measure of human goodness. Whatever goodness is humanly possible is grown into, and part of that task involves acknowledging and redressing failure, error, cruelty, carelessness, ignorance, etc. Moreover, living with a certain amount of guilt and shame seems honest. But I will not speculate about all cases. I can imagine some where one might forgive oneself for poor life choices and wasted stretches of time, and in a catalystic manner, thus enabling the pursuit of better aims. But these are not paradigmatic scenes and should not distort our feel for forgiveness's utopian energies, which are principally interpersonal, resolving a disjointed relation into a renewed, consonant one.

OFF THE HOOK

How would you have replied if Karl had asked you to forgive him? Can one forgive him? May one forgive him? Should one? I cannot answer the first on behalf of anyone. As many observe, people find forgiveness in their heart in the most surprising ways and under the most intense circumstances, including prolonged torture, unlawful imprisonment, etc. As an empirical phenomenon, forgiveness, like hope and trust, is mercurial. I am thus reticent to answer the "can" question outside a living context. Philosophy should shy away from fortune telling.

I wonder how often strong theological currents underwrite the most surprising acts of forgiveness. Does one forgive because God will take care of the revenge part—namely, through eternal damnation? I find it hard to admire that smoke and mirrors scenario, which renders forgiveness its opposite. Or does one forgive because one has no right to cast away what God has made? In this scene, strength to forgive comes from the almighty command that one should. Here, too, I have my qualms. I sense a vassal acting nervously near the throne. And yet, I am not so daft as to doubt that experiences of love are transformative. The thought that X is loved admirably by another may be a catalyst toward seeing them in a fuller, more fulsome light.

Because one cannot forgive on behalf of others, I do not think that I could forgive Karl if he had asked this of me. I could report the fact that a victim had forgiven a perpetrator, but one cannot assume the role of the victim and exercise discretion on their behalf. One might hazard a guess about what another would say and do if they were still alive, in right mind, etc. But that is to speak from an objectivating attitude in which acts of forgiveness are impossible because resentment is impossible. In other words, much like a sedative, such remarks could have the perlocutionary effect of attenuating perpetrator guilt, but they would lack any illocutionary force.

"But Karl's crimes were directed against a group as well as the persons involved. Does that set among the wronged anyone who is also a member of that group, or would have been regarded as such at that time?" I see why the question arises. Karl's acts and general conduct certainly rendered the world hostile to and unsafe for Jewish folk. And putting someone in harm's way is its own harm. But that was not what haunted Karl. His soul raged from his role in the grisly murder of innocents, some of whose faces he saw as his death drew near. Also, it is perilous in moral matters to speak for a group, arrogating the role of representative. Other members of the group will feel differently, and in matters of forgiveness no one has the right to usurp their say in the matter. So, one may say something as a member of a targeted group—"You have made the world less safe for me, but I forgive you (or not)"—but one may not speak for that group. But again, Karl sought forgiveness for other wrongs for which neither you nor I may forgive him.

THESE THINGS TAKE TIME

Because I consider the wronged to wield an accountable discretion in matters of forgiveness, I resist any categorical sense of "the unforgiveable." The decision to withhold forgiveness, to the degree it is something as seemingly simple as a "decision," needs to be worked out every time. I presume, however, that certain cases will be easier for and on us.

I suggested that Karl's request of Simon is philosophically disoriented. But it also indicates that Simon is still very much a Nazi in certain respects—no need to differentiate among "the Jews." Karl has therefore not yet fully grasped his crime. Even were I permitted to forgive him I do not think I should. Yes, he seems genuinely contrite, but not about the full depth of his awfulness. I would thus be forgiving him for something that is a bit different than what he did. It isn't just that he killed innocents, including children, who happened to be Jewish; he did all that because they were Jewish, intensifying his villainy with race hatred. If that thick slice of evil remains lodged in his contrition, he is not yet worthy of forgiveness.

I also think that certain deeds should be marked with condemnation, namely those that profoundly violate a life, whether through murder or rape, torture, or profound abuse. Such acts indelibly mark lives, sometimes by ending them. The wrong is ongoing, therefore, and our resentment has the right to keep pace. One has not moved on because the wrong persists. Violations linger as the loss of who we were before the deed. Withholding forgiveness announces, "Your having done that is now part of who you are. Live with it, as I live with its perverse effects."

Importantly, withholding forgiveness from profoundly violating acts need not entail maintaining a feverish resentment, which most likely will exhaust someone already suffering. Contempt can be a matter-of-fact disposition that does not consume one from within and that one does not proactively visit upon those they deem to deserve it. Nor does it exile the contemptible for any moral consideration. It does not even reduce the doer to the deed any more than a profound violation need be the sole, defining feature of a life so wronged. But it remains a defining feature. In other words, forgiveness is not the only way to see more to a person than their failures. This is evident in Hayes's love without forgiveness for Wallace Stevens. But love is not the only regard with which we let others go about their business, unforgiven. In fact, one need only encourage them to dim the light of their crimes with deeds to the contrary. The question "Who is not more than his limitations?" can also be heard as a provocation to be proven down a road that recontextualizes a past without denying it or its continued effects.

THE BALL IS IN YOUR COURT

My sense of forgiveness, like King's, is catalystic. But unlike his, mine is theologically unmoored. Forgiveness on my account occurs through the exercise of a sovereign discretion that nevertheless does not derive from autonomy as a moral ideal or from a psychological capacity for total self-control. Neither the ego nor the superego is master in its own house.

A feel for the singularizing energies of forgiveness, and for their fragile, even unpredictable character, renders me proximate to Derrida's thought that forgiveness takes place in a manner that "exceeds all institution, all power, all juridical-political authority" (Derrida 2001, 54). Whatever calls for forgiveness, it is other than a categorical duty or even, I would add, the insistence of convention. But the decision to forgive, if it is even that, is responsive to whatever forces effect a change of heart. A forgiver is both cause and effect, or confounds the distinction.

But my grasp of this scene is somewhat different from Derrida's. He agrees that each "time forgiveness is effectively exercised, it seems to suppose some sovereign power" (Derrida, 59). But this compromises forgiveness as he sees it or longs for it. "What I dream of," he says, "what I try to think as the 'purity' of a forgiveness worthy of its name, would be a forgiveness without power: *unconditional but without sovereignty*" (Derrida, 59). To the degree that "sovereignty" names a set of powers whose exercise is delimited and legitimated by an explicit juridical order, I agree. But is this all that is implied when he also says:

> And since we are speaking of forgiveness, what makes the "I forgive you" sometimes unbearable and odious, even obscene is the affirmation of sovereignty. It is often addressed from the top down, it confirms its own freedom or assumes for itself the power of forgiving, be it as victim or in the name of the victim. (Derrida, 59)

On my view, forgiveness is inseparable from this power, this freedom of sorts, one that no one can exercise for us. To not assume this power and stand accountable for how one wields it is tantamount to a refusal to enter a scene of forgiveness in its mortal singularity. Forgiveness individuates us, subjects us by leaving it to us to forgive another, or not. Whether we go on as before or in some enlarged sense, or whether we diminish as a *we*, is, to an appreciable degree, up to the wronged. That is the plight of finite beings in nontheological moral spaces, but also their power, one no doubt generated, in part, by the historical unfolding of forgiveness practices.

But that is probably not Derrida's chief concern, if it is even his concern.

(I am never sure of him, which is why I am always rereading him.) More on point is his worry about what comes between us, as it were, when we deliberate about forgiveness—namely, conditions, which always have their roots in cultural orders that typify us and so threaten to efface singularity. His dream thus concerns a *pure forgiveness*, one bereft of orders of substitutability. But that would be inconceivable, as he observes in a manner that embraces the paradox: "Forgiveness must announce itself as impossibility itself" (Derrida, 39, 33).

The concern, as I understand it, is that all concerned parties ironically go missing when a scene of forgiveness opens. Derrida writes, "For, if pure forgiveness cannot, if it *must* not *present itself* as such, and thus exhibit itself in consciousness without at the same time denying itself, betraying or reaffirming a sovereignty, then how to know what is an act of forgiveness, if it never takes place, and who forgives whom, what from whom?" (Derrida, 49). To the degree I rely on semantic orders of intelligibility, I become "one of those," from "the wronged" to "a wrongdoer" to all the universals that could characterize us. In Derrida's words, "As soon as the victim 'understands' the criminal, as soon as she exchanges, speaks, agrees with him, the scene of reconciliation has commenced, and with it this ordinary forgiveness which is anything but forgiveness" (Derrida, 49).

I appreciate the logic of Derrida's argument even if I do not feel its force. We do meet and conspire in terms that are not of our making and that typify us at our own expense, and that only intensifies situations that aspire to intimacy. But such terms and their grammar also give us back to ourselves as possibilities for further improvisation. Moreover, the pragmatic dimensions of language institute us as more than a moment in a semantic field, say as the one who asserts, contests, questions, recounts, promises, apologizes, forgives, etc. In other words, we both are and are not immanent to those fields or horizons of meaning, and in that *not*, understood in part through our bearing, in part through our being-in-common, arises the best answer to the question "Who are you?" I thus find the extraordinary demands of forgiveness quite ordinary, and to the degree that forgiveness only takes place if it remains resolutely ordinary in this manner, you and I, in the company of us, committing, accounting, and recounting, prepared to pivot.

It is telling that Derrida opts for a rhetoric of purity when he dreams of forgiveness freed from sovereign acts. "Purity" initiates a purging operation at the expense of finitude (our dependencies, our limits), here marked by the challenge (the opportunity, too) of collaborative improvisation across the folds of ethical life. That no doubt says too much, however. Derrida does state, "Forgiveness is thus mad. It must plunge, but lucidly, into the night of the unintelligible" (Derrida, 49). But this also overstates the matter, gesturing toward an order of sanity and intelligibility whose only appreciable effect is to cast deliberation as a nighttime moo, to replay Hegel's dig at Schelling in an inverse gesture.

One might argue that appreciating the madness of forgiveness humbles those who find themselves in a scene of forgiveness. Addressing the more general concern of responsibility, François Raffoul writes, "The issue is thus to free 'the pure eventfulness of the event' [the singularity of the occurrence] . . . by breaking the power of the ego and its attempts to neutralize it. As event, an event is said to be im-possible in the sense that it happens outside the horizon of preparedness of the subject as 'I can'" (Raffoul 2010, 301). But to what end? Will this realization render us humbler or more alert to what has transpired and/or might yet be? Might the resulting vertigo somehow prove generative? One cannot say on the terms orienting the analysis. That would pull the realization back within the anticipations of the deliberative subject. But isn't that our lot?

My impatience intensifies when I think of how Gonsalves found his way back to Ellington, and of how Ellington received him. If anything, their willingness to play together was what made a possible future intelligible to both, and its pursuit "sane" to Ellington in the sense of being worth the risk that his forgiveness acknowledges. But such apparent successes should not obscure the fact that the terms with which forgiveness scenes open are in flux and contestable. I am thus somewhat happier when I read, "A 'finalized' forgiveness is not forgiveness; it is only a political strategy or a psycho-therapeutic economy" (Derrida 2001, 50). Unlike the earlier invocation of madness, this remark orients: forgiveness is never really said and done. Resentment might linger or the wrong might be repeated, or its fuller depth discovered. Or we might rediscover each other because of what the wrong disclosed or what appeared as we acknowledged it. And even if the scene of forgiveness is resolved to our satisfaction, we less conclude than turn a corner.

Acknowledgments

Every name bears the echo of others. Paul Taylor, Kevin Corrigan, and Andrew Mitchell helped me locate passages or navigate specific words. Late in the game, Lynne Huffer read the Preface and helped it along by way of interrogation and affirmation. Their willingness to think with me, and to help me, remains much appreciated. Two different classes read and discussed texts engaged here, and they worked with me on each phenomenon as if it were their own, which it is. Profound thanks, therefore, to the students in PHIL 415 (fall 2021) and PHIL 515 (fall 2020). Thanks also to Linda Li, who helped me proof and correct the draft I submitted to the press, and to Sara Saba, who helped me with the bibliography, index, and proofing. Two reviews solicited by the press led to the Preface and other changes in tone and stage setting. Disagreements no doubt persist, but I took to heart most of the concerns conveyed. Doing so made this a better book, as did the detailed efforts of my copyeditor, Mariah Gumpert. My editor, Kyle Wagner, was receptive and encouraging throughout and a helpful sounding board as I drafted the Preface. I am grateful to have such a thoughtful interlocutor who can respond from a perch outside the confines of specialist debates. Some initial thoughts on hope and trust were shared with the American Philosophies Forum, which John Stuhr convenes with indomitable energy and creativity, and which many make an annual rite of thinking. Each has been reworked, including the lines on hope that appeared in the *Journal of Speculative Philosophy*, but my gratitude remains to that venue and to the many who have made the American Philosophies Forum a vital scene of thought and conversation. Finally, just before copyedits arrived, I had the good fortune to participate in a seminar on democratic faith convened by Melvin Rogers and Ryan Preston-Roedder. Seven other participants shared work and responded to a lengthy excerpt from my hope chapter. The whole event made this a better book at the eleventh hour. In addition to Melvin and Ryan, thanks to Andrew Chignell, Mark Lance, Ainsley LeSure, Vincent Lloyd, and Katie Stockdale.

Through many encounters, and now over many years, I have been struck by the proximity of my thoughts to the work of Eddie Glaude and Melvin Rogers. Both have been generous with their energy, whether by visiting a class or visiting with me via Zoom for a handful of hours. I hope they know that their distinct ways of working and thinking orient and cheer me. Sometimes it's a blessing for another to get inside your head. An argument throughout is that ethical life pulses across culture, and that philosophy should unfold in dialogue with the full breadth of that culture, including poems and pop songs. I thus have quoted a handful of works that furthered my reflections and mentioned even more in passing. I would have quoted those as well, but the permission process is overly slow and, in most cases, unnecessarily expensive. I am thus all the more grateful for those who responded to my queries and worked with my budget, which was modest. They are as follows:

Lucille Clifton, "turning," from *How to Carry Water: Selected Poems*. Copyright © 1974, 1987 by Lucille Clifton. Reprinted with the permission of The Permissions Company, LLC, on behalf of BOA Editions, Ltd., boaeditions.org.

Sage Francis, lyrics from three tracks from *A Healthy Distrust*, "Lie Detector Test," "Gunz Yo," and "The Buzz Kill." © 2005. Epitaph: reprinted with the permission of Sage Francis.

Terrance Hayes, "Snow for Wallace Stevens," from *Lighthead*. © 2010. Penguin Books. Reprinted with the permission of Terrance Hayes.

Aimee Mann, lyrics from "It's Not," from *Lost in Space*. © 2002. Super Ego Records. Reprinted with the permission of Aimee Mann via Downtown Music Publishing LLC.

In length and manner, this is an indulgent book. I hope it is never just that, but it takes risks and so no doubt stumbles. I ran this route given the subject matter and what I set out in *Philosophy, Writing, and the Character of Thought*: those who aspire to philosophy should write aspirationally. My decision to continue in this vein was buoyed when Scott Parker responded so insightfully to that initial effort by way of a thoughtful interview, which appeared in *Rain Taxi*. I also am grateful to Eduardo Mendieta for his distinct and overlapping work on form and genre, for our conversations, and for being such a delight as a human being. Without ever being didactic, he never fails to instruct.

I have the good fortune of sharing my life with Hilary Hart. Her feel for and commitment to intimacy has intensified my interest in and concern for these dynamic eddies of ethical life. What she has made possible for us compels me to be philosophically responsive to its radiant, vulnerable currents. It seems only natural that she came to mind so often when I began to think, "For example . . ."

But in the end, it's my mother's fault. When I am asked how it is that I ended up doing this—namely, aspiring to philosophy—she always comes to mind. As far back as I remember, she has taken me seriously—my questions, my ruminations, my wish to preach the story of the prodigal son in our house basement at the age of seven. (I shit you not.) One needs to take oneself seriously to aspire to philosophy, to think that one might account for oneself in a manner that rings true and provides another with good enough reasons for furthering the experiment in their own way. For me, that aspiration, a second birth as it were, also began with my mother and her love. I dedicate this to her to memorialize, in some small fashion, that unrepayable gift.

Bibliography

Abu-Nimer, Mohammed, and Ilham Nasser. 2013. "Forgiveness in the Arab and Islamic Contexts: Between Theology and Practice." *Journal of Religious Ethics* 41, no. 3 (September): 474–94.

Adorno, Theodor. 1974. *Minima Moralia*. Translated by E. F. N. Jephcott. London: New Left Books.

———. 1991. *Notes to Literature*. Vol. 1. Edited by Rolf Tiedemann. Translated by Shierry Weber Nicholsen. New York: Columbia University Press.

———. 1997. *Aesthetic Theory*. Edited by Gretel Adorno and Rolf Tiedemann. Translated by Robert Hullot-Kentor. Minneapolis: University of Minnesota Press.

Alcoff, Linda Martín. 2006. *Visible Identities: Race, Gender, and the Self*. New York: Oxford University Press.

Arendt, Hannah. 1958. *The Human Condition*. Chicago: University of Chicago Press.

Aronson, Ronald. 2017. *We: Reviving Social Hope*. Chicago: University of Chicago Press.

Arsić, Branka. 2010. *On Leaving*. Cambridge, MA: Harvard University Press.

Babich, Babette E. 2003. "Nietzsche's Imperative as a Friend's Encomium: On Becoming the One You Are, Ethics, and Blessing." *Nietzsche-Studien* 32, no. 1: xx–yy.

Baier, Annette C. 1995. *Moral Prejudices: Essays on Ethics*. Cambridge, MA: Harvard University Press.

———. 2010. *Reflections on How We Live*. Oxford: Oxford University Press.

Baldwin, James. 2010. *The Cross of Redemption: Uncollected Writings*. Edited by Randall Kean. New York: Random House.

Benjamin, Walter. 2003. *Selected Writings*. Vol. 1, 1913–1926. Edited by Marcus Bullock and Michael W. Jennings. Cambridge, MA: Belknap Press.

Berg, Joyce, John Dickhaut, and Kevin McCabe. 1995. "Trust, Reciprocity, and Social History." *Games and Economic Behavior* 10: 122–42.

Bloch, Ernst. 1986. *The Principle of Hope*. Vol. 1. Translated by Neville Plaice, Stephen Plaice, and Paul Knight. Cambridge, MA: MIT Press.

Blöser, Claudia. 2020. "Hope in Kant." In *The Moral Psychology of Hope*. Edited by Claudia Blöser and Titus Stahl. London: Rowman & Littlefield.

Blöser, Claudia, and Titus Stahl. 2017. "Fundamental Hope and Practical Identity." *Philosophical Papers* 46, no. 3: 345–71.

Blöser, Claudia, and Titus Stahl, eds. 2020. *The Moral Psychology of Hope*. London: Rowman & Littlefield.

Boleyn-Fitzgerald, Patrick. 2002. "What Should 'Forgiveness' Mean?" *Journal of Value Inquiry* 36: 483–98.

Braudel, Fernand. 1977. *Afterthoughts on Material Civilization and Capitalism*. Translated by Patricia Ranum. Baltimore, MD: Johns Hopkins University Press.

Butler, Joseph. 1850. *The Works of the Right Reverend Father in God Joseph Butler, D. C. L., Late Lord Bishop of Durham*. 2 vols. Oxford: Oxford University Press.

Butler, Judith. 2005. *Giving an Account of Oneself*. New York: Columbia University Press.

Campbell, Marvin. 2017. "Stevens and Race: 'Like Decorations in a Nigger Cemetery' Revisited." *Wallace Stevens Journal* 41, no. 2 (Fall): 177–87.

Carse, Alisa. 2010. "Trust as Robustly Moral." *Philosophic Exchange* 40, no. 1, article 3.

Cavell, Stanley. 1981. *Pursuits of Happiness: The Hollywood Comedy of Remarriage*. Cambridge, MA: Harvard University Press.

———. 1990. *Conditions Handsome and Unhandsome: The Constitution of Emersonian Perfectionism*. Chicago: University of Chicago Press.

———. 2002. *Must We Mean What We Say? Updated Edition*. Cambridge: Cambridge University Press.

———. 2003. *Emerson's Transcendental Etudes*. Edited by David Justin Hodge. Stanford, CA: Stanford University Press.

———. 2005. *Philosophy the Day after Tomorrow*. Cambridge, MA: Harvard University Press.

Chignell, Andrew. 2023. "The Focus Theory of Hope." *Philosophical Quarterly* 73, no. 1 (January): 44–63.

Clifton, Lucille. 1987. *good woman: poems and a memoir 1969–1980*. Brockport, NY: BOA Editions.

Colapietro, Vincent. 2006a. "Practice, Agency, and Sociality: An Orthogonal Reading of Classical Pragmatism." *International Journal for Dialogical Science* 1, no. 1 (Spring): 23–31.

———. 2006b. "Toward a Pragmatic Conception of Practical Identity." *Transactions of the Charles S. Peirce Society* 42, no. 2: 173–205.

———. 2009. "A Revised Portrait of Human Agency: A Critical Engagement with Hans Joas's Creative Appropriation of the Pragmatic Approach." *European Journal of Pragmatism and American Philosophy* 1, no. 1/2: 1–25.

———. 2013. "Time as Experience/Experience as Temporality: Pragmatic and Perfectionist Reflections on Extemporaneous Creativity." *European Journal of Pragmatism and American Philosophy* 1.

Cornell, Drucilla, Michel Rosenfeld, and David Gray Carlson, eds. 1992. *Deconstruction and the Possibility of Justice*. New York: Routledge.

Crouch, Stanley. 2006. *Considering Genius*. New York: Basic Civitas Books.

Culbreth, Andrew. 2020. "Good Hope and Happiness in Plato and Aristotle." PhD diss., Emory University.

Davidson, Donald. 2006. *The Essential Davidson*. New York: Oxford University Press.

Derrida, Jacques. 1979. *Spurs: Nietzsche's Styles*. Chicago: University of Chicago Press.

———. 2001. *On Cosmopolitanism and Forgiveness*. Translated by Mark Dooley and Michael Hughes. London: Routledge.

Dewey, John. 1983. *The Middle Works: 1899–1924*. Vol. 14, *1922: Human Nature and Conduct*. Edited by Jo Ann Boydston. Carbondale: Southern Illinois University Press.

Dickinson, Emily. 1979. *The Poems of Emily Dickinson*. Edited by Thomas H. Johnson. Cambridge, MA: Harvard University Press.

Dormandy, Katherine, ed. 2020. *Trust in Epistemology*. New York: Routledge.

Dyson, Michael Eric. 2006. *Pride*. New York: Oxford University Press.

Eagleton, Terry. 2017. *Hope without Optimism*. Charlottesville: University of Virginia Press.

Ellison, Ralph Waldo. 2001. *Living with Music: Ralph Ellison's Jazz Writings*. Edited by Robert G. O'Meally. New York: Modern Library.

Emerson, Ralph Waldo. 1971. *The Collected Works of Ralph Waldo Emerson: Nature, Addresses, Lectures*. Edited by Joseph Slater and Robert E. Spiller. Cambridge, MA: Harvard University Press.

———. 1972. *The Early Lectures of Ralph Waldo Emerson*. Vol. 3, *1838–1842*. Edited by Robert E. Spiller and Wallace E. Williams. Cambridge, MA: Harvard University Press.

———. 1979. *The Collected Works of Ralph Waldo Emerson: Essays; First Series*. Edited by Joseph Slater, Alfred Ferguson, and Jean Ferguson Carr. Cambridge, MA: Harvard University Press.

———. 1983. *The Collected Works of Ralph Waldo Emerson: Essays; Second Series*. Edited by Alfred R. Ferguson, Jean Ferguson Carr, and Joseph Slater. Cambridge, MA: Harvard University Press.

———. 1987. *The Collected Works of Ralph Waldo Emerson*. Vol 4, *Representative Men*. Edited by Wallace E. Williams and Douglas Emery Wilson. Cambridge, MA: Harvard University Press.

———. 1996. *Essays and Poems*. New York: Literary Classics of America.

———. 2003. *The Collected Works of Ralph Waldo Emerson*. Vol. 6, *The Conduct of Life*. Edited by Barbara Packer, Joseph Slater, and Douglas Emery Wilson. Cambridge, MA: Harvard University Press.

Epictetus. 1928. *The Discourses as Reported by Arrian, the Manual, and Fragments*. 2 vols. Translated by W. A. Oldfather. Cambridge, MA: Harvard University Press.

Faulkner, Paul, and Thomas Simpson, eds. 2017. *The Philosophy of Trust*. Oxford: Oxford University Press.

Finch, Aisha K. 2015. *Rethinking Slave Rebellion in Cuba: La Escalera and the Insurgencies of 1841–1844*. Chapel Hill: University of North Carolina Press.

Fisher, Mark. 2009. *Capitalist Realism: Is There No Alternative?* Winchester, UK: O Books.

Foley, Richard. 2001. *Intellectual Trust in Oneself and Others*. Cambridge: Cambridge University Press.

Foucault, Michel. 1984a. *The Foucault Reader*. Edited by Paul Rabinow. New York: Random House.

———. 1984b. *The History of Sexuality*. Vol. 1, *An Introduction*. Translated by Robert Hurley. New York: Random House.

———. 2021. *Speaking the Truth about Oneself*. Edited by Henri-Paul Fruchaud and Daniele Lorenzini. Chicago: University of Chicago Press.

Francis, Sage. 2005. *A Healthy Distrust*. Compact Disc. Epitaph. 86709-2.

Frankfurt, Harry. 2005. *On Bullshit*. Princeton, NJ: Princeton University Press.

Fromm, Erich. 1970. *The Revolution of Hope*. New York: Harper and Row.

Gabriel, Markus. 2015. *Why the World Does Not Exist*. Cambridge: Polity Press.

Gillespie, Dizzy. 1971. Interview by Dick Cavett. *The Dick Cavett Show*. ABC. August 12, 1971.

Glaude, Eddie S., Jr. 2007. *In a Shade of Blue*. Chicago: University of Chicago Press.

———. 2016. *Democracy in Black: How Race Still Enslaves the American Soul*. New York: Crown.

———. 2020. *Begin Again: James Baldwin's America and Its Urgent Message for Our Own*. New York: Crown.

Gleason, Toby, ed. 2016. *Conversations in Jazz: The Ralph J. Gleason Interviews*. New Haven, CT: Yale University Press.

Govier, Trudy. 1998. *Dilemmas of Trust*. Montreal: McGill–Queen's University Press.

Green, Rochelle M., ed. 2019. *Theories of Hope*. Lanham, MD: Lexington Books.

Griswold, Charles L. 2007. *Forgiveness: A Philosophical Exploration*. Cambridge: Cambridge University Press.

Griswold, Charles L., and David Konstan, eds. 2012. *Ancient Forgiveness: Classical, Judaic, and Christian*. Cambridge: Cambridge University Press.

Grumet, Robert S. 2013. *Manhattan to Minisink: American Indian Place Names in Greater New York and Vicinity*. Norman: University of Oklahoma Press.

Gumbs, Alexis Pauline. 2016. *Spill: Scenes of Black Feminist Fugitivity*. Durham, NC: Duke University Press.

Habermas, Jürgen. 1984. *Philosophical Discourse of Modernity*. Translated by Frederick Lawrence. Cambridge, MA: MIT Press.

Halloran, S. Michael. 1982. "Aristotle's Concept of Ethos, or if Not His Somebody Else's." *Rhetoric Review* 1, no. 1 (September): 58–63. Published online May 2009. https://doi.org/10.1080/07350198209359037.

Hamm, J. A., B. L. Leonhardt, R. L. Fogley, and P. Lysaker. 2014. "Literature as an Exploration of the Phenomenology of Schizophrenia: Disorder and Recovery in Denis Johnson's *Jesus' Son*." *Medical Humanities* 40: 84–89.

Hansen, Jenny. 2008. "What's So Great about Nature?" *Journal of Speculative Philosophy*, n.s. 22, no. 3: 183–90.

Harding, Sandra, ed. 2004. *The Feminist Standpoint Theory Reader: Intellectual and Political Controversies*. New York: Routledge.

Hass, Robert. 1989. *Human Wishes*. New York: Ecco.

Havel, Václav. 1990. *Disturbing the Peace*. New York: Alfred A. Knopf.

———. 1997. *The Art of the Impossible: Politics as Morality in Practice*. New York: Alfred A. Knopf.

Hawley, Katherine. 2012. *Trust: A Very Short Introduction*. Oxford: Oxford University Press.

Hayes, Terrance. 2010. *Lighthead*. New York: Penguin Books.

Hegel, G. W. F. 1977. *Phenomenology of Spirit*. Translated by A. V. Miller. Oxford: Oxford University Press.

———. 1991. *Elements of the Philosophy of Right*. Edited by Allen Wood. Translated by H. B. Nisbet. Cambridge: Cambridge University Press.

Heidegger, Martin. 1962. *Being and Time*. New York: Harper and Row.

———. 1993. *Basic Writings: Revised and Expanded Edition*. Edited by David Farrell Krell. San Francisco: HarperCollins.

Heller, Michael C. 2017. *Loft Jazz: Improvising New York in the 1970s*. Oakland: University of California Press.

Holmgren, Margaret. 2002. "Forgiveness and Self-Forgiveness in Psychotherapy." In *Before Forgiving*. Edited by Sharon Lamb and Jeffrie Murphy. Oxford: Oxford University Press.

Horkheimer, Max. 1995. *Between Philosophy and Social Science*. Translated by G. Frederick Hunter, Matthew S. Kramer, and John Torpey. Cambridge, MA: MIT Press.

Horkheimer, Max, and Theodor Adorno. 2002. *Dialectic of Enlightenment: Philosophical Fragments*. Edited by Gunzelin Schmid Noerr. Translated by Edmund Jephcott. Stanford, CA: Stanford University Press.

Hoxie, Frederick E. 1995. *Parading through History: The Making of the Crow Nation in America, 1805–1935*. Cambridge: Cambridge University Press.

Jackson, Jesse. 1988. "1988 Democratic National Convention Address." Omni Coliseum, Atlanta, GA, July 19, 1988. Accessed June 18, 2018. http://www.americanrhetoric.com/speeches/jessejackson1988dnc.htm.

James, William. 1978. *Pragmatism and the Meaning of Truth*. Cambridge, MA: Harvard University Press.

Johnson, Noel D., and Alexandra Mislin. 2011. "Trust Games: A Meta-Analysis." *Journal of Economic Psychology* 32: 865–89.

Jones, Karen. 1996. "Trust as an Affective Attitude." *Ethics* 107, no. 1: 4–25.

———. 2004. "Trust and Terror." *Moral Psychology: Feminist Ethics and Social Theory*. Edited by Peggy DesAutels and Margaret Urban Walker. Lanham, MD: Rowman & Littlefield.

———. 2012. "Trustworthiness." *Ethics* 123, no. 1: 61–85.

Kahn, Ashley. 2002. *A Love Supreme: The Story of John Coltrane's Signature Album*. New York: Viking Penguin.

Kant, Immanuel. 1983. *Perpetual Peace and Other Essays*. Translated by Ted Humphrey. Indianapolis, IN: Hackett.

King, Martin Luther, Jr. 1957. "King Asks Non-Violence in Little Rock School Crisis." *Martin Luther King, Jr. Papers Project*. Accessed September 2021. https://kinginstitute.stanford.edu/king-papers/documents/dr-king-asks-non-violence-little-rock-school-crisis.

———. 1963. *Strength to Love*. Boston: Beacon Press.

———. 1986. *A Testament of Hope*. Edited by James M. Washington. New York: HarperCollins.

Kirkham, Richard L. 1992. *Theories of Truth*. Cambridge, MA: MIT Press.

Lear, Jonathan. 2006. *Radical Hope: Ethics in the Face of Cultural Devastation*. Cambridge, MA: Harvard University Press.

Lebron, Christopher. 2012. *The Color of Our Shame*. New York: Oxford University Press.

Lehrer, Keith. 1997. *Self-Trust: A Study of Reason, Knowledge and Autonomy*. Oxford: Oxford University Press.

Leiris, Michel. 1987. *Nights as Days, Days as Nights*. Translated by Richard Sieburth. Hygiene, CO: Eridanos.

Lerner, Akiba. 2019. "Redemptive Transgressions: The Dialectical Evolution of Hope and Freedom in the West." In *Theories of Hope: Exploring Alternative Affective Dimensions of Human Experience*. Edited by Rochelle M. Green. Lanham, MD: Lexington Books.

Levy, Lilyana. 2021. "Contested Illness and Embodied Knowing: On Medical Gaslighting." PhD diss., Emory University.

Linderman, Frank B. 1960. *Pretty-Shield*. Lincoln: University of Nebraska Press.

Lingis, Alphonso. 2004. *Trust*. Minneapolis: University of Minnesota Press.

Locke, John. 1988. *Two Treatises of Government*. Edited by Peter Laslett. Cambridge: Cambridge University Press.

Lugones, María. 2003. *Pilgrimages/Peregrinajes: Theorizing Coalition against Multiple Oppressions*. Lanham, MD: Rowman & Littlefield.

Luhmann, Niklas. 2017. *Trust and Power*. Edited with a revised translation by Christian Morgner and Michael King. Originally translated by Howard Davies, John Raffan, and Kathryn Rooney. Cambridge: Polity Press.

Lysaker, John. 1996. "The Shape of Selves to Come: Rorty and Self-Creation," *Philosophy and Social Criticism* 22, no. 3: 39–74.

———. 1999a. "On What is to be Done with What Has Always Already Happened." *Studies in Practical Philosophy* 1, no. 1: 86–113.

———. 1999b. "Lenin, Nancy, and the Politics of Total War." *Philosophy Today* 43: 186–95.

———. 2002. *You Must Change Your Life: Poetry, Philosophy, and the Birth of Sense*. State College: Penn State University Press.

———. 2008. *Emerson and Self-Culture*. Bloomington: Indiana University Press.

———. 2017. *After Emerson*. Bloomington: Indiana University Press.

———. 2018. *Philosophy, Writing, and the Character of Thought*. Chicago: University of Chicago Press.

Lysaker, John, and Paul Lysaker. 2005. "Being Interrupted: The Self and Schizophrenia." *Journal of Speculative Philosophy* 19, no. 1: 1–21.

Lysaker, Paul, Louanne Davis, and John Lysaker. 2006. "Enactment in Schizophrenia: Capacity for Dialogue and the Experience of the Inability to Commit to Action." *Psychiatry* 69, no. 1 (Spring): 81–93.

Lysaker, Paul, and John Lysaker. 2017. "Metacognition and the Prospect of Enhancing Self-Management in Schizophrenia Spectrum Disorders." *Philosophy, Psychiatry & Psychology* 24, no. 2 (June): 169–78.

Lysaker, Paul, and John Lysaker. 2021. "Disturbances in Dialogue and Metacognition: A Renewed Way to Understand and Respond to Alterations in Self-Experience in Psychosis." *Theory and Psychology* 31, no. 3: 335–54.

MacLachlan, Alice. 2009. "Practicing Imperfect Forgiveness." In *Feminist Ethics and Social and Political Philosophy: Theorizing the Non-Ideal*. Edited by Lisa Tessman. Dordrecht: Springer Science+Business Media B.V.

———. 2012. "Mercy and Forgiveness." In *Encyclopedia of Applied Ethics*. 2nd ed. Edited by Ruth Chadwick. London: Academic Press.

Manguso, Sarah. 2015. *Ongoingness: The End of a Diary*. Minneapolis: Graywolf Press.

Mann, Aimee. 2002. *Lost in Space*. Super Ego Records. Compact Disc. SE 1007.

Marriott, David. 2020. "Blackness: N'est Pas?" *Propter Nos* 4 (Fall): 27–51.

Martin, Adrienne M. 2014. *How We Hope: A Moral Psychology*. Princeton, NJ: Princeton University Press.

May, Herbert G., and Bruce M. Metzger, eds. 1962. *The New Oxford Annotated Bible with the Apocrypha*. Revised Standard Version. New York: Oxford University Press.

Mayo Clinic. n.d. "Radiation Sickness." Accessed September 2021. https://www.mayoclinic.org/diseases-conditions/radiation-sickness/symptoms-causes/syc-20377058.

McGeer, Victoria. 2004. "The Art of Good Hope." *Annals of the American Academy* 592 (March): 100–127.

———. 2009. "Moral Travel and the Narrative Work of Forgiveness." Paper presentation. Text provided courtesy of the author.

McLeod, Carolyn. 2002. *Self-Trust and Reproductive Autonomy*. Cambridge, MA: MIT Press.

Medicine Crow, Joseph. 1992. *From the Heart of the Crow Country*. New York: Orion.

Mikkelsen, Jon M. 2013. *Kant and the Concept of Race*. Albany, NY: SUNY Press.

Monson, Ingrid. 1996. *Saying Something: Jazz Improvisation and Interaction*. Chicago: University of Chicago Press.

Moten, Fred. 2003. *In the Break: The Aesthetics of the Black Radical Tradition*. Minneapolis: University of Minnesota Press.

———. 2017. *Black and Blur*. Durham, NC: Duke University Press.

Murphy, Jeffrie G., and Jean Hampton. 1988. *Forgiveness and Mercy*. Cambridge: Cambridge University Press.

Murray, Albert. 2017. *Stomping the Blues*. 25th anniversary ed. Minneapolis: University of Minnesota Press.

Nancy, Jean-Luc. 1991. *The Inoperative Community*. Edited by Peter Connor. Translated by Peter Connor, Lisa Garbus, Michael Holland, and Simona Sawhney. Minneapolis: University of Minnesota Press.

———. 1993. *The Birth to Presence*. Translated by Brian Holmes et al. Stanford, CA: Stanford University Press.

NCVC (National Center for the Victims of Crime). 2021. "Child Sexual Abuse Statistics." Accessed October 2021. https://victimsofcrime.org/child-sexual-abuse-statistics/.

Nelson, Maggie. 2009. *Bluets*. Seattle: Wave Books.

Nietzsche, Friedrich. 1966. *Beyond Good and Evil*. Translated by Walter Kaufmann. New York: Random House.

———. 1974. *The Gay Science*. Translated by Walter Kaufmann. New York: Random House.

———. 1988. *Kritische Studienausgabe 3: Morgenröte, Idyllen aus Messina, Die fröhliche Wissenschaft*. Edited by Girgio Colli and Mazzino Montinari. Berlin: Walter de Gruyter.

———. 2001. *The Gay Science*. Edited by Bernard Williams. Translated by Josefine Nauckhoff. Cambridge: Cambridge University Press.

———. 2005. *The Anti-Christ, Ecce Homo, Twilight of the Idols, and Other Writings*. Edited by Aaron Ridley and Judith Norman. Translated by Judith Norman. Cambridge: Cambridge University Press.

———. 2013. *The Complete Works of Friedrich Nietzsche*. Vol. 4, *Human, All Too Human II*. Translated by Gary Handwerk. Stanford, CA: Stanford University Press.

Nisenson, Eric. 1993. *Ascension: John Coltrane and His Quest*. New York: St. Martin's.

Norlock, Kathryn, J. 2009. *Forgiveness from a Feminist Perspective*. Lanham, MD: Lexington Books.

———, ed. 2017. *The Moral Psychology of Forgiveness*. London: Rowman & Littlefield International.

Nussbaum, Martha. 2016. *Anger and Forgiveness: Resentment, Generosity, Justice*. Oxford: Oxford University Press.

Nyman, Michael. 1999. *Experimental Music: Cage and Beyond*. 2nd ed. Cambridge: Cambridge University Press.

Obama, Barack. 2006. *The Audacity of Hope: Thoughts on Reclaiming the American Dream*. New York: Crown.

O'Brien, Tim. 1990. *The Things They Carried*. Boston: Houghton Mifflin Harcourt.

OED (*Oxford English Dictionary*) Online, s.v. "Trust," December 2022. Oxford University Press, https://www-oed-com.proxy.library.emory.edu/view/Entry/207004?rskey=gWGvQs&result=1.

O'Neill, Onora. 2002. *A Question of Trust: The BBC Reith Lectures 2002*. Cambridge: Cambridge University Press.

Ortega, Mariana. 2016. *In-between: Latina Feminist Phenomenology, Multiplicity, and the Self*. Albany: SUNY Press.

Page, Clarence. 2016. "My 'Implicit Bias' against Black People." *Chicago Tribune*. October 7, 2016. Accessed December 2019.

Parker, Scott. 2018. *A Way Home: Oregon Essays*. Portland, OR: Kelson Books.

Pindar. 1990. *Odes*. Edited and translated by Diane Arnson Svarlien. Accessed September 2021. http://www.perseus.tufts.edu/hopper/textdoc=Perseus%3Atext%3A1999.01.0162%3Abook%3DP.%3Apoem%3D2.

———. 2007. *The Complete Odes*. Translated by Anthony Verity. Oxford: Oxford University Press.

Pope Francis. 2017. *On Hope*. Chicago: Loyola Press.

Potter, Nancy Nyquist. 2002. *How Can I Be Trusted? A Virtue Theory of Trustworthiness*. Lanham, MD: Rowman & Littlefield.

Raffoul, François. 2010. *The Origins of Responsibility*. Bloomington: Indiana University Press.

Rawls, John. 1971. *A Theory of Justice*. Cambridge, MA: Harvard University Press.

———. 1996. *Political Liberalism*. New York: Columbia University Press.

Rhees, Rush, ed. 1984. *Recollections of Wittgenstein*. Oxford: Oxford University Press.

Roberts, Robert. 1995. "Forgivingness." *American Philosophical Quarterly* 32, no. 4: 289–306.

Rogers, Melvin. 2014. "Race and the Democratic Aesthetic: Whitman Meets Billie Holiday." In *Radical Future Pasts: Untimely Political Theory*. Edited by Romand Coles, Mark Reinhardt, and George Schulman. Lexington: University of Kentucky Press.

———. 2015. "David Walker and the Political Power of the Appeal." *Political Theory* 43, no. 2: 208–33.

———. Forthcoming. *The Darkened Light of Faith: Race, Democracy, and Freedom in African American Political Thought*. Princeton, NJ: Princeton University Press.

Rorty, Richard. 1989. *Contingency, Irony, and Solidarity*. Cambridge: Cambridge University Press.

Rorty, Richard, and Pascal Engel. 2007. *What's the Use of Truth?* New York: Columbia University Press.

Segev, Tom. 2010. *The Life and Legends of Simon Wiesenthal*. New York: Doubleday.

Sexton, Anne. 1981. *The Complete Poems*. Boston: Houghton Mifflin.

Shade, Patrick. 2001. *Habits of Hope: A Pragmatic Theory*. Nashville, TN: Vanderbilt University Press.

———. 2019. "Shame, Hope, and the Courage to Transgress." In *Theories of Hope: Exploring Alternative Affective Dimensions of Human Experience*. Edited by Rochelle M. Green. London: Lexington Books.

Sharpe, Christina. 2016. *In the Wake: On Blackness and Being*. Durham, NC: Duke University Press.

Shipp, Matthew. 2020. "Black Mystery School Pianists." December 18, 2020. https://nmbx.newmusicusa.org/black-mystery-school-pianists/.

Simic, Charles. 1989. *The World Doesn't End*. San Diego: Harcourt Brace Jovanovich.

Simon, Sidney B., and Suzanne Simon. 1990. *Forgiveness: How to Make Peace with Your Past and Get on with Your Life*. New York: Grand Central Publishing.

Smith, Adam. 1981. *An Inquiry into the Nature and Cause of the Wealth of Nations*. Vol. 1, edited by R. H. Campbell, A. S. Skinner, and W. B. Todd: Indianapolis, IN: Liberty Fund.

Snow, Nancy. 2019. "Faces of Hope." In *Theories of Hope: Exploring Alternative Affective Dimensions of Human Experience*. Edited by Rochelle M. Green. Lanham, MD: Lexington Books.

Solnit, Rebecca. 2016. *Hope in the Dark: Untold Histories, Wild Possibilities*. Chicago: Haymarket.

Spillers, Hortense J. 2003. *Black, White, and in Color: Essays on American Literature and Culture*. Chicago: University of Chicago Press.

Steinbock, Anthony J. 2014. *Moral Emotions: Reclaiming the Evidence of the Heart*. Evanston, IL: Northwestern University Press.

Stevens, Wallace. 1971. *The Palm at the End of the Mind: Selected Poems and a Play*. Edited by Holly Stevens. New York: Alfred A. Knopf.

Stockdale, Katie. 2020. "Emotional Hope." In *The Moral Psychology of Hope*. Edited by Claudia Blöser and Titus Stahl. London: Rowman & Littlefield.

———. 2021. *Hope under Oppression*. New York: Oxford University Press.

Strawson, Peter. 2008. *Freedom and Resentment and Other Essays*. New York: Routledge.

Stuhr, John. 1997. *Genealogical Pragmatism: Philosophy, Experience, and Community*. Albany: SUNY Press.

Tanesini, Alessandra. 2020. "Virtuous and Vicious Intellectual Self-Trust." In *Trust in Epistemology*. Edited by Katherine Dormandy. New York: Routledge.

Tarski, Alfred. 1983. *Logic, Semantics, Metamathematics*. 2nd ed. Edited by John Corcoran. Translated by J. H. Woodger. Indianapolis, IN: Hackett.

Taylor, Paul. 2018. "Moral Perfectionism." In *To Shape a New World: Essays on the Political Philosophy of Martin Luther King, Jr*. Edited by Tommie Shelby and Brandon M. Terry. Cambridge, MA: Harvard University Press.

Thoreau, Henry David. 2008. *Walden, Civil Disobedience, and Other Writings*. 3rd ed. Edited by William Rossi. New York: W. W. Norton.

Vattimo, Gianni. 2011. *A Farewell to Truth*. Translated by William McCuaig. New York: Columbia University Press.

Vice, Samantha. 2020. "Pessimism and the Possibility of Hope." In *The Moral Psychology of Hope*. Edited by Claudia Blöser and Titus Stahl. London: Rowman & Littlefield.

Walker, Margaret Urban. 2006. *Moral Repair: Reconstructing Moral Relations after Wrongdoing*. Cambridge: Cambridge University Press.

Wall, Steven. 2017. "Perfectionism in Moral and Political Philosophy." *Stanford Encyclopedia of Philosophy*. Accessed March 2020. https://plato.stanford.edu/search/searcher.py?query=perfectionism.

Warren, Calvin. 2015. "Black Nihilism and the Politics of Hope." *CR: The New Centennial Review* 15, no. 1 (Spring): 215–48.

Webb, Darren. 2019. "Education and the Construction of Hope." In *Theories of Hope: Exploring Alternative Affective Dimensions of Human Experience*. Edited by Rochelle M. Green. Lanham, MD: Lexington Books.

Wenz, John. 2016. "This Planet Has One of the Weirdest Orbits We've Ever Seen." *Popular Mechanics*. March 21, 2016. https://www.popularmechanics.com/space/news/a20025/hd-20782b-wildly-eccentric-orbit/.

West, Cornel. 1997. *Restoring Hope: Conversations on the Future of Black America*. Edited by Kelvin Shawn Sealey. Boston: Beacon Press.

———. 2018. "Hope and Despair: Past and Present." In *To Shape a New World: Essays on the Political Philosophy of Martin Luther King Jr*. Edited by Tommie Shelby and Brandon M. Terry. Cambridge, MA: Harvard University Press.

Wiesenthal, Simon. 1997. *The Sunflower: On the Possibilities and Limits of Forgiveness*. Revised and expanded edition. New York: Shocken Books.

Williams, Bernard. 1993. *Morality: An Introduction to Ethics*. Cambridge: Cambridge University Press.

Williams, Patricia, J. 1992. *The Alchemy of Race and Rights: Diary of a Law Professor*. Cambridge, MA: Harvard University Press.

Wilmer, Val. 2018. *As Serious as Your Life: Black Music and the Free Jazz Revolution, 1957–1977*. London: Profile Books.

Winters, Joseph R. 2016. *Hope Draped in Black: Race, Melancholy, and the Agony of Progress*. Durham, NC: Duke University Press.

Wittgenstein, Ludwig. 1951. *Tractatus Logico-Philosophicus*. Translated by C. K. Ogden. New York: Humanities Press.

Yancy, George. 2012. *Look, a White!* Philadelphia: Temple University Press.

Index

O'Neill, Onora, 98
ontology, 12–13, 22, 63–66, 82, 174
ordinary language, xv–xvi, 5–6, 24, 97,
    102–4
Ortega, Mariana, 65, 82

Page, Clarence, 117
Parker, Scott, 8–10
partiality, 55, 76–77, 82, 128, 159, 176
perfectionism, xix, 44, 143, 150–65,
    167–69; aesthetic, xiii, 12–13, 79,
    170, 174, 177, 186; and "become
    who you are," 37, 158–59; experi-
    ment, xiv–xvii, 161, 164, 167,
    169–78, 195, 200; humanist, 158;
    and improvisation, xvi, 112, 148,
    172–76, 200, 223
phenomenology, 77
Pindar, 35, 158–63, 167, 172
Potter, Nancy Nyquist, 93, 106, 117–
    18, 134–40
pragmatism, xiii, 47–48, 68, 82, 161,
    169, 172, 227

race, 64, 83, 131, 153–54, 174, 202,
    221, 225
Raffoul, François, 228
Rawls, John, 156–57
Rhees, Rush, 87
Roberts, Robert, 204, 217–18
Rogers, Melvin, 44–45, 157
romanticism, 49, 78, 80–82
Rorty, Richard, xvi, 67–68, 74–75

scripture, 185, 194–95
self-knowledge, 79, 141, 157
Sexton, Anne, 41–42, 47
Shade, Patrick, 24, 40, 47–48
Sharpe, Christina, 12
Shipp, Matthew, 173
Simon, Sidney B., 223
Simon, Suzanne, 223
Simpson, Thomas, 95–98, 100, 108,
    113, 118, 122
singularity, xviii, 49, 100, 193, 197,
    214, 226–28

Smith, Adam, 14
Snow, Nancy, 10–11
Solnit, Rebecca, 28, 34
Spillers, Hortense J., 164–66
Steinbock, Anthony J., 6, 45, 46
Stevens, Wallace, 12–13, 28–29, 57, 78,
    216–17, 225
Stockdale, Katie, 3, 16
Strawson, Peter, 188
Stuhr, John, 84

Tanesini, Alessandra, 124, 130
Tarski, Alfred, 69
Taylor, Paul, 151, 157, 168
theology, 34–37, 42–43, 49, 52, 57,
    63, 88–89, 152, 155, 158, 179, 181,
    196–97, 209, 224
Thoreau, Henry David, xiv, 9, 151, 159;
    and perfectionism, 171–72; and
    the self, 177; Walden, xix, 28, 48–
    49, 55–56, 118, 142–44, 155
trust: and agency, 81–82, 97–98, 102–
    3, 107, 109, 111, 119–22, 125, 136,
    138–39; and betrayal, 91–94, 98,
    101, 105, 108–9, 138; and charac-
    ter, 87, 92, 110, 116, 118, 122, 138;
    and convention, 108–9, 136, 145,
    148, 173–74; and deliberation,
    94–95, 97, 99, 103, 105–6, 127; and
    dependence, 88–89, 97–100, 102,
    108, 122, 136; and desire, 77, 99,
    115, 118, 120, 123; distrust, 87, 90,
    92–93, 96, 98–102, 107, 110, 114,
    117, 119, 121, 123, 127–34; and
    ethical life, 108, 145; and friend-
    ship, 92–94, 104–5, 108–9, 135–36;
    and the future, 55, 87, 92, 94, 98,
    109–10, 124, 127, 129, 145–46, 152,
    172, 177; versus gambling, 96, 170;
    and goodwill, 118, 122, 129, 131,
    140; as intersubjective, 96–97, 102,
    109–11, 120, 124; and the past,
    87, 99, 109, 122, 126–27; and the
    present, 146, 156, 168; and reason,
    126, 128, 132–35; and reliance, 95,
    97–99, 102–3, 114, 117, 126; self-